AF560743

COLONIALISM AND URBANIZATION IN INDIA: THE PUNJAB REGION

Colonialism and Urbanization in India

The Punjab Region

REETA GREWAL

MANOHAR
2009

First published 2009

ISBN 81-7304-619-0

Published by
Ajay Kumar Jain *for*
Manohar Publishers & Distributors
4753/23 Ansari Road, Daryaganj
New Delhi 110 002

Typeset by
Kohli Print
Delhi 110 051

Printed at
Salasar Imaging Systems
Delhi 110 035

To my parents

Harjinder Grewal
and
J.S. Grewal

Contents

Figures, Tables and Appendices

FIGURES

*Maps pertaining to the British Punjab are based largely on James Douie's *The Punjab, North West Frontier Province and Kashmir*, originally published in 1916.

TABLES

APPENDICES

Preface

In a classic statement on urbanism Louis Wirth refers to urbanization as 'one of the most impressive facts of modern times'. Social scientists had begun to take interest in urban studies by the middle of the twentieth century. The historians appeared on the scene a little later.

As a young researcher at Guru Nanak Dev University, I was inspired by the activities of the Urban History Association of India, which had just been founded in Amritsar for promoting the study of urban history in the Indian context. I began with the assumption that, though a global development, urbanization was a regional phenomenon, tied not only to the region's geography and economy, but also to its polity. As a process, it impinged on the region's society as a whole, enveloping its cities and towns as well as the people living in the villages.

My early research dealt with the interplay of geography, economy and polity in the pre-colonial context, and brought out the bearing of the political processes on urbanization. The present work takes the story further, highlighting the interrelations between the processes of urbanization, modernization and social change within the colonial context. My assumption is that the impact of the colonial power was probably more pervasive in the Punjab as the last region to be annexed than in the rest of British India.

Since the historical studies of urban processes in a regional setting were relatively late in emerging, I had to chart my own course, borrowing from allied disciplines, particularly geography, sociology, social anthropology, economics, political science, and public administration. Though interdisciplinary in orientation, the present work remains embedded in the discipline of history. Based on extensive and rigorous use of sources available at various archives and repositories, this work is largely an empirical study of the processes involved in urbanization in north-western India, covering the British province of the Punjab (excluding the Delhi territory, and the North West Frontier Province), from 1849 to 1947, that is from annexation by the British to independence and partition of the region.

Beginning with the pre-colonial background, the study focuses upon the bearing of the evolving colonial context on the changes in the relative size and distribution of urban centres over time, and the proportion and composition of urban population; physical growth and planning of urban areas in the plains and the hills; reorientations in urban functions and institutions; visible and invisible modes of colonial control and management of urban people and their cultural reorientations and political articulation. Wherever made possible by the available evidence, questions of urban-rural interactions and subregional and subcontinental variations have been kept in view. I would feel gratified if this endeavour provides the basis for more in-depth and specific studies of the urban processes in different regions of the subcontinent, including the Punjabs on both sides of the international border.

I have taken long to publish this work, but I feel happy that I have been able to revise it thoroughly in the light of the recent researches in urban history. In the course of doing this work, I received help from several of my teachers, colleagues and students. Professor J.S. Grewal, the founder secretary of the Urban History Association of India (UHAI), was unsparing in his constructive criticism, and generous with his insights. Professor Indu Banga, my former teacher and senior colleague at present, has been no less exacting, and she too has continued to take interest in this work and share her ideas and unpublished work with me. I am indebted to them both. I cherish my association with my former teachers at the Departments of History, Economics, Political Science, and Guru Ram Das School of Planning at Guru Nanak Dev University, Amritsar. My senior colleagues in history, geography, sociology, and public administration at the Panjab University allowed me access to their personal collections and department libraries. I am thankful to them all. I am gratful to Professor Gurdev Singh Gosal, the eminent geographer, for his thought-provoking comments whenever I happened to discuss the subject with him.

I thank Shri Ramesh C. Jain and Shri Ajay Kumar Jain of Manohar Publishers who have been extremely patient and accommodating. Their insistence on quality has been most helpful. I am happy to acknowledge the assistance received from Shri Mohan Singh who prepared the maps and diagrams with care.

I would like to acknowledge the responses of my researchers and MA students who obliged me to reflect deeply on urban processes. I shall feel rewarded if they find this book of some interest.

Finally, I thank my parents for their affectionate support and encouragement all through this work, and my husband and children for their love, understanding, and help from time to time.

6 December 2007 REETA GREWAL

Abbreviations and Spellings

ABBREVIATIONS

DG	:	*District Gazetteer*
GNDU	:	Guru Nanak Dev University (Amritsar)
PIHC	:	*Proceedings Indian History Congress*
IIAS	:	Indian Institute of Advanced Study (Shimla)
JRH	:	*Journal of Regional History* (GNDU, Amritsar)
NAI	:	National Archives of India (New Delhi)
NWFP	:	North West Frontier Province
OUP	:	Oxford Univesity Press (New Delhi)
PPP	:	*Panjab Past and Present* (Punjabi University, Patiala)
PSA	:	Punjab State Archives (Patiala and Chandigarh)
UHAI	:	Urban History Association of India (Chandigarh)

SPELLINGS

Place names are not spelt uniformly in the publications and records of the colonial period. For the reader's convenience, I have tried to stay close to the spellings current today in the text and endnotes, and give the actual spellings in the bibliography. For spellings in general, and Indian words and terms in particular, as well as their italicization and capitalization, I have generally followed *The New Oxford Dictionary of English* (2000). The Glossary mostly contains non-English words and terms. The guiding principles at any rate have been consistency and closeness to the sources and regional usage.

1

Theoretical and Historiographical Context

Urban centres have existed in various parts of the world for thousands of years, but it is only in the modern times that urbanization has emerged as a dominating force in human history. This is not to underestimate the tremendous influence of ancient cities in all spheres of civilization, though the scale on which this phenomenon has grown in the last few hundred years remains unprecedented. The study of urban processes and their ramifications has become one of the foremost concerns of social scientists in the developing as well as industrialized countries today to 'help solve difficulties that have already arisen and to help forestall difficulties that may arise in the future'.[1]

Urbanization is generally seen as a behavioural, structural or demographic process, depending on the inclinations of the observer.[2] Sociologists view urbanization in relation to the changing patterns of individual behaviour and increasing diffusion of modernization traits. In India they have been particularly concerned with social change and social movements located in urban areas.[3] Louis Wirth gives the 'minimal definition' of a city as 'a relatively large, dense and permanent settlement of socially heterogeneous individuals'.[4] Furthermore, theories of urbanism deal with relations between members of the urban society and their rural counterparts in terms of the urban-rural dichotomy.[5] Urban anthropology is interested in the changing institutions, roles, and relationships in specific urban situations and their interactions with the countryside.[6] Economists interpret urbanization in terms of economic development and shifts from agricultural to secondary and tertiary production and functions.[7] Literature has been delineating the complex social relations in the rapidly changing urban environment and grappling with the elusive questions of urban values and ethos.[8] Geographers view urbanization mainly as a process of the movement, concentration and composition of population in large human settlements, increase in the size and number of such settlements, and their interrelations and functions.[9] Demographers statistically analyse and interpret the changing structure of urban population in terms of proportions, distribution, density, age, sex and occupations.[10] Among some other disciplines, town planning is concerned with the city plans and their application on the ground; and political science and public administration deal mainly with forms of urban politics, management and governance.[11]

Urbanization is thus the concern of several disciplines. It is a multifaceted process that 'reveals itself through temporal, spatial and sectoral changes in demographic, social, economic, technological and environmental aspects of life'.[12] However, most of the social science disciplines are concerned more with recent times, contemporary problems, future projections, application of theories, and with individual cities and metropolises. Moreover, when they do go back in time and trace the urban phenomena historically in the Indian context, the tendency is to depend on the easily available secondary works and leave out the areas that later went to Pakistan.[13]

While sharing most of the concerns of the social scientists and also some of their methods, the historian generally tries to take as total a view of the urban past as possible. The domain of the historian extends as much to the cities as to the small towns; it deals as much with the general and theoretical as with the specific and empirical; and it incorporates both the statistical and the human aspects of an urban situation. Like fellow practitioners of history, urban historians also study change in a given space and time and are bound by the constraints of the availability and reliability of evidence.[14]

The multi-dimensional nature of the urban process defies a single definition of an 'urban centre'. There has been a continuous debate involving legal, economic and social elements in the definition of what constitutes a town, city or urban place. The oldest definition of a city would undoubtedly be the ideogram of a cross within a circle denoting an enclosed trading place.[15] The Latin roots of the words 'city' and 'urban' are shared by the words 'civilization' and 'urbanity', implying that the world outside the city was uncivilized. The economic and social opportunities distinguishing an urban from a rural setting, thus, were present in the earliest cities.[16] By about the fourteenth century in

West Asia, stress began to be laid on the political status of the city as the seat of government which demarcated it from the surrounding countryside.[17] In Western Europe, by the seventeenth century, the economic element acquired primacy in the definition of a city.[18]

Viewed historically, there could be two bases for defining a city or a town: the natural and the legal. As a natural social entity an urban centre constituted a unit which was distinct from neighbouring areas by virtue of its size, density of population, dominant means of livelihood, and social relations. The legal entity was a kind of governmental unit consisting of a legally incorporated or designated area within which the population exceeded a specified minimum and a local government exercised authority as delegated by the State. The natural and legal bases were generally integrated into a single whole.

It is possible to identify the characteristics that made urban centres distinct from rural settlements. Firstly, the population in urban centres was generally much larger and more densely clustered than in other settlements. The urban people were more mobile and heterogeneous as a group. They followed a multitude of non-agricultural occupations which catered to both urban and rural centres. Occupational specialization developed a larger economic base and led *inter alia* to increase in production, trade and transportation. In the social sphere arose specializations related to religious, recreational and educational activities, including relatively better healthcare. The administrative personnel based in urban areas and their functions too were more diversified and specialized. A variety of services became an essential characteristic of a city; and its internal organization, both spatial and social, was determined by the nature of services it performed. At the same time, a city or a town or a townlet, could not exist without its villages which supplied the necessary food, raw materials and skilled and unskilled labour. This mutually sustaining, mutually dominating and mutually exploiting town-countryside relationship was a complex one, varying over time and place.[19]

Compared to the early 'city', the city in modern times has been large and dynamic. Its changing role has been influenced by a combination of factors having varying degrees of impact on the urban phenomena. Besides agricultural development, these factors include trade and commerce, transportation, industrialization, technological innovations, and socio-cultural developments.[20] In a formulation, labelled POET, the process of urbanization is seen as determined by the variables of Population, Social Organization, Physical Environment and Technology.[21] However, the model of urbanization constructed on the basis of the POET framework is statistically oriented and its application gets limited to the recent past because of the nature and availability of the data. Moreover, it does not take into account the important variable of polity and is not suitable to grapple with the complexities of economy and society. A historically meaningful study of the process of urbanization can be made in terms broadly of geography, polity and economy.[22] Geography takes into account the physical nature of the area, its topography, soil, climate and vegetation, all of which affect the pattern of settlements. The political conditions, warfare, structure of power, administrative arrangements, and policies of the State modify the physical form and accelerate or retard the pace of urbanization which is sustained and even expanded by trade and commerce, manufacturing activity, communications and technology. The social structure remains related essentially to these three basic variables of geography, polity and economy.

The degree and pattern of urbanization has varied according to the times and conditions under which it developed—whether in medieval or modern times, in an agricultural or industrial economy, in a free or colonial society, in an emerging nation or post-colonial country.[23] The pace of urbanization within the same territory may vary over a period of time. Furthermore, centres within the same urban system may develop at different rates. Growth and decline can occur simultaneously, and deurbanization can become a part of the process of growth. Rather, when deurbanization is on a small scale then overall urbanization takes place. The ongoing change in the fortunes of a town or city remains linked to the overall pattern of urbanization in a region.

Some kind of urban hierarchy is integral to the process of urbanization. To quote Braudel, 'a town never exists unaccompanied by other towns; some dominant, others subordinate . . . , all are tied to each other. . . '.[24] Over a period of time, the combination of various factors resulted in the development of some units to a higher level than others. These dominant units having the largest urban population and the widest range of functions then became the primary centres of the region. Relatively less developed urban units remained at the middling level, between the primate city and the small town. Together, towns of different sizes constituted the regional and inter-regional markets, having links also with towns outside the subcontinent. In fact, movement was 'vital' to them: 'without markets and roads, there would be no towns'.[25]

Thus, the urban centres of a region may be seen as forming a pyramid, (Figure 1.1), constituted by a large number of small basal towns, a smaller number of middle-level urban units, and a very small number of cities at the apex. Such vertical links could result in several urban pyramids, each having its own apex. Through horizontal linkages the apical cities connected the region as a whole with other regions having similar urban pyramids.[26] As they moved towards the apical city, the number of units at each level decreased and variety in urban functions increased. Urban centres formed a network that could, in theory, link the remotest hamlet to the metropolis.[27]

II

Urbanization in India has received attention from the social scientists in the post-independence period. It was in the 1950s that substantial urban studies in sociology, geography, demography and some other disciplines began appearing, but serious works in urban history took longer to make their mark. By now, however, a large number of monographs and articles have appeared with different takes on the urban situation. The aspects covered vary according to the interest of the researcher. Put together, they inform the present understanding of urbanization and the urban phenomena in historical perspective.[28]

As a part of the widening sphere of urban as well as historical studies, urban history has received considerable attention from Indian historians in the past three decades or so. Their work can be divided into three main categories: the first, dealing with individual centres; the second, relating to the process of urbanization; and the third, focusing on one or another specific aspect of the urban phenomena. All the three foci of enquiry are interlinked and they are essential for the totality of perspective on urban studies. However, like most other branches of history, urban history too has developed gradually over the past century.[29]

The nature of early research in urban history may be illustrated with reference to the studies of individual centres. One of the earliest studies of Calcutta by A.K. Ray (1902) takes up the city in legend, tradition and literature and also dwells on its morphology, population, and trade

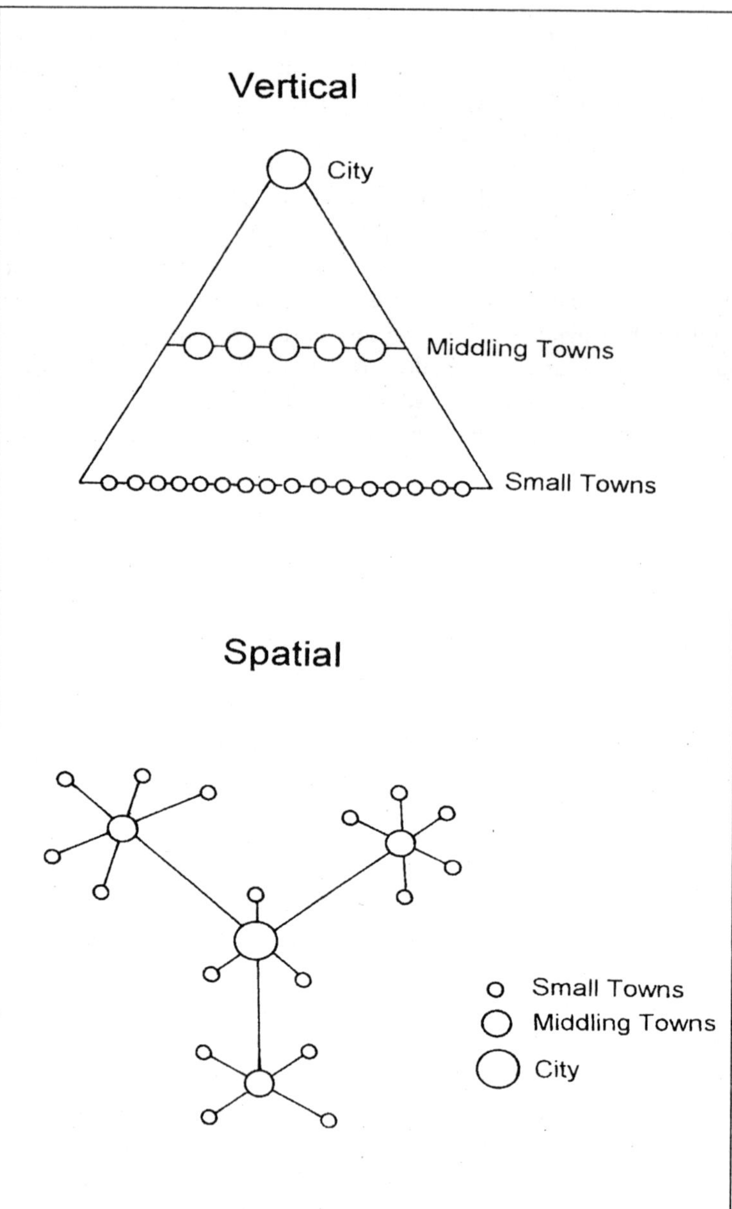

Figure 1.1: Urban Pyramid: Theoretical

as a port. In his work on Benares (1933), E.B. Havell describes the city, its *ghats*, temples and sacred wells in the context of Hinduism. In an altogether different approach, D.R. Gadgil (1965) is interested particularly in the population, employment, migration, occupational structure, and housing of Sholapur. A. Mitra (1970) looks at Delhi in terms of its historical evolution and physical, demographic, economic, and social growth. R. Nath (1977) focuses only on the architecture and monuments of Agra. Surendra Gopal's monograph on Patna (1982) describes the people, festivals, fairs, literature, painting, calligraphy, and trade in the city. As narratives mostly of disparate urban aspects, the concerns in these works do not extend to the pattern and process of urbanization, or to variations over time.

The works dealing with the processes of urbanization have a wider perspective and are interdisciplinary in character. Among such studies focusing on recent centuries may be mentioned that of Ahmedabad by Kenneth L. Gillion (1968), Delhi by Narayani Gupta (1981), Lucknow by Veena Talwar Oldenburg (1984), and Burdwan by Indrani Ganguly (1987). They cover the changing physical and human aspects of urban centres over time in relation to the interrelated influences of geography, economy and polity, specifically bringing out the bearing of colonial rule. Anthony D. King dwells on the theoretical aspects of colonial urban development (1976). The interaction between the theoretical and the empirical in a north Indian situation is particularly evident in Narayani Gupta's *Delhi Between Two Empires 1803–1931*. After tracing the history of the city from the end of the Mughal period to the aftermath of the uprising of 1857, she dwells on the subsequent changes in its administration and morphology, and the various aspects of its society which turned Delhi in to a new entity, psychologically as well as physically. These changes are linked to the changing social and political milieu and the character of the urban government. Gupta's study is based on a considerable number of primary sources, including the records of the Delhi Municipality, the Chief Commissioner's Office, the local Christian missions, and contemporary newspapers in English and Indian languages, in addition to the official records of the departments of Home, Internal Trade, Education, and Local Self-Government.

The third category of studies are mainly in the form of articles on specific aspects like morphology, demography, social structure, occupational structure, social mobility, and city administration in a particular town or group of towns. Their focus on a specific aspect brings out the role of that particular variable in the process of urbanization. Such studies are included largely in the collections of incisive essays on different facets of the urban phenomena in the subcontinent. The bulk of these essays pertain to the bearing of colonial situation on urban economy and life.[30] To illustrate, M.J. Mehta's essay on Ahmedabad in the nineteenth century shows how the British policies arrested the urban potentialities of the city and ruined its traditional industry. The British did create certain infrastructural facilities in the form of the modern means of communication and transportation, but mainly to serve their own economic needs and not to aid the traditional manufactures.[31] On the other hand, Indu Banga's essay shows how Karachi as a port and a city grew in direct relation to the growing wheat trade of the Punjab which got linked to the global economy under colonial rule.[32] Serious studies of individual centres, groups of urban units, particular urban regions, and specific urban aspects as well as conceptual issues have enriched our understanding of the processes of urbanization in India. Also, the programmes of the Urban History Association of India (UHAI) have made a significant contribution towards drawing attention to this relatively new area of historical research. Founded in Amritsar and presently based in Chandigarh, the impact of the UHAI has been felt both at the pan-Indian and regional levels.

III

The beginning of the study of urbanization in the Punjab region goes back to the late 1960s.[33] The pioneering study of Amritsar by V.N. Datta (1967) broke fresh ground in a comprehensive approach to this important urban centre. The next decade saw the study of some other individual urban centres like Sarhind (1972), Faridkot (1976), Amritsar (1977), and Patiala (1981)—all edited by Fauja Singh. By and large, these studies exhibit the 'biographical approach' which is 'primarily narrative and descriptive, tracing the history of the town through time, pausing on noteworthy events, noteworthy persons, and places of historical interest'.[34]

A different, and distinctly integrated and interdisciplinary approach to urban studies is first noticed in the study of Batala by J.S. Grewal (1975) who, as mentioned earlier, later became the founder-secretary of the UHAI. Somewhat misleadingly titled *In the By-lanes of History*, this seminal work is based on literary sources, judicial documents, inscriptions, and fieldwork. While analysing the process of urban growth of Batala during the sixteenth and seventeenth centuries, the author traces the morphology of Batala, its demographic history, its economic activities, and its linkages with the immediate hinterland and the region. The life in the town is reconstructed in terms of its social structure, occupations, social relations, and cultural scene. The study of Batala is related to the geography of the area, and the polity and economy of the times. In another study, J.S. Grewal brings out the bearing of religion and politics on the growth of Amritsar (1981) and its rise into the foremost city of the region. The relevance of polity and economy for the process of urbanization in the Punjab is underlined by Indu Banga with reference to the Upper Bari Doab (1981). Ravinder Kumar (1997) analyses the texture of urban society and politics in Lahore in 1919. In addition to several essays including those by the present author, there are full-length studies of Amritsar by A. Gauba (1988) and of Jalandhar by Kanchan Jyoti (1988).

Two aspects of the work done so far on the urban history of the Punjab may be pointed out. Essentially interdisciplinary in nature, these studies facilitate a better understanding of the history of the region in its political, social, economic and cultural spheres and bring out the linkages of the region with other parts of the country. Furthermore, a recent collection of essays (2005) breaks out of the constraints of conventional periodization. Stretching from the Harappan to the contemporary times, the sixteen contributions to this volume cover facets of urbanization in the broad north-western region. They are based on a variety of sources and informed by a diversity of perspectives. Five of these essays, including one by the present author (jointly with J.S. Grewal), focus on the colonial period, relating it, at the same time, with the pre- and post-colonial times.[35]

While attempting to take the story further within the historical specificities of the Punjab region, the present study postulates a close connection between urbanization as a process and the colonial situation as a totality.[36] Colonialism 'as a power relationship enforced by an alien culture',[37] reached its apogee under the Crown (1858–1947), following the uprising of 1857–8. The Punjab entered the scene during this last century of colonial rule. It probably bore the maximum impact of the interplay between political and military domination and the processes of industrialization, capitalism, and Westernization, tinged with the modernizing and evangelizing impulses, and a deepening of the racial line.

The cities and large towns of the Punjab region became the spearhead of the new political, military, economic, and cultural penetration, with significant implications for urban society. There were alterations in the size and structure of the urban population, hierarchy and distribution of urban centres, and their physical forms and buildings. The traditional pattern of urban functions and interaction with the countryside were reoriented. A new framework for cultural domination, social control and governance was introduced in urban areas through the systems of education and health, printing presses, municipalities, and other cultural and political institutions. Merely responding, initially, to the new environment and stimuli, the people, particularly in cities and large towns, eventually came to have their own social, cultural and political institutions whose concerns increasingly diverged from those of the colonial state. To appreciate the nature and magnitude of change thus brought about, the present study begins with the pre-British background and the colonial context in the Punjab.

NOTES

1. Kingsley Davis, 'Foreword', in Jack P. Gibbs (ed.), *Urban Research Methods*, New Delhi: Affiliated East West Press, 1966, p. xiv.
2. Harold Carter, *The Study of Urban Geography*, London: Arnold Hienemann, 1972, p. 26.
3. R. Ramachandran, *Urbanization and Urban Systems in India*, New Delhi: Oxford University Press (OUP), 1997, p. 10.
4. Louis Wirth, 'Urbanism as a Way of Life', *The American Journal of Sociology*, vol. XLIV, no. 1, July 1938, p. 8.
5. The changing behaviour pattern in the urban sphere, according to Louis Wirth, includes the following features: heterogeneity and segregation of population; breakdown of caste boundaries; weak or absent folk tradition; superficial, anonymous and transitory social relations; and reliance on formal control mechanisms. Ibid., pp. 8–24. Also, H.J. Gans, 'Urbanism and Suburbanism as Ways of Life', in R.E. Pahl (ed.), *Readings in Urban Sociology*, Oxford: Pergamon, 1969, pp. 95–118.

6. See, for example, Aidan Southall (ed.), *Urban Anthropology: Cross-Cultural Studies of Urbanization*, New York: Oxford University Press, 1974, pp. 3–14.
7. Carter, *Study of Urban Geography*, p. 29. Also, Ramachandran, *Urbanization and Urban Systems*, pp. 10–11.
8. For example, Kshama Goswamy, *Nagarikaran aur Hindi Upanyas* (Hindi), Delhi: Jayashri Prakashan, 1981, pp. 65–269. In fact, the author sees a direct connection between urbanization and the development of the novel as a mature literary form. Ibid., pp. 30–64.
9. R.P. Mishra, *Million Cities of India*, Delhi: Vikas, 1978, p. 15. Also, Ramachandran, *Urbanization and Urban Systems*, pp. 7–9.
10. Ashish Bose, *Studies in India's Urbanization, 1901–71*, New Delhi: Tata McGraw Hill, 1973, p. 5.
11. Ramachandran, *Urbanization and Urban Systems*, pp. 12–13.
12. Mishra, *Million Cities of India*, p. 16.
13. Ibid., pp. 22–74, as an illustration of this approach to 'the history of urbanization'.
14. This is noted, for example, by Henry Pirenne, *Medieval Cities*, New Jersey: Princeton, 1969, p. 58.
15. Emrys Jones, *Towns & Cities*, London: Oxford University Press, 1966, p. 7.
16. Alcaeus of Lesbos, a Greek poet (*c.* 600 BC), described the city as 'not the house finely roofed nor the stones of walls well builded, nay canals and dockyards make the city but men able to use their opportunity'. Quoted in Pahl (ed.), *Readings in Urban Sociology*, p. 3.
17. Bert F. Hoselitz, *Sociological Aspects of Economic Growth*, Delhi: Amerind Publishing Company, 1975, p. 104.
18. In his 'Treatise on the Causes of the Magnificence and Greatness of Cities' Giovanni Botero defines a city as 'an assembly of people, a congregation drawn together to the end that they may thereby live better at their ease in wealth and plenty'. Quoted in G.S. Ghurye, *Cities and Civilization*, Bombay: Popular Prakashan, 1962, p. 4.
19. This has been emphasized particularly by Fernand Braudel. See Satish Chandra, *Fernand Braudel on Towns*, Occasional Papers Series 11, Chandigarh: Urban History Association of India, 1992, pp. 4–5.
20. Factors influencing the urban processes have been underlined by historians and other social scientists. See, for example, Kingsley Davis, 'The Origin and Growth of Urbanization in the World', *American Journal of Sociology*, vol. XL, no. 5, March 1955, pp. 429–37. D.R. Gadgil, *The Industrial Evolution of India in Recent Times 1860–1939*, New Delhi: Oxford University Press, 1979, pp. 145–9. Pranabranjan Ray, 'Urbanization in Colonial

Situation: Serampore', in M.S.A. Rao, (ed.), *Urban Sociology in India*, New Delhi: Orient Longman, 1974, pp. 119–50. Ian J. Kerr, 'Urbanization and Colonial Rule in 19th Century India', *Panjab Past and Present*, vol. XIV, pt. I, April 1980, pp. 210–24.

21. This formulation put forth by human ecologists has been developed into a model by Stanley K. Shultz: 'An Approach to a Theory of Urbanization', in J.S. Grewal and Indu Banga (eds.), *Studies in Urban History*, Amritsar: Guru Nanak Dev University (GNDU), 1981, pp. 8–17.
22. This approach is evident in the author's first research publication entitled, 'Polity, Economy and Urbanization: Early 19th Century Punjab', *Journal of Regional History* (*JRH*), vol. IV, 1983, pp. 56–72. Cf. Shultz, 'An Approach to a Theory of Urbanization', pp. 15–16.
23. Gerald Breese, *Urbanization in Newly Developing Counties*, New Delhi: Prentice Hall of India, 1978, pp. 32–6.
24. Quoted in Satish Chandra, *Fernand Braudel on Towns*, p. 5.
25. Braudel, quoted in ibid., p. 4.
26. For the application of the idea of an 'urban pyramid' to historical study, see Ravinder Kumar, 'The Changing Structure of Urban Society in Colonial India', *Indian Historical Review*, vol. V, nos. 1–2, 1978–9, pp. 201–4.
27. A theoretical construct of the urban pyramid is presented in Figure 1.1.
28. An idea of the growing field of urban history can be had from the bibliographies published by the Urban History Association of India, Amritsar/Chandigarh: *Newsletter 1*, pp. 1–35; *Newsletter 3*, pp. 11–28; *Newsletter 4*, pp. 12–21. Indu Banga (ed.), *The City in Indian History*; rpt., New Delhi: Manohar/UHAI, 2005, pp. 279–95. Idem (ed.), *Ports and Their Hinterlands in India (1700–1950)*, New Delhi: Manohar/UHAI, 1992, pp. 375–9.
29. For further detail on works included in this historiographical review, see the Bibliography given at the end of the book.
30. For some of these collections refer to note 28 above. Also, J.S. Grewal and Indu Banga (eds.), *Studies in Urban History*, Amritsar: GNDU, 1981; Makrand J. Mehta (ed.), *Urbanization in Western India (Historical Perspective)*, Ahmedabad: Gujarat University, 1988. Then there are collections on urbanization in the wider context of colonialism, such as Robert Ross and Gerard J. Telkamp (eds.), *Colonial Cities*, Dordrecht: Martinus Nijhoff Publishers for the Leiden University Press, 1985; and Dalip K. Basu (ed.), *The Rise and Growth of the Colonial Port Cities in Asia*; rpt, Berkeley: University of California Press, 1983.
31. M.J. Mehta, 'Business Environment and Urbanization: Ahmedabad in the 19th Century', in *Studies in Urban History*, pp. 123–34.
32. Indu Banga, 'Karachi and its Hinterland under Colonial Rule', in *Ports and Their Hinterlands in India (1700–1950)*, pp. 337–58.

33. For details on works listed in this section see Bibliography.
34. S.C. Misra, 'Urban History in India: Possibilities and Perspectives', in *The City in Indian History*, p. 4. Misra goes on to say that 'in an earlier age, such studies were undertaken as a labour of love, the tribute of proud devoted citizens to their city. In more recent times they have been supported by city authorities and other public bodies'. An early example of this kind of work is Syed Muhammad Latif's *Lahore—Its History, Architectural Remains and Antiquities*, published in 1892.
35. Reeta Grewal (ed.), *Five Thousand Years of Urbanization: The Punjab Region*, New Delhi: Manohar/Institute of Punjab Studies, 2005. The authors of the remaining four contributions are Indu Banga, Surya Kant, J.S. Rahi, and Kusum Chopra, Atiya Habeeb Kidwai and Subhash Marcus, representing among themselves, the disciplines of history, geography, literature, economics and development studies.
36. For some idea of the characteristics of urbanization under colonial rule, see in particular Anthony D. King, *Colonial Urban Development: Culture, Social Power and Environment*, London: Routledge & Kegan Paul, 1976, pp. 22–96. Idem in 'Colonial Cities: Global Pivots of Change', Robert Ross and Gerard J. Telkamp (eds.), *Colonial Cities*, pp. 7–32. Also Georges Balandier, 'The Colonial Situation: A Theoretical Approach', in Immanuel Wallerstein (ed.), *Social Change: The Colonial Situation*, New York: John Wiley, 1966, pp. 34–61.
37. King, 'Colonial Cities', p. 27.

2

The Pre-Colonial Background and the Colonial Situation

The British established their paramountcy over the kingdom of Lahore in 1846 and annexed it in 1849. After the decline of the Mughal empire, this region had seen the emergence of a large number of new centres of power, particularly under the Sikhs, followed by their absorption into the expanding state of Ranjit Singh (1780–1839) in the early nineteenth century. The new state stretched across the Punjab plains from the river Sutlej to Peshawar and also extended into the hills and Kashmir. It covered the whole of the Mughal provinces of Lahore and Kashmir and parts of the provinces of Multan and Kabul. The urbanscape in this vast regional state under Ranjit Singh became substantially different from what it had been under the Mughals only a century earlier.[1] This urbanscape was qualitatively altered in the colonial situation during the late nineteenth and early twentieth centuries. This chapter identifies the relevant aspects of the new context that had a close bearing on urbanization and traces its antecedents in the immediately preceding period.

The early nineteenth-century background can be gleaned through the eyes of Ganesh Das, a Wadera Khatri and a hereditary *qanungo* of Gujrat in the Chaj Doab, that is the interfluve between the rivers Chenab and Jhelum.[2] He wrote his *Char Bagh-i Panjab* in 1849 at the behest of the new rulers of the Punjab, tracing the history of the region, and providing extremely valuable data on its polity and society in the pre-British period.[3] In the course of his topographical description of each of the five *doabs*, which at times reads like a gazetteer, Ganesh Das throws light on the urban situation, particularly how it was affected by political change, and provides information on aspects of life in cities and towns that distinguished them from the villages around.

I

Generally, Ganesh Das was sure about the difference between a rural and an urban settlement.[4] He uses three terms for his urban centres: *qasba*, *shahr* and *balda*. The term *shahr* is used by him for more than 30 urban centres. However, for many of these, for instance Kunja and Gujrat, he uses the term *qasba* as well. On the whole, it appears that Ganesh Das uses both these terms primarily to distinguish urban centres from villages.[5] In any case, it cannot strictly be maintained that he uses the term *qasba* for a town and *shahr* for a city. Nevertheless, he has his own way of indicating the size of urban centres by using the term *qasba* for a middling town and *shahr* for a middling city, along with using terms like *qasba-i-khurd* (a small town), *qasba-i-kalan* (a large town), *shahr-i-khurd* (a small city), and *shahr-i-kalan* (a large city). For a very large city, he uses the term *balda*.

In the territories covered by the former Mughal province of Lahore, with which Ganesh Das tends to equate his 'Punjab', there were only two cities *par excellence* (*bulad-i-kalan*): Amritsar and Lahore. Outside this area, he uses the term *balda* for Peshawar and Multan. The number of *shahrs* and *qasbas* mentioned by him in the *Char Bagh* is more than 90. Over 60 of these were situated in the three *doabs* of Sindh Sagar, Chaj and Rachna. Only about 20 of these were situated in the *doabs* of Bari and Bist Jalandhar. In all probability, the number of urban centres in these two *doabs* was larger than the number that can be listed on the basis of the *Char Bagh* alone.[6]

Ganesh Das did not look upon his towns and cities as unchanging entities. They were subject to decline and decay. The city of Attock, for instance, lay deserted in his days.[7] The small city of Ban had become a village, and the town of Buchcha was no more an urban centre.[8] In some cases, Ganesh Das indicates the cause of decline or decay. The city of Daulatnagar declined because many of its inhabitants migrated to the new township of Gujrat founded by Akbar.[9] The city of Aurangabad was lying deserted since 'the inception of the Khalsa rule'.[10] The Khalsa sacked the city of Sialkot and razed its mansions to the ground: 'Its houses were deserted and its population was dispersed'.[11] The town of Sodhra lay depopulated since the beginning of Sikh rule in the last quarter of the eighteenth century, and the population of Wazirabad dwindled for the same reason.[12] On the whole, thus, the decline of some urban centres could be attributed to political change.

Conversely, the revival of certain urban centres could also be ascribed to political change and state policy. Sialkot presented an interesting example of repopulation by its conquerers—Sardars Jiwan Singh, Sahib Singh, Natha Singh Shahid and Mohar Singh Atariwala.

> All these four from amongst the Sikhs occupied the city and the fort of Sialkot and turned their attention to populating the city. They divided the city of Sialkot amongst themselves, covering each locality, lane and shop. They brought back the dispersed people to rehabilitate the town. In Sammat 1865 [AD 1808] Maharaja Ranjit Singh besieged and occupied the fort and forcibly seized the town from its masters. He reconstructed and repaired the towers, the old wall and the fort. He reassured the people and gave dresses of honour to prominent persons, and caused the place to be populated.[13]

The revival of Wazirabad could be attributed to Sardar Gurbakhsh Singh and his son Jodh Singh who 'repopulated the city and it became a flourishing place again'. In the time of Ranjit Singh, one of his European officers, Avitabile, as the governor of Wazirabad, built a new quarter (*katra*), widened its bazaar, and added to the beauty of the town according to his taste.[14] The best known example of revival was that of Lahore.

> During the invasions of Ahmad Shah and the upsurge of the Khalsa as the Singhs, the city of Lahore became totally deserted. The twelve localities which were outside the city wall were razed to the ground and in the nine localities inside the city wall only a few mansions survived. However, when the chiefs of the Khalsa came into possession of Lahore, they paid attention to populating the city and induced people of various places to settle down here. When this capital city fell into the hands of Maharaja Ranjit Singh, new impetus was given to its development. The fort, the towers, the royal mansions, the octagonal tower and the throne were all beautified to a high degree. The city wall which had been built by Akbar was repaired in Sammat 1870 [AD 1813]. The residents of the city were thus made safe against thieves. Furthermore, a ditch, battlements and many *deodis* [*sic*] adjoining the gates were constructed to add strength to the city.[15]

Nobles and officials of the state purchased large houses (havelis) or plots from their proprietors to build beautiful mansions, adding much to the busy life of the city. Ranjit Singh repaired the Shalamar Bagh, and many a noble laid out his own garden, enabling Ganesh Das to list about 40.[16]

The relevance of the actions of rulers and members of the ruling class to the fortunes of urban centres can be seen in some other cases also. Haripur in the Hazara area, for instance, was founded by Hari Singh Nalwa, the well-known general of Ranjit Singh, as an administrative centre, with the fort of Harkishangarh adjoining the 'city' to serve as a garrison post (thana).[17] The fortunes of Gujrat came to be linked with Sardar Gujjar Singh who adopted it as his capital, 'giving encouragement and satisfaction to people from all places'.[18] Eminabad owed some of its palatial buildings and splendid gardens to those of its inhabitants who rose to be eminent administrators. Diwan Moti Ram, Ram Dayal and Kirpa Ram, the illustrious descendants of Diwan Mohkam Chand, built 'many fine buildings and tanks and laid out gardens' in Kunja.[19] A much more conspicuous example was that of Amritsar. With the coming of Sikh rule many a man of consequence founded a *katra* or separate locality in his own name around the original town of Ramdaspur. The new rulers of the Punjab were keen to construct rest houses (*bungas*) of their own around the sacred tank (*amritsar*). During the reign of Ranjit Singh, a wall with towers and *deodhis* was built around the place, enclosing all the *katras*. 'It thus became a single city.' Ranjit Singh built the fort of Gobindgarh for his residence and laid out the garden palace of Ram Bagh for his comfort. Following his example, many of the nobles laid out their own gardens within and outside the wall. The city came to be known as Amritsar, and served as the second capital of Ranjit Singh.[20]

If some of the old urban centres suffered due to the indifference of the new rulers of the Punjab during the late eighteenth and the early nineteenth centuries, some others gained due to their policies and measures. There were still others which acquired the status of towns for the first time during this period. Rawalpindi, for example, was a small village before Sardar Milkha Singh adopted it as his headquarters. 'Since he was considerate of the well-being of its inhabitants, traders and merchants and other people came from various places and settled here.'[21] Gujranwala was a small village before it was adopted by Sardar Charhat Singh as his capital. 'It then became a large town.' In the reign of Ranjit Singh, Hari Singh Nalwa, added to the population and prosperity of Gujranwala. 'He laid out a garden, constructed a tank and built new *samadhs* of the ancestors of Maharaja Ranjit Singh and made them places of reverence.'[22] Dera Baba Nanak rose to be an urban centre because of its association with Guru Nanak and the residence of his descendants at that place. 'People come for pilgrimage to the place of Guru Nanak and give offerings', observes Ganesh Das.[23]

What was common to Dera Baba Nanak and Gujranwala was the presence of Khatris and *sahukars* who in Ganesh Das's presentation provide the economic backbone to an urban centre. Amritsar, for example, grew into 'a city of distinction' when it became the centre of commerce for the traders of all countries. Like the Khatris of Lahore, merchants from many countries adopted Amritsar as their home, and no other city in the Punjab was so large now as the city of Amritsar.[24] The artisans were as important for an urban centre as traders and shopkeepers. The town of Gujrat was marked by the presence of artisans who were 'skilful in all kinds of crafts'. Its blacksmiths made swords of good quality.[25] Dinga was transformed from a village into a town when its headman (*muqaddam*) 'brought Khatris and others, particularly craftsmen, from all over to populate the place'.[26] Similarly, Jalalpur rose to be a town when its zamindar, who was also the revenue farmer (*ijaradar*) of Gujrat and Herat, succeeded in bringing to this place 'Khatri families of all classes and craftsmen of all kinds'.[27]

Indeed, Ganesh Das appears to give considerable importance to the manufactures of his towns. Kunja and Bajwara were famous for turbans known for their exceptional whiteness.[28] Miani was a gift of the salt mines, known appropriately as Lun-Miani. Salt was sold in this town and custom was levied on it.[29] Sahiwal was known for its *salus* and fine vessels of copper and brass.[30] Chiniot was known for the excellence of its bow-makers.[31] Paper of fine quality and great variety, all white and clean and durable, was manufactured in the suburbs of Sialkot. It was also known for its embroidery work. 'The Bhabra women use coloured silken threads on white cloth to embroider floral pattern of excellent artistic quality. The weavers of Sialkot make very fine *susi* cloth of all varieties in green and blue and they weave fine *lachas* and *lungis*.'[32] The context of manufactures makes the references to artisans and craftsmen in the pages of the *Char Bagh* rather significant. The city of Lahore, for instance, had its Khatris, its merchants and its *sahukars*, but it also had a large number of 'craftsmen of many subcastes, both Hindu and Muslim'.[33] The reference to 'subcastes' here is in fact a reference to their different skills and occupations.

However, the affluent traders and merchants contributed much more to the striking morphology of their towns than the craftsmen. The leading *sahukars* of Gujrat, for instance, dug tanks and step wells (*baolis*) and constructed temples for the use of the people as 'memorials' for future generations.[34] This was in addition to their own mansions and gardens. Pasrur had its wealthy traders who left similar 'memorials' behind.[35] The *sahukars* of Amritsar were extremely rich, like Rama Shah Bania and Samadju, the Kashmiri. They all left 'memorials' behind in the form of tanks and gardens, besides their mansions (havelis).[36] The collaterals of Ganesh Das built impressive mansions and laid out spacious gardens in Sialkot.[37] It is in this context that Ganesh Das's references to Khatris and *sahukars* become significant. Wazirabad was the abode of Khatris of 'almost all subcastes', and there were many *sahukars* and wealthy merchants in the city.[38] Chiniot too had many Khatris, and among its *sahukars* were many Khojas and Parachas.[39] Shahdara had several rich *sahukars*.[40] Among the merchants of Bhera, Qutbuddin and Imam Bakhsh were men of wealth and their business was flourishing.[41]

Polity and economy did not exhaust the factors which contributed to urbanization and urban life before the advent of British rule in the Punjab. Raja Gulab Singh, as the administrator of Gujrat in the reign of Ranjit Singh, built a temple of Mahadev in Dinga and it became 'a place of worship for the Hindus'.[42] Wazirabad had the honour of having a *sati* whose *samadh* on the road to Gujrat was 'a place of worship for the people of Hindustan'. The 'city' was also marked by a number of dharmsalas and temples, and there were a number of *khanqahs* and *mazars*.[43] Jhelum had a number of places associated with Hindu worship.[44] Makhad was associated with Jogi Birandi Nath, and Bhera was associated with Pir Dhiraj Nath and Pir Azam Shah, apart from its reciters of the Koran who enjoyed revenue-free lands.[45] Eminabad had the *khanqah* of Sayyid Mansur 'who was famous for his austerities'.[46] The *khanqah* of Shah Burhan in Chiniot was a place of pilgrimage, like the tomb of Mian Barkhurdar in Pasrur.[47] Naina Kot had the *samadh* of Ram Kaur, an Udasi, which served as a place of pilgrimage, and Shahdara was associated with Shah Husain, 'a pearl among the men of miracles'.[48]

The largest cities of the Punjab had also the largest number of religious places. There were many temples called Shivdwaras and Thakurdwaras in Lahore. There were many *khanqahs* too which were associated with *walis* and fakirs and which had become centres of pilgrimage. The oldest among these was the *khanqah* of Khawaja Ali al-Hujwiri, the chief of the fakirs, popularly known as Data Ganj Bakhsh. People thronged to his *mazar* on Fridays. Another place of pilgrimage was the mausoleum of Shah Abu al-Ma'ali. At the *mazar* of Madho Lal Husain a large fair was held every year. The beautiful mausoleum of Hazrat Mian Mir was another place held sacred. Equally popular was the edifying place of Chajju Bhagat.[49] The city of Amritsar was studded with places of worship. There were many temples, *akharas* and gurdwaras. The foremost among these was the Har Mandir or the Golden Temple. It was 'the most important centre of pilgrimage for the Sikhs of Guru Nanak'. They visited the Har Mandir every morning and evening. 'On two occasions every year people come here for worship in unusually large numbers: the day of the Waisakhi and the night of the Diwali.'[50]

The towns and cities of the Punjab had their men of letters and learning too. The learned men of Gujrat included scholars of Islamic Law. There were poets, hakims and masters of composition in the city.[51] The well-known Punjabi poet Ahmad Yar was a resident of Jalalpur, and there were poets of Persian and Hindi also in the town. It had its masters of composition and calligraphy. The eunuch Baru of Jalalpur was 'unrivalled' in the art of dancing.[52] The 'city' of Sialkot had its men of letters and learning, its masters of composition, its men of medicine, its mathematicians, and its philosophers.[53] Many a learned man of Wazirabad cultivated the science of astronomy, mathematics, philosophy and medicine, and the arts of composition and calligraphy.[54] Qazi Zainuddin and his son Qazi Ali Asghar Hasni in Eminabad had earned distinction in medicine as well as law.[55] In Amritsar, Bhai Sant Singh Giani was a great exponent of the Granth Sahib, and Bhai Buddh Singh was a distinguished poet.[56] Shahdara had a peculiar kind of cultural attraction. It had the mausoleum of Jahangir known for its aesthetic beauty.[57]

The reliance on Ganesh Das for the early nineteenth-century background is not because he is the only contemporary writer who gives information on urban centres, but because he gives the most authentic information and a flavour of his times, largely based on first-hand knowledge. In his description, the urban centres of the early nineteenth-century Punjab do not come out as mere conglomerates, but as centres of flourishing economic life and noteworthy learning and piety, patronized by the new rulers and their ruling class.

Ganesh Das's evidence can be supported by two kinds of studies based on a variety of contemporary sources. One of these relates to the town of Batala in the Upper Bari Doab, outlining its history up to the middle of the nineteenth century.[58] The other is the unpublished M. Phil. dissertation of the author relating to the Punjab as a whole during the early-nineteenth century.[59] There are a few essays too which are relevant,[60] but these two studies sufficiently reinforce the evidence presented by Ganesh Das on the pre-colonial background.

II

Before turning to the specific context of colonial rule for urbanization in the Punjab, the impressionistic statements of Ganesh Das may be compared with the figures available for the population of his 'cities' and towns in the earliest census taken by the British in 1855. Amritsar, his premier city, had indeed over 120,000 persons while Lahore had a population less than 95,000 in 1855. The population of the 'cities' of Sialkot, Gujranwala and Rawalpindi ranged between 20,000 and 15,000 persons. However, Jalandhar and Batala, about which Ganesh Das did not know as much as about the urban centres of the Chaj and Rachna Doabs, had a population of more than 25,000. The population of some of his other 'cities', like Gujrat, Bhera, Kasur, Jalalpur and Chiniot, ranged between 15,000 and 10,000. Interestingly, while Ganesh Das's 'town' of Pind Dadan Khan had more than 13,000 persons in 1855, his 'city' of Sahiwal had a population of less than 10,000. Some of his other 'towns', like Jhelum and Miani, had about 6,000 persons each. A place like Kartarpur in the Jalandhar Doab, which is not mentioned by him as a town or a city, had a population of over 11,500 in 1855. Nurmahal, similarly, had over 8,800 persons.[61] Thus, in terms of population, Ganesh Das was not always clear about the status and the relat ive positions of his urban centres (Figure 2.1).

Considering the opportunities available to him for observation and collecting information, the number of urban centres enumerated by Ganesh Das in the former Mughal province of Lahore is nonetheless remarkable (see Appendix 2A). Even in the first detailed census of 1881 the number of urban centres, including a large number of towns of the lowest class, in corresponding districts was only about 90. This number was almost the same 60 years later, in the census of 1941. It

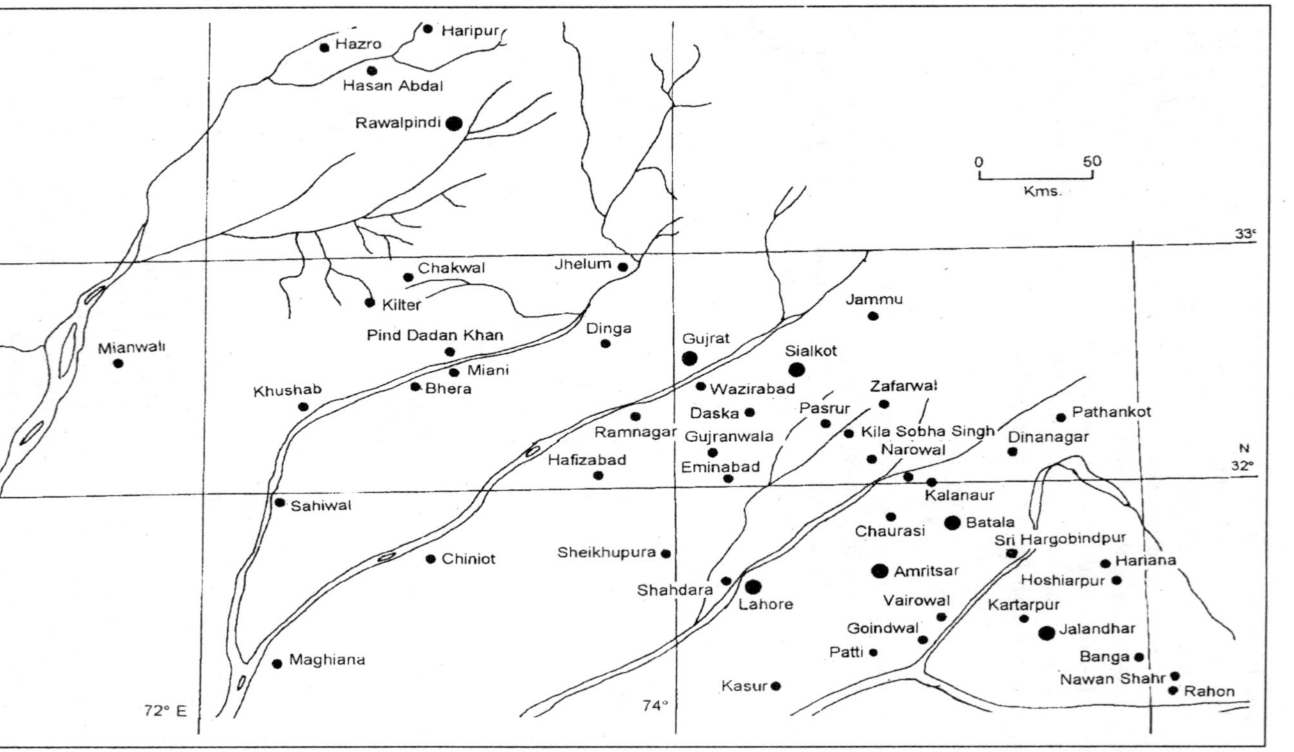

Figure 2.1: Towns and Cities of the *Char Bagh*: Early-Nineteenth Century

would be wrong to assume, however, that there was no change in the pattern of urbanization in this part of the Punjab under colonial rule. Merely the number of urban centres is no safe indicator of urbanization. The size of population, the relative position of urban centres and their location become as important as their number in a study of urbanization.

A comparison between some of the urban centres common to Ganesh Das and the census of 1855 would show that their population and relative position did not remain the same under the British. For example, the population of both Amritsar and Lahore increased considerably during this period, but it increased more in the case of Lahore than in the case of Amritsar, and consequently, their relative positions also changed. Both these cities came to have a population of about 150,000 each in 1881. In 1931, however, Lahore had nearly 430,000 persons whereas Amritsar had only about 265,000. Thus, Lahore emerged as the largest city of the colonial Punjab. The population of Rawalpindi shot up from 16,000 in 1855 to nearly 120,000 in 1931; and that of Sialkot shot up from about 20,000 to over 100,000. They became, respectively, the third and the fourth largest cities in the province in 1931. Jalandhar, in contrast, became the fifth largest urban centre in 1931, down from its third position in 1855, though its population increased nearly three times. The increase in the population of Batala during this period was rather small; it remained less than 34,000 in 1931, registering a decline in its relative position over the period. The population of Pind Dadan Khan and Sahiwal decreased from 1855 to 1931. Gujranwala and Miani retained their relative positions through the period, but the population of Miani increased by only a few hundreds and that of Gujranwala by tens of thousands. This change in the pattern of urbanization defies any monocausal explanation, though it may be safe to assume that the colonial context cumulatively had a bearing on the process as well as the pattern of urbanization in the region.

III

The colonial context may be outlined in terms of politico-administrative, economic and cultural changes after annexation. Initially, the Punjab was enlarged as a politico-administrative unit and placed in the larger context of the British empire. The province encompassed the plains between the rivers Yamuna and Indus, besides a large part of the Western Himalayas and plains and hills across the river Indus. Delhi territory, including parts of the present Haryana area, was added after the uprising of 1857–8. Nearly 40 princely states of different sizes were politically attached to the province. The process of contraction began when the state of Jammu and Kashmir was placed directly under the Government of India in 1877. In 1901, the North-West Frontier Province (NWFP) was created by separating five districts placed under a Chief Commissioner. In 1911, the city of Delhi with a surrounding enclave was separated from the Punjab to accommodate the imperial capital. The Punjab became smaller by more than 3,15,000 sq km. Still, it had an area of about 3,47,000 sq km. The British territory, excluding the princely states, covered about 2,52,000 sq km. This territory was more than double the area covered by the Punjab of Ganesh Das[62] (Figure 2.2).

The British territory in the Punjab was divided into tahsils, districts and divisions for the purpose of administration (see Appendix 2B). Generally, four or five tahsils constituted a district and five or six districts formed a division. After excluding the NWFP and Delhi, there were 5 divisions, 28 districts and 114 tahsils in the Punjab province, giving the average of about 5.5 districts for a division and about 4 tahsils for a district. Subsequently, in 1919, Sheikhupura district was created, taking the number to twenty-nine.[63] The basic unit of administration in the pre-British times in the Punjab was the pargana which in the early nineteenth century was synonymous with the 'taluka'. The number of such units in the territory covered by the British districts was several hundreds.[64] Evidently, the British district was many times larger than the earlier administrative unit at the secondary level. In fact, every district was constituted by combining a number of former parganas or talukas. Therefore, the near equivalent of the former pargana in size was actually the British tahsil. Even the average tahsil was larger than the average pargana. An average British district covered 5,500 to 7,800 sq km, and contained 1,000 to 2,000 villages.

Even the princely states attached to the province attempted to conform broadly to the territorial subdivisions in the British administered area. For instance, the whole of the Patiala State, covering an area of about 14,000 sq km and equal to about two British districts, was divided into 5 *nizamats* which consisted of 16 tahsils. Thus, the area of a *nizamat* on an average was less than half the area of a British district and the

Figure 2.2: The Coloniai Punjab: Political

average area of a Patiala tahsil was less than half the area of a British tahsil. The Nabha State, extending over an area of less than 2,600 sq km, was divided into three *nizamats*, with an average area less than that of a British tahsil. This was partly due to the fact that the territories of the Nabha State were more scattered than those of Patiala. In the large state of Bahawalpur, by contrast, a *nizamat* covered over 13,500 sq km, equal to about two British districts. But it was a semi-desert and sparsely populated area. On the whole, the relatively larger urban centres in a princely state served as *nizamat* headquarters and the smaller ones as tahsils.[65]

In the British territory, the existing large towns and cities which had facilities and services required by the new rulers were chosen as administrative headquarters. Such centres were located in all parts of the Punjab region and included, among others, Lahore, Amritsar, Jalandhar, Multan, Peshawar, Rawalpindi, Gujrat, Jhelum and Karnal. Some of the towns were comparatively small, but their location dictated selection as district headquarters, notably Hoshiarpur, Panipat, Bannu, Kohat, Jhang, Attock and Rohtak. The British also laid out new towns like Lyallpur, Montgomery, Gurdaspur and Gurgaon to specifically function as the administrative centre of the district. All the district headquarters served as tahsils, and some of them served as divisional headquarters. Other tahsils were established in small urban centres like Phillaur, Nakodar, Palwal, Pasrur, Ramnagar, Haripur, Dadri, Miani, Dipalpur and Kaithal.[66] More important than the size was the nature of functions and the number and kind of personnel employed at the administrative headquarters.

Three main branches of administration evolved in the Punjab by the early twentieth century: executive, revenue and judicial. At the head of all these three was the Lieutenant Governor. On the executive side, he had under him Commissioners, Deputy Commissioners, Assistant and Extra-Assistant Commissioners, Tahsildars and Naib Tahsildars. On the revenue side, there were Financial Commissioners above the Commissioners. For the administration of justice, there was the Chief Court with its Divisional and Sessions Judges, assisted by District Judges, Subordinate Judges and Munsifs. To a considerable degree, however, the three branches of administration were dovetailed. All the executive officers mentioned above performed revenue duties as well. The Deputy Commissioners and Tahsildars performed judicial duties also in criminal cases. The Assistant and Extra-Assistant Commissioners and Naib Tahsildars performed judicial duties in both the civil and criminal spheres.[67] This structure continued throughout the period, with the difference that under the Government of India Act of 1919, the Lieutenant Governor was replaced by the Governor and the Chief Court by the High Court. At the district level, the Deputy Commissioner was assisted also by the Superintendent of Police, Civil Surgeon and the Inspector of Schools. The Financial Commissioners looked after departments and aspects related to revenues and other resources.[68] The basic administrative structure through which colonial rule came to impinge on the people by the beginning of the twentieth century is presented in Figure 2.3:

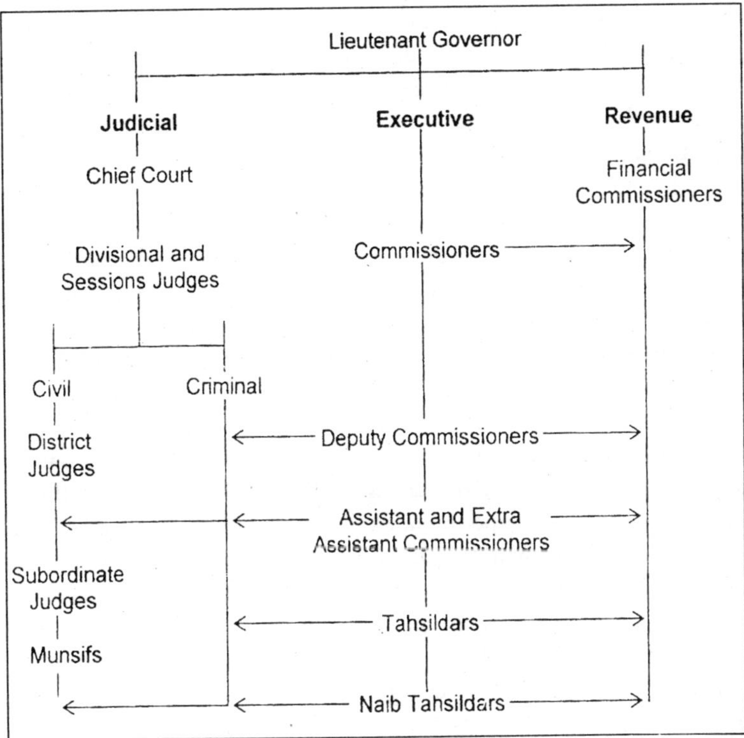

Source: Sir James Douie, *The Panjab, North-West Frontier Province and Kashmir*; rpt., Delhi: Low Price Publications, 1994, p. 213.

Figure 2.3 : Structure of British Administration before 1919

Much of the administrative personnel continued to be concentrated at the district headquarters.[69] In the divisional headquarters and the capital city of the province this concentration was even larger. Several of these centres also housed substantial cantonments. This 'centralization' of administration and military authority had a direct bearing on the character and growth of towns and cities. An important aspect of the colonial polity was enlargement in the sphere of governance and corresponding proliferation in government departments. The Government of India had in the province the departments of railways, post and telegraphs, customs and accounts, including income tax. The principal departments of the provincial government dealt with roads and buildings, irrigation, police, education, health and forests, the last having been mentioned already. In due course, electricity was added to the Public Works Department. For local administration or local self-government, municipalities of different grades were created in a large number of urban centres, more than 180 before 1900; and the offices of district boards were also located in the district headquarters. The departments of agriculture, cooperative societies and industries were created in the twentieth century. The system of jails too became important with time.[70]

It is relevant to add that the capital city, the divisional and district headquarters and, to a much smaller extent, the tahsil headquarters came to have in-residence administrative personnel who did not belong to the three branches of administration already mentioned. Thus not to talk of Lahore which had the largest concentration of the government departments, Multan came to have the headquarters of the Forest Division, and also had offices of the Railway Traffic Superintendent, Superintending Engineer of Canals, Superintendent of Post Offices, Inspector of Schools, Superintendent of Canals as well as the Executive Engineer of Military Works. Lyallpur had, among others, a Colonization Officer, Extra Colonization Officer, Superintending Engineer of Executive Division and Irrigation, Superintendent of Post Offices and Sub-Divisional Officer of Revenues. Among the small urban centres, Gurgaon had the Horse Breeding Department; Mianwali had offices of the Assistant of Customs Patrol, and Kahror housed the Assistant Engineer of Canals; Rewari had the offices of the Assistant Traffic Superintendent of Railways; and Pinjaur came to have the headquarters of the Conservator of Patiala State Forests.[71]

The new administration was made possible largely by the new means of communication and transportation which were needed for military and commercial purposes as well (Figure 2.4). The main lines of railways were developed before the end of the nineteenth century: between Lahore and Amritsar in 1862; between Lahore and Multan in 1865; between Amritsar and Delhi in 1870; and between Lahore and Peshawar in 1883. Lahore was also linked with Karachi. Branch lines from Lala Musa, Gogera and Campbellpur converged on Kundian near Mianwali and from there a single line ran along the Indus to join the trunk line to Karachi at Sher Shah near Multan. Delhi was linked with Karachi through Samasata in the south of Bahawalpur, and also through Rewari and Merta. There were three alternative routes from Delhi to Lahore: up to Ambala through Karnal or Saharanpur, and then from Ludhiana through Jalandhar or Ferozepore. For strategic considerations, Rawalpindi was linked with Kohat with a bridge over the Indus at Khushalgarh. For administrative purposes, Ambala was linked with Simla through Kalka, and Amritsar was linked with Pathankot. Different lines converged on Khanewal for the export of enormous quantities of wheat and cotton from the canal irrigated tracts to Karachi.[72]

The extension of railways in the twentieth century was meant primarily to forge linkages for the export and import of goods for trade, though these lines promoted passenger traffic as well. For example, Amritsar was linked with Dera Baba Nanak, and Dera Baba Nanak with Jassar. Shahdara was linked with Narowal, and Narowal with Jassar. Batala was connected with Kadian, Chak Jhumra with Chiniot, and Lyallpur with Jaranwala. Sarhind was linked with Ropar, Kasur with Pakpattan, and Pakpattan with Mailsi. Bahawalpur was linked with Fort Abbas. A narrow gauge line linked Pathankot with Joginder Nagar. By 1912, there were 6,400 km of railways in the Punjab. In the 20 years following, about 2,400 km were added, partly to double a few main lines, but largely to connect small towns with the main lines.[73] The networking of towns and cities through the railways created an indirect link between the productive countryside of the Punjab on the one hand and the cities outside the province, especially the ports (Figure 2.4).[74]

The railways were the carriers *par excellence* of heavy goods and long distance passengers. The annual average of persons travelling by railways in the region in the 1920s was well over 817 million. The quantity of goods carried was even more significant. To Karachi alone in 1930–1,

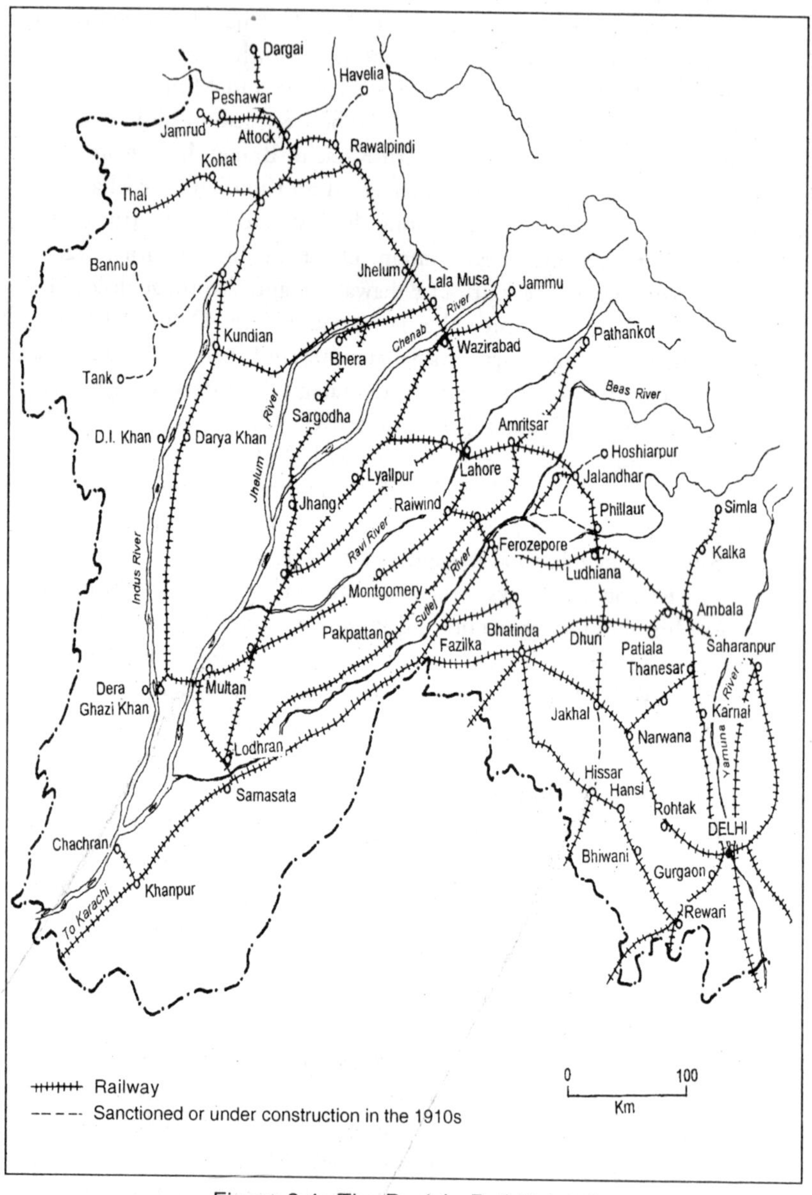

Figure 2.4: The Punjab: Rail Network

for instance, were sent over 384,000 tons of wheat, nearly 208,000 tons of other grains, and about 190,000 tons of cotton. In addition to these were sent hides and skins, bones, wool, and several other items in smaller quantities. The value of foreign trade of the Punjab by the 1920s was equally noteworthy, being nearly Rs. 3 billion a year on an average.[75]

There was no serious competition between the railways and the roads till the end of colonial rule. They supplemented or complemented each other (Figure 2.5). The roads were meant primarily for short distance passengers and light goods. The most important metalled road to be completed was the Grand Trunk Road from Calcutta to Peshawar. The stretch from Delhi to Karnal had been built before the annexation of the kingdom of Lahore. The stretch from Karnal to Lahore was completed before 1857–8. Lahore was linked with Peshawar in 1863–4; the road crossed the Indus near Attock. Peshawar was linked with Kohat, Bannu and Dera Ismail Khan. Ambala was connected by road with Kalka, and Kalka with Simla. A loop from Ludhiana linked it with Ferozepore, and Ferozepore with Lahore. Many other linkages were forged. By 1930, there were about 6,400 km of metalled roads in the Punjab. These were supplemented by more than 32,000 km of unmetalled roads. Consequently, nearly all the urban centres in the province got linked with one another. There were about 18,000 cars and lorries on the roads by 1930–1.[76] To roads and railways were added post and telegraph, bringing the towns and cities of the region metaphorically closer. On the whole, the colonial context created for a faster pace of change, particularly in the towns and cities.

One of the most important reasons for annexing the Punjab to the British empire was its potential for economic exploitation. The three most important planks of British agrarian policy in the province during the nineteenth century were recording of rights in land, periodic settlements of land revenue, and extension of agriculture through canals (Figure 2.6). In the long run, the last of these proved to be the most important. The 'magnificent system' of canals came to be looked upon as one of 'the greatest achievements of British rule' in the Punjab.[77] Already, before the annexation of the kingdom of Lahore, the Delhi and Hansi branches of the Western Jamna Canal had been completed. Both these branches were remodelled in the 1890s when the Sirsa Branch was opened for irrigating parts of the districts of Karnal and

Figure 2.5: The Punjab: Road Network

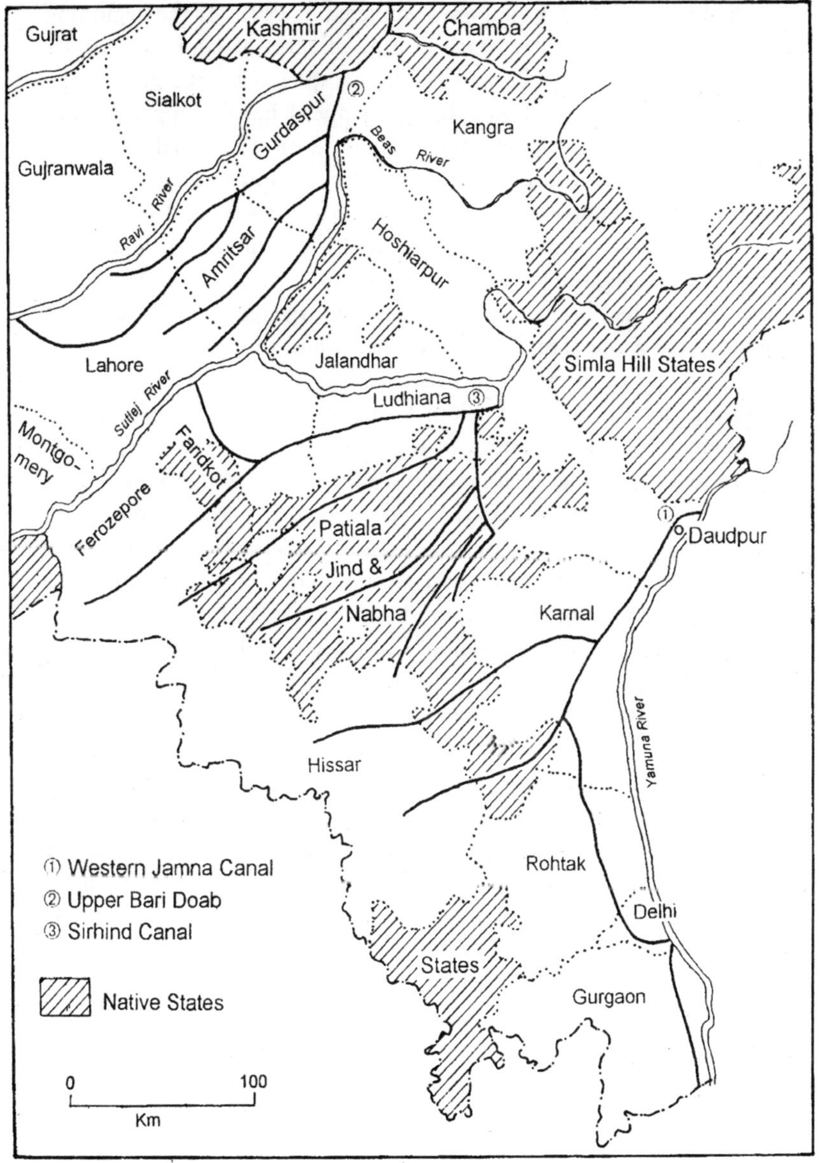

Figure 2.6: The Punjab Canals: Eastern

Hissar. By then, the Upper Bari Doab Canal had proved to be a great success, and work on the Sirhind Canal had been completed.

The Lower Chenab Canal was completed in 1905. At the beginning of the twentieth century, nearly 6 million acres of land were under canal irrigation in the Punjab. To be completed by the end of the second decade were the Lower Jhelam, Upper Chenab, Upper Jhelam, and the Lower Bari Doab Canals (Figure 2.7). The canal irrigation schemes undertaken but not completed in the inter-war period were known as the Sutlej Valley, Haveli and Thal Projects. In 1930–1, the area under canal irrigation was about 12.5 million acres which rose to around 14 million acres by the end of colonial rule.[78] By this time, nine colonies had been set-up in the newly irrigated areas.[79] Vast areas of cultivable waste came under cultivation and thousands of new villages came into existence which needed the services of urban centres.

Thanks to the nature of colonial economy, industry lagged behind commerce. The manufactures in towns and cities of the Punjab suffered a setback during the nineteenth-century due mainly to the British policy of taking out raw materials and importing finished goods.[80] Before long, however, new industries began to develop in subordination to the needs of the metropolitan economy, like cotton ginning and baling. By restraining the transfer of agricultural land to the non-agriculturists, the Punjab Alienation of Land Act of 1900 obliged many an urban moneylender to seek new fields for investing his surplus wealth. A beginning had been made in modern banking in 1895 with the foundation of the Punjab National Bank. More swadeshi banks and insurance companies came up in the next decade and a half to add to the foreign banks in the region.[81] An increasing number of factories were established during the twentieth-century as a result of change in the policy of the government after World War I for reasons of 'political expediency, economic advantage and military security'.[82] Under the Act of 1919 industry became a provincial subject and steps were taken to promote the setting up of factories.[83] Consequently, between 1921 and 1931 the number of factories rose from 297 to 647, and more followed.[84] The new factories were located almost entirely in towns and cities, which made significant difference to the character as well as the size of the urban centres.

The cultural fall out of the colonial situation in the Punjab was the sizeable presence of Christian missionaries who looked upon the Punjab

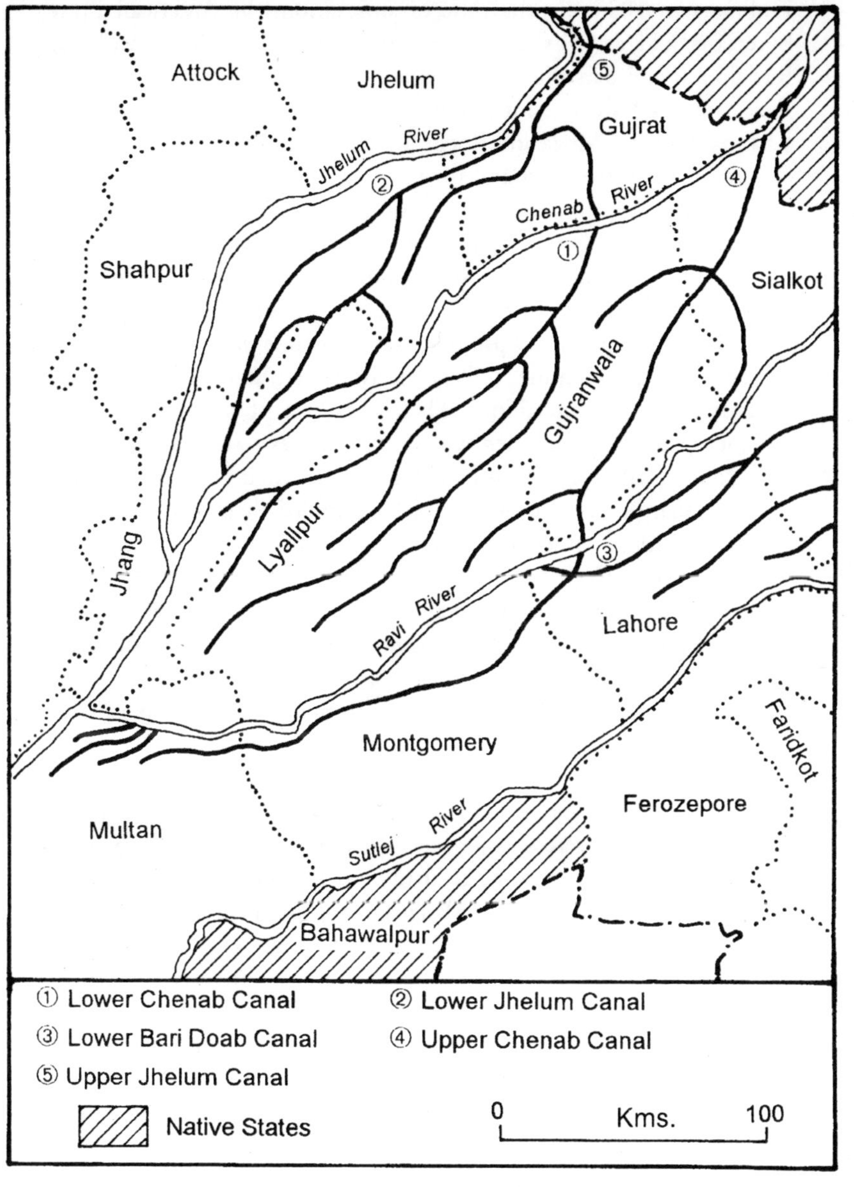

Figure 2.7: The Punjab Canals: Western

region as a test case for the spread of Christianity.[85] The first to come was the American Presbyterian Mission which began its activities in Ludhiana in 1834. By the time of annexation, the American Presbyterians had established centres at Lahore, Jalandhar, Ambala, Rawalpindi and Sabathu in the Simla hills. In the next half a century they came to have missions at Ferozepore, Kapurthala, Hoshiarpur, Khanna, Phillaur, Moga and Ropar. By the beginning of the twentieth-century, many more cities and towns came to have the mission organizations belonging to another half a dozen denominations.[86]

The main objective of the missionaries was evangelical. They chose to concentrate initially on the towns and cities, because they aimed at influencing the leaders first. The mission compounds, houses, schools and colleges, hospitals, and printing presses became the symbols of their presence and programme.[87] They received tacit, and often tangible, support from the officialdom. Their criticisms of the Indian socio-religious practices, combined with initial successes in winning upper class converts alarmed the urban Punjabis. In their effort to counter the missionaries, the educated Punjabis founded their own socio-religious associations which replicated the institutions and strategies of the missionaries.[88]

Western education was integral to the cultural context of colonial rule. The humanistic underpinnings notwithstanding, the missionaries had initiated the process of the spread of education primarily to obtain converts, and the government followed suit mainly to obtain personnel for the middle and lower rungs of administration and public forces. In due course, government Anglo-vernacular schools came to be established in the large urban centres and most of the small towns.[89] In addition, the municipalities were encouraged to maintain or aid schools within their jurisdiction.[90] It became clear to all that education embedded in Western knowledge and English language was indispensable for upward mobility in the colonial context. In view of the growing popularity of the missionary schools among the upcoming Punjabis, and their increasing exposure to Christianity, provision of culturally 'safe' English education became the dominant concern of the voluntary associations established by the educated Punjabis under the Societies Registration Act 1860.[91] By the early twentieth century, the cities and large towns came to have institutions of higher education affiliated to the University of the Punjab, established at Lahore in 1882. The new education, aided by the growing use of the printing press, contributed towards the emergence of a sizeable professional middle class both within and outside the government service.[92] The urban areas were the natural setting for the new middle classes.

With the emergence of the urban middle classes arose, finally, new socio-cultural ideologies which became the basis for political articulation in the province.[93] The British sought to contain the situation by creating a nominated legislative council in the Punjab for the first time in 1897. An element of election was introduced in 1909 for Muslims when the council was enlarged. The principle of election became far more prominent in 1919 when the franchise as well as the council was enlarged on a communal basis for Muslims and Sikhs. A few government departments were placed under responsible ministers, but much greater autonomy was given to the province in 1935, with a far larger increase in the number of voters. However, the number of urban voters remained much less compared to the rural voters.[94] This enabled the pro-rural Unionist Party to participate in constitutional politics and form the government in the Punjab until the elections of 1946.[95] Furthermore, the Punjabis participated in agitational politics, and the region had its share of militancy too. Cities and towns were also the cradle of communal tension and communal riots. Though the masses were sought to be mobilized in the countryside as well as the towns, the leadership in politics remained largely middle class and substantially urban.[96] The context for the present study may be summed up by saying that the urban centres were the matrix as much of colonial domination as of social change and Indian resurgence.

NOTES

1. J.S. Grewal and Veena Sachdeva, 'Urbanization in the Mughal Province of Lahore (*c.* 1550–1850)', in Reeta Grewal (ed.), *Five Thousand Years of Urbanization: The Punjab Region,* New Delhi: Manohar/Institute of Punjab Studies, 2005, pp. 107–27.
2. It may be of interest to know that it was the Mughal emperor Akbar who coined the name 'Chaj Doab' by joining the first letters of the rivers bounding this interfluvial tract. The remaining four *doabs* were also named by him in this manner as the Bist Jalandhar, Bari, Rachna, and the Sindh Sagar.

Finally, the name 'Punjab' as the land of five *doabs* (and six rivers, of course) was also given by Akbar. Indu Banga, 'Ecology and Land Rights in the Punjab', *Journal of Punjab Studies*, vol. 11, no. 1, Spring 2004, pp. 60 and 71 n. 5. For a concise description of the geography of the north-western region, see O.H.K. Spate and A.T. Learmonth, *India and Pakistan: A General and Regional Geography*, 3rd edn., London: Methuen, 1967, pp. 513–29.

3. Ganesh Das, *Char Bagh-i Panjab* (Persian), Kirpal Singh (ed.), Amritsar: Khalsa College, 1965. A section of this work providing rich social, administrative and topographical data has been translated and edited by J.S. Grewal and Indu Banga as *Early Nineteenth Century Panjab* (From Ganesh Das's *Char Bagh-i Panjab*), Amritsar: GNDU, 1975 (cited hereafter as *Char Bagh*).
4. It must, however, be pointed out that the difference between village and town does not always come out clearly in Ganesh Das's work. He refers to Lakhanwal in the Chaj Doab as 'a large village, almost a town'; some other places also appeared to be towns as well as villages. *Char Bagh*, pp. 68 and 88.
5. Ibid., pp. 56, 59 and 71. At places, Ganesh Das gives the impression that he was clear about the distinction between a *qasba* and a *shahr*. The *qasba* of Jalalpur, for instance, was 'almost a small city'. Ibid., p. 68.
6. The urban centres mentioned by Ganesh Das as *qasbas* and *shahrs* are given in alphabetical order in Appendix 2A.

   Ganesh Das admits that he did not possess adequate information about the Bist Jalandhar Doab. Based as he was in the Chaj Doab, it is not surprising that he fails to mention several towns of this *doab*, like Kapurthala, Sultanpur, Kartarpur, Nakodar, Mukerian and Hoshiarpur. There are indications that in some cases the term pargana is meant to convey the urban status of a place. Ganesh Das does not say so, but his information on the Bari Doab too is not very adequate. In any case, he fails to mention towns like Pathankot, Hargobindpur, Fatehgarh, Jandiala and Sujanpur. Whereas he can mention nearly 60 towns and cities in the other three *doabs*, he refers to only about a dozen in the Bari and Bist Jalandhar Doabs. It is almost certain, therefore, that the number of urban centres in the Punjab during the 1840s was larger than the number listed here on the basis of the *Char Bagh* alone. By the same logic, however, its information about towns in the Rachna, Chaj and Sindh Sagar Doabs can be taken to be generally reliable.
7. Ibid., p. 39.
8. Ibid., pp. 79 and 106.
9. Ibid., p. 53.
10. Ibid., p. 78.
11. Ibid., p. 83.

12. Ibid., pp. 92 and 93.
13. Ibid., p. 84.
14. Ibid., p. 93.
15. Ibid., pp. 115–16.
16. Ibid., pp. 116–17.
17. Ibid., p. 41. According to the biographer of Hari Singh Nalwa, the fort and the town were founded in AD 1822 Baba Prem Singh Hoti, *General Hari Singh Nalwa*, rpt., Ludhiana: Lahore Book Shop, 1937, pp. 166–7.
18. Ibid., p. 58.
19. Ibid., pp. 71 and 98.
20. Ibid., pp. 132–4.
21. Ibid., p. 42.
22. Ibid., p. 105.
23. Ibid., pp. 135–6.
24. Ibid., p. 133.
25. Ibid., p. 62.
26. Ibid., p. 67.
27. Ibid., pp. 68–9.
28. Ibid., p. 71.
29. Ibid., p. 72.
30. Ibid., p. 73.
31. Ibid., p. 109.
32. Ibid., p. 85.
33. Ibid., p. 122.
34. Ibid., pp. 58–9.
35. Ibid., p. 78.
36. Ibid., p. 134.
37. Ibid., p. 84.
38. Ibid., pp. 58–9.
39. Ibid., p. 109. The Khojas and Parachas were generally the Muslim converts from amongst the Khatris, Aroras and Bhatias who constituted the traditional mercantile communities in the Punjab region. They were 'fairly numerous' in Lahore, Sialkot, Gujrat and several other places in the Punjab For detail see J.S. Grewal, *Maharaja Ranjit Singh: Polity, Economy and Society*, Amritsar: GNDU, 2001, pp. 91–2.
40. *Char Bagh*, p. 111.
41. Ibid., p. 73.
42. Ibid., p. 67.
43. Ibid., pp. 95–7.
44. Ibid., pp. 45–6.
45. Ibid., pp. 47 and 73. Some Udasi 'dervishes' were enjoying revenue-free lands in Jalalpur. Ibid., p. 69.

46. Ibid., p. 99.
47. Ibid., pp. 78 and 109.
48. Ibid., pp. 76 and 111.
49. Ibid., pp. 118–22.
50. Ibid., p. 133.
51. Ibid., pp. 57–8.
52. Ibid., pp. 68 and 69.
53. Ibid., p. 87.
54. Ibid., pp. 96–7.
55. Ibid., p. 98.
56. Ibid., p. 134.
57. Ibid., p. 111.
58. J.S. Grewal, *In the By-Lanes of History: Some Persian Documents from a Punjab Town*, Shimla: Indian Institute of Advanced Study (IIAS), 1975, pp. 3–24.
59. Reeta Grewal, 'Polity, Economy and Urbanization: Early Nineteenth Century Punjab', M.Phil. dissertation, GNDU Amritsar 1983.
60. For example, the essays by J.S. Grewal, Indu Banga, Anand Gauba and the present author, listed in the Bibliography.
61. A list of selected urban centres from the census of 1855 is given below, with figures of population in brackets in the descending order:
    Amritsar (122,184), Lahore (94,143), Peshawar (53,294), Ludhiana (47,191), Jalandhar (28,422), Batala (26,208), Gujranwala (17,650), Dera Ghazi Khan (15,899), Rawalpindi (15,813), Gujrat (14,724), Bhera (13,913), Kasur (13,905), Pind Dadan Khan (13,588), Pindigheb (13,364), Jalalpur (12,369), Kartarpur (11,539), Maghiana (10,768), Nurpur (10,531), Sahiwal (9,437), Nurmahal (8,891), Ropar (7,110), Jhelum (6,060), and Miani (6,005).
    General Report on the Administration of the Punjab Territories, No. 6, Selections of Records of the Government of India, 1855.
62. Sir James Douie, *The Panjab, North-West Frontier Province and Kashmir*, rpt., Delhi: Low Price Publications, 1994 (cited hereafter as *Panjab, NWFP*), pp. 224–70. D.C. Verma and Sukhbir Singh, *Haryana*, 4th edn., New Delhi: National Book Trust, 2001, pp. 42–3. Since 1803, the Delhi territory had been attached with the North-West Provinces.
63. The administrative headquarters of the early twentieth-century are listed in Appendix 2B.
64. There were more than 230 parganas in the province of Lahore towards the end of the sixteenth century, and by the end of the seventeenth century their number was about 300. Veena Sachdeva, *Polity and Economy of the Punjab during the Late Eighteenth Century*, New Delhi: Manohar, 1993, p. 85. It may be pointed out that some urban centres were included in the

list of parganas or *mahals* as fiscal units. Nevertheless, even in the *Char Bagh* the number of parganas and talukas in the former province of Lahore is more than one hundred.

65. Douie, *Panjab, NWFP*, pp. 274–8 and 280–3.
66. Some of the tahsils were not in urban areas for reasons of convenience and practicability. For example, tahsil headquarters of Kharian, Phalia, Kadirabad, Mailsi, Lodhran, Sarai Sidhu, Ajnala, Mansehra, Terri, Hangu and Punahana, were not considered as towns during this period. Lodhran, however, became an important railway station on the way to Karachi.
67. The locally influential people were also associated with governance as Honorary Civil Judges. In 1922 their number was reported to be nearly 13,000. Sukhdev Singh Sohal, *The Middle Classes in the Punjab (1849–1947)*', Jalandhar: ABS Publications, 2008, p. 145, n, 115.
68. Douie, *Panjab, NWFP*, pp. 214, 215 and 216.
69. The Deputy Commissioner's office staff consisted of a Superintendent, Readers, Record Keeper, Deputy Record Keeper, Revenue Accountant, Superintendent of village accountants, and departmental clerks. The Superintendent Coordinated the activities of the English language and vernacular branches of the office. The tahsil offices were similar but smaller. J. Royal Roseberry, III, *Imperial Rule in Punjab*, New Delhi: Manohar, 1987, pp. 115–16.
70. Douie, *Panjab, NWFP*, pp. 216–18.
71. Based on *District Gazetteers*.
72. Douie, *Panjab, NWFP*, p. 130.
73. *Census of Punjab 1931: Report*, pp. 50–2.
74. For commercialization of agriculture and foreign trade, see Himadri Banerjee, *Agrarian Society of the Punjab (1849–1901)*, New Delhi: Manohar, 1982, pp. 47–76.

    The extensive rail net of the Punjab, fed by its roads, 'enabled Karachi to become the "natural port" for the immense grain production in the canal-irrigated tracts in the region'. Indu Banga, 'Karachi and its Hinterland under Colonial Rule', in Indu Banga (ed.), *Ports and Their Hinterlands in India (1700-1950)*, New Delhi: Manohar, 1992, p. 343.
75. *Census of India 1931*, pp. 40–1.
76. Ibid., 49-50. Also Douie, *Panjab, NWFP*, pp. 127–8.
77. Douie, *Panjab, NWFP*, p. 132.
78. *Census of India 1931*, pp. 38–40. See also, Imran Ali, *The Punjab under Imperialism, 1885–1947*, New Delhi: OUP, 1989, pp. 9–10.
79. For a list of the canal irrigation projects and colonies, Ali, *Punjab under Imperialism*, p. 9. Cf. Sukhwant Singh, *Agricultural Growth under Colonial Constraints 1849–1947*, Delhi: Manpreet Prakashan, 2000, pp. 102–9.
80. For colonial economy in relation to the Punjab, Richard G. Fox, *Lions of the*

Punjab: Culture in the Making, Berkeley: University of California Press, 1985, pp. 14–78.

81. For some detail: Sheena Pall, 'Lala Lajpat Rai and the Punjab National Bank', in J.S. Grewal and Indu Banga (eds.), *Lala Lajpat Rai in Retrospect: Political, Economic, Social and Cultural Concerns*, Chandigarh: Panjab University, 2000, pp. 40–50. Amiya Kumar Bagchi, *The Evolution of the State Bank of India: The Era of the Presidency Banks, 1876–1920*, New Delhi: Sage/State Bank of India, 1997, vol. II, pp. 236-7.
82. Secretary of State to the Governor-General, quoted in Harminder Singh, 'Industrial Development in the Punjab (1901–1947)', M. Phil. dissertation, GNDU, Amritsar, 1981, p. 188.
83. Ibid., pp. 187–225.
84. Ibid., p. 146 n. 2; *Census of India*, 1931, p. 41. For more information, see Chapter VI.
85. Hopes of an easy victory of the Punjab for Christianity were entertained on the bases of the impact of Sikhism [and Islam] and the frontier location of the Punjab region, with a large tribal and non-Brahmanical population which did not observe idolatory and caste restrictions. C.H. Loehlin, 'The History of Christianity in the Punjab', *The Panjab Past and Present*, vol. VII, pt. 1, 1973, pp. 208–10.
86. Ibid., pp. 218–19 and 224–7. John C.B. Webster, *The Christian Community and Change in Nineteenth Century North India*, New Delhi: Macmillan, 1976, p. 16.
87. Several senior administrators figure in the annals of the Church Missionary Society of the Church of England as 'Christian heroes in the Punjab' who regarded their work as 'a sort of civil lay mission', and contributed energy, funds, and land to the cause of Christianity. Loehlin, 'History of Christianity in the Punjab', pp. 210-11. See also, Kenneth W. Jones, *Arya Dharm: Hindu Consciousness in 19th Century Punjab*, New Delhi: Manohar, 1989; rep., p. 8.
88. J.S. Grewal, 'Christian Presence and Cultural Reorientation: The Case of the Colonial Punjab', *Proceedings Indian History Congress*, Calcutta: 1990, p. 537.
89. Amrit Walia, *Development of Education and Socio-Political Change in the Punjab 1882–1947*, Jalandhar: ABS Publications, 2005, pp. 26–55. See also, Surinder Kaur, 'British Policy Towards Education in the Punjab, 1849–1947', M. Phil. dissertation, GNDU, Amritsar 1981, pp. 1–22. B.S. Saini, *Social & Economic History of the Punjab, 1901–39*, New Delhi: Ess Ess Publications, 1975, pp. 141–76. For more information see Chapter 6.
90. For example, Anand Gauba, *Amritsar: A Study in Urban History (1840–1947)*, Jalandhar: ABS Publications, 1993, pp. 193–9. Also, Kanchan

Jyoti, 'Jullundur 1846–1947: An Urban History', Ph.D. thesis, GNDU, Amritsar, 1988, pp. 259–60 and 262–5.

91. Much of the educational activity of the Punjabis was inspired by the socio-religious movements initiated in the region by the leaders of the Brahmo and Arya Samajes, the Singh Sabhas and the Islamic Anjumans. For the educational concerns of these movements: Kenneth W. Jones, *Arya Dharm*, pp. 67–94; Ganda Singh (ed.), *The Singh Sabha and Other Socio-Religious Movements in the Punjab, 1850–1920, Punjab Past and Present* (*PPP*), vol. VII, pt. 1, 1973, pp. 68–9, 76–9, 86–94 and 110–24. Edward D. Churchill Jr. 'Muslim Societies of the Punjab, 1860-1890', *PPP*, vol. VIII, pt. 1, 1974, pp. 69–91.

92. Sukhdev Singh (Sohal), 'Professional Middle Classes in the Punjab', *Journal of Regional History*, vol. III, 1982, pp. 72–86. Idem, 'Emergence of the Middle Classes and Forms of Political Articulation', in Indu Banga (ed.), *Five Punjabi Centuries: Polity, Economy, Society and Culture*; rpt., New Delhi: Manohar, 2000, pp. 462–9.

93. For the process of social change and the emergence of new ideologies which became the basis of political articulation among the Sikhs, Hindus and Muslims, respectively: J.S. Grewal, 'The Making of the Sikh Self-Image before Independence', in P.C. Chatterjee (ed.), *Self-Image, Identity and Nationality*, Shimla: IIAS, 1989, pp. 187–200. Indu Banga, 'The Emergence of Hindu Consciousness in Colonial Punjab', in ibid., pp. 201–17. David Gilmartin, *Empire and Islam: Punjab and the Making of Pakistan*, Berkeley: University of California Press, 1988, pp. 73–107.

94. Under the Act of 1919, there were 13 urban constituencies against a total of 51 rural and 7 special constituencies. Under the Act of 1935, this number rose to 19 urban and 138 rural and 18 special constituencies. Kirpal C. Yadav, *Elections in Panjab 1920–1947*, New Delhi: Manohar, 1987, respectively Tables 4 and 8, pp. 11 and 16.

95. For the Unionist policies and measures, Raghuvendra Tanwar, *Politics of Sharing Power: The Punjab Unionist Party 1923–47*, New Delhi: Manohar, 1999, pp. 46–167.

96. This was despite the marked preference of the colonial state for the leadership of the landed classes. Moreover, even when the Unionist and Akali leadership had their support bases in the countryside, their spheres of activity tended to be urban. This was true of both legislative and agitational politics as gleaned, for example, from Satya M. Rai, *Legislative Politics and Freedom Struggle in the Punjab, 1897–1947*, New Delhi: ICHR, 1984, pp. 93–214.

APPENDIX 2A

Qasbas and *Shahrs* of Ganesh Das (in alphabetical order)

Ahmadabad, Ahmadnagar, Akhnur, Akya, Amritsar, Bahlolpur, Basoli, Batala, Bhera, Bhimbar, Bilaspur, Bishanpur, Chakwal, Chamba, Chiniot, Daud Khel, Dera Baba Nanak, Dera Ghazi Khan, Dera Ismail Khan, Dhan, Dinanagar, Dinga, Dipalpur, Diwal, Eminabad, Faridabad, Garjakh, Goindwal, Gujrat, Hafizabad, Haranpur, Hariana, Haripur, Hasan Abdal, Hazro, Helan, Jalalpur, Jalalpur Bhattian, Jalandhar, Jandiala Sher Khan, Jhelum, Kabula, Kalanaur, Kallar, Kalyana, Kasur, Khata, Khaun, Khewa, Sial, Khushab, Kila Sobha Singh, Kila Suba Singh, Kirana, Kullu, Kunja, Lahore, Machhiwara, Maghiana, Makhad, Mamdot, Mandi, Mauj, Miani, Mianwali, Muraliwala, Musa Khel, Nadaun, Nainakot, Narowal, Naunar, Nawan Shahr, Nurpur, Pakpattan, Pasrur, Patti, Pind Dadan Khan, Qadirabad, Rahela (Sri Hargobindpur), Rahon, Ralyala, Ramnagar, Rawalpindi, Riasi, Ropar, Sahiwal, Shahdara, Shahpur, Sheikhupura, Sialkot, Sodhra, Takht Hazara, Takht Pari, Talwan, Tulamba, Vairowal, Wal Sacharan, Wazirabad, and Zafarwal.

APPENDIX 2B

Administrative Headquarters (in alphabetical order)

The administrative status of a place during the period of British rule did not remain the same in all cases. For instance, Amritsar had the headquarters of a division from 1849 to 1884, but not afterwards. Similarly, Hissar enjoyed this status from 1858 to 1884. On the other hand, Lahore, Multan, Jalandhar and Rawalpindi served as divisional headquarters throughout the period. Batala was the headquarters of a district only up to 1852, yielding this status to Gurdaspur afterwards. Similarly, Gugera remained the seat of district administration from 1852 to 1865. Attock became the headquarters of a district in 1904, and Sheikhupura in 1919. Most of the places, however, retained their status as district headquarters throughout the British period. The districts of Hazara, Peshawar, Kohat, Bannu and Dera Ismail Khan constituted the North-West Frontier Province in 1901. The tahsil headquarters, including boundaries, changed more frequently than the divisional or districts headquarters. In 1931, for instance, five tahsils stood abolished and four new tahsils were created. Moreover, not all tahsil headquarters were in towns. While the change in the administrative status of a place affected its position for better or worse, an improvement or decline in the position of an urban centre became the criterion of change in some cases.

The administrative headquarters in the Punjab region (including North-West Frontier Province), are listed below and show the position in the first decade of the twentieth century. Both the district and divisional headquarters, including Peshawar as the headquarters of the NWFP, are given in capital letters. In addition, the headquarters of divisions and the NWFP are given in italics:

Ajnala, Alipur, *AMBALA*, AMRITSAR, ATTOCK, Ballabhgarh, BANNU, Batala, Bhakkar, Bhera, Bhiwani, Chakwal, Chiniot, Chunian, Daska, Dasuya, Dera (Gopipur), DERA GHAZI KHAN, DERA ISMAIL KHAN, Dharmsala, Dipalpur, Fatehabad, Fatehjang, Fazilka, FEROZEPORE, Firozepur (Jhirka), Garhshankar, Gohana, Gugera, Gujar Khan, GUJRANWALA, GUJRAT, GURDASPUR, GURGAON, Hafizabad, Hamirpur, Hansi, HAZARA, HISSAR, HOSHIARPUR, Isakhel, Jagadhri, Jagraon, *JALANDHAR*, Jampur, Jaranwala, Jhajiar, JHANG, JHELUM, Kabirwala, Kahuta, Kaithal, KANGRA, KARNAL, Kasur, Khangarh Dogran, Kharian, Khushab, KOHAT, Kulu, *LAHORE*, Leia, Lodhran, LUDHIANA, LYALLPUR, Mailsi, MIANWALI, Moga, MONTGOMERY, Muktsar, *MULTAN*, Murree, MUZAFFARGARH, Nakodar, Naraingarh, Nawan Shahr, Nuh, Nurpur, Pakpattan, Palampur, Palwal, Panipat, Pasrur, Pathankot, *PESHAWAR*, Phalia, Phillaur, Pind Dadan Khan,

Pindigheb, Rajanpur, *RAWALYPINDI,* Rayya, Rewari, ROHTAK, Ropar, Samrala, Samundri, Sargodha, SHAHPUR, Shakargarh, Sharakpur, Shorkot, Shujabad, SIALKOT, SIMLA, Sinawan, Sirsa, Talagang, Tarn Taran, Taunsa, Thanesar, Toba Tek Singh, Una, Wazirabad, Zafarwal, and Zira.

3

Pattern of Urbanization under Colonial Rule

Pattern of urbanization may be studied in terms of variations in the number, sizes, spacing, and interrelationships of towns and cities over time.[1] The development of new urban centres and the relative position of growing and declining towns underline the spatial dynamics of urbanization which was significantly altered in the colonial context. The urban pattern in the pre-colonial Punjab had been the result largely of the terrain, climate and the existing level of technology. The towns and cities were located mostly along trade routes and rivers, in the valleys of mountains, and at points of contact between the hills and the plains. The plain areas of the well-endowed upper *doabs* had the maximum concentration of urban centres in the early nineteenth century.[2]

At the time of the first detailed census of the British province of the Punjab in 1881, the cultivated areas in its sub-regions ranged from about 18 to about 60 per cent. In the mountainous zone of Kangra and the Simla hill states cultivation was scattered and inferior, covering about 10 to 14 per cent of the area. The submontane zone along the foothills, with ample rain and fertile soil, had nearly 70 per cent of its area under cultivation. The eastern plain had considerable rainfall, and between the Jhelum and the Sutlej, the area cultivated was over 85 per cent. The Sutlej-Yamuna Divide which had long been prone to droughts and famines had started receiving irrigation by this time. On the other hand, the western plain, separated by a meridian running through Lahore, continued to suffer from inadequate rain and occasionally saline soil which accounted for scarce cultivation largely confined to the river valleys.[3] The Salt Range tract had ample rainfall but cultivation was of inferior kind, covering barely 20 per cent of the tract. There was a corresponding variation in the density of population. In 1881 the submontane tract had 449 persons to a square mile (or 2.8 sq km), followed by the eastern plain with 296 persons. The Salt Range area had a density of 139 and the western plain had 82 persons to a square mile. The Himalayan zone was the least populated with 78 persons to a square mile.[4]

I

The distribution of urban centres in the Punjab during the late nineteenth-century largely corresponded to these natural divisions (Figure 3.1). In 1881, 'towns' were generally concentrated in the eastern plain, and closely aggregated in the Upper Bari and Bist Jalandhar Doabs.[5] In this zone were located also the two 'cities' of the region, Lahore and Amritsar, and most of the middling towns, such as Batala, Kasur, Jalandhar, Hoshiarpur, Ferozepore, Ludhiana, Ambala, and Karnal. Some urban centres were scattered in the Upper Rachna, Chaj and Sindh Sagar Doabs, and near the confluence of the rivers in the south-west. They were located largely along the rivers and were mostly small, with the exception of the middling towns of Peshawar, Rawalpindi, Gujrat, Sialkot and Multan.[6] The lower areas along the rivers Indus, Chenab and Jhelum had only a few urban settlements which formed a cluster of small towns near the confluence of the five rivers.

On the whole, the Himalayan tract had approximately 5 per cent of the total number of towns in the Punjab; the submontane had over three; the Salt Range tract had about 4 per cent; the western plain had about 35; and the eastern plain had over 52 per cent of the urban centres of the region.[7] Furthermore, the mountainous zone had only about 2 per cent of the urban population; the submontane areas slightly less than two; the Salt Range had over 3 per cent of the urban people; the western plain had over 28 per cent; whereas more than 64 per cent of the urban population lived in the eastern plain.[8] There was no exact correspondence between the number of urban centres, level of cultivation, and the proportion of people living in towns and cities of the sub-regions of the province.[9] The largest urban units were located in the eastern plain, and the smallest towns were in the mountainous and submontane zones. In terms of the concentration of urban centres, the eastern plain formed the maximum concentration zone; the submontane zone was an area of notable concentration; the western plain formed a

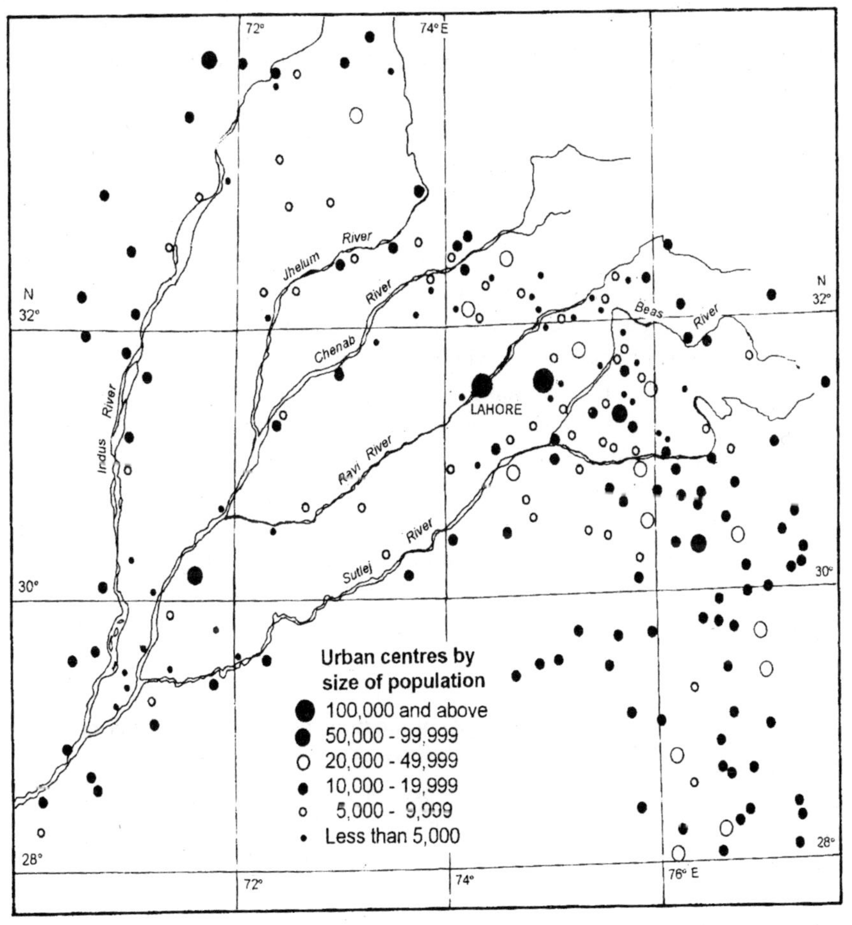

Figure 3.1: The Punjab: Distribution of Urban Centres, 1881

zone marked by relatively scarce and widely spaced units; and the central parts of the western plain, and the southern extreme of Bahawalpur, formed a zone of almost negative urbanization.

The pattern of urbanization became appreciably different in 1941 (Figure 3.2). The most striking variation was in the size of towns. The number and location of urban centres on the whole also changed. By this time, 'cities' with over a lakh of population came to be located not only in the eastern plain but also in the peripheral areas like Multan, Peshawar and Rawalpindi. In the eastern plain four more middling towns got upgraded as cities: Sialkot, Jalandhar, Ludhiana and Ambala. Urban centres sprang up in the newly irrigated western plain constituting the lower Bari, Rachna and Chaj Doab.[10] The towns in this region were confined no more to the river valleys. Among these new urban centres were the canal colony towns of Sargodha, Lyallpur, Montgomery, Toba Tek Singh, Gojra, Okara and Chichawatni. Nearly a score of new towns were in other areas where too irrigational facilities had been made available, most notably the Sutlej-Yamuna Divide. These new centres serving as *mandi* towns included Farukhnagar, Hodal, Abohar, Mansa, Jaito, Gidderbaha and Bhatinda.

Some small towns with even less than 5,000 population also came up just below the confluence of the rivers in the Bahawalpur state. With the addition of the cantonments, hill resorts, and the summer capital of Simla, the Himalayan zone now had 6.7 per cent of the urban units, 2 per cent more than the proportion in 1881; the submontane had only 1.65 per cent compared to an earlier 3.30, while the Salt Range tract had 4.37 per cent in place of 3.41 per cent.[11] The western plain had a much larger proportion now, at over 46 per cent. The corresponding proportion of urban centres in the eastern plain came down from over 52 to 41 per cent. On the whole, the relative proportion of towns and cities increased in the mountainous zone, the Salt Range tract and the canal irrigated western plain, and declined in the already well populated eastern plain and the submontane zone. The zone of maximum concentration was still the eastern plain, with over 57 per cent population; the western plain remained a zone of notable concentration with slightly over 35 per cent (Figure 3.3). The central areas of the Sindh Sagar Doab and a large part of Bahawalpur tract below the Sutlej remained negative zones with only a few urban centres.

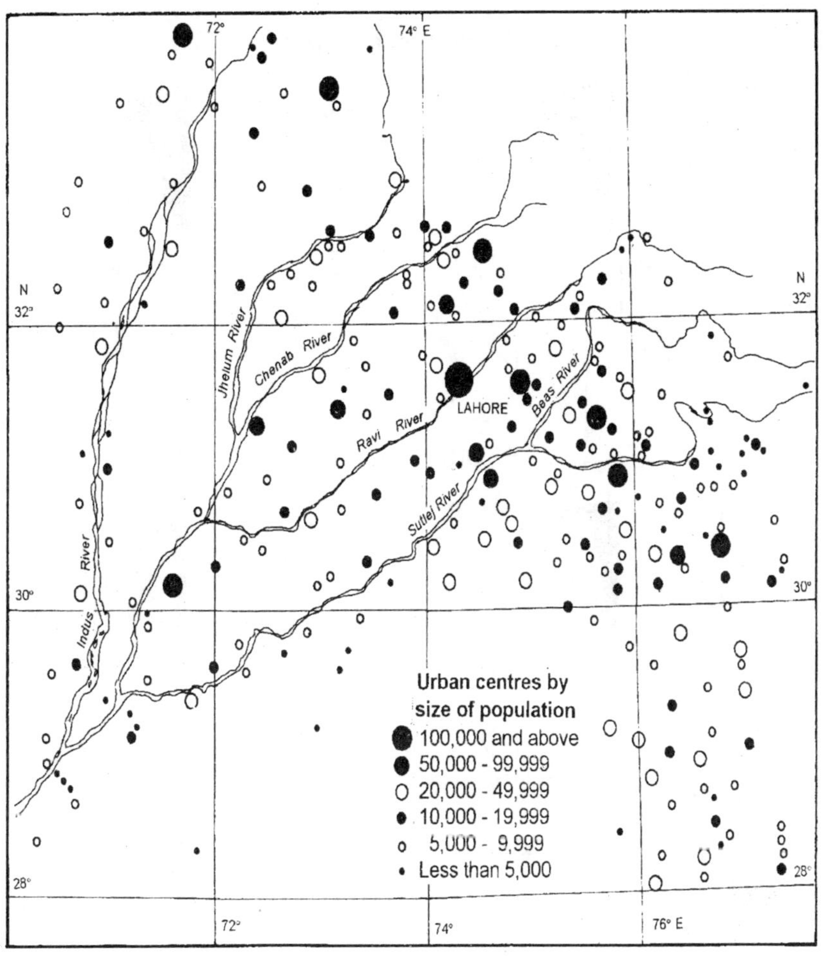

Figure 3.2: The Punjab: Distribution of Urban Centres, 1941

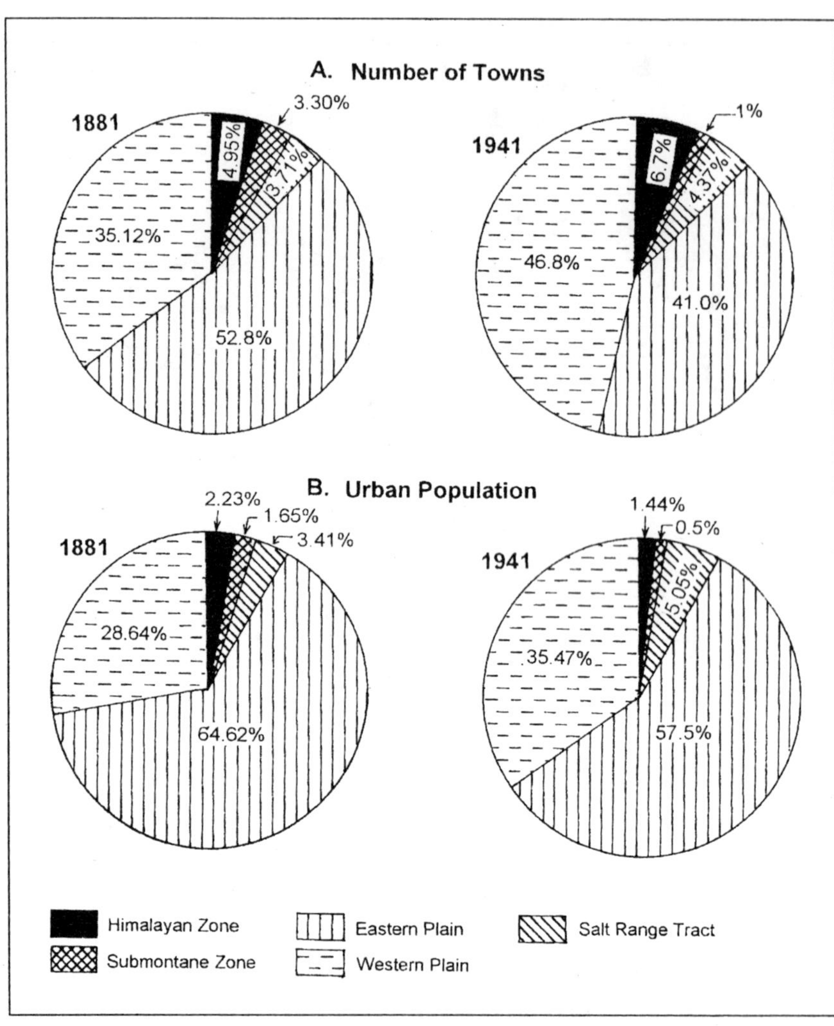

Figure 3.3: Proportion of Towns and Urban Population, 1881–1941

The total number of urban centres during this period witnessed an appreciable increase. Between 1881 and 1941, the number of towns increased from 240 in 1881 to 292 in 1941 (see Appendix 3A), though the urban units remained less than 1 per cent of the total settlements of the region, being 0.46 and 0.56 per cent respectively.[12] However, this increase had not been steady: the number went down to 220 in 1891, rose to 238 in 1901, fell to 208 in 1911, and further to 205 in 1921, and rose again to 249 in 1931.[13] It is interesting to note that in the 1880s there was one town for every 1540 sq km, whereas in 1941 this average was one for every 518 sq km.[14] Significantly, the total number of the formally designated 'towns' in the Punjab was smaller now than what it had been in the early nineteenth century.

II

In the Census Reports from 1881 to 1941, the 'town' included every municipality, civil lines and cantonment. In addition, every contiguous collection of houses inhabited by not less than 5,000 persons was deemed 'a town' by the provincial census superintendent.[15] On the criteria of predominantly non-agricultural character of population, relative density of dwellings, and importance of the place as a centre of trade, the overgrown villages stood excluded from this definition. The 'urban' places were classified into six categories on the basis of the size of population. Centres with over one lakh people were designated as cities, forming the class I category. Centres with 50,000 to 99,999 residents were categorized as class II towns. Class III towns had 20,000 to 49,000 people, and class IV units had 10,000 to 19,999 inhabitants. Class V towns had 5,000 to 9,999 persons, whereas places with less than 5,000 people, but with definite 'urban' elements like manufactures, communication linkages, and educational institutions, were categorized as class VI.

The number of urban settlements at each hierarchical level in the Punjab region changed considerably over time (see Figure 3.4). This is evident also from Table 3.1.

In 1881, there were only two 'cities' in the region; in 1941 there were nine, their proportion rising from less than 1 to over 3 per cent.[16] At the middling level, that is in classes II-III, the percentage rose from over 7 in 1881 to nearly 17 by the end of the period.

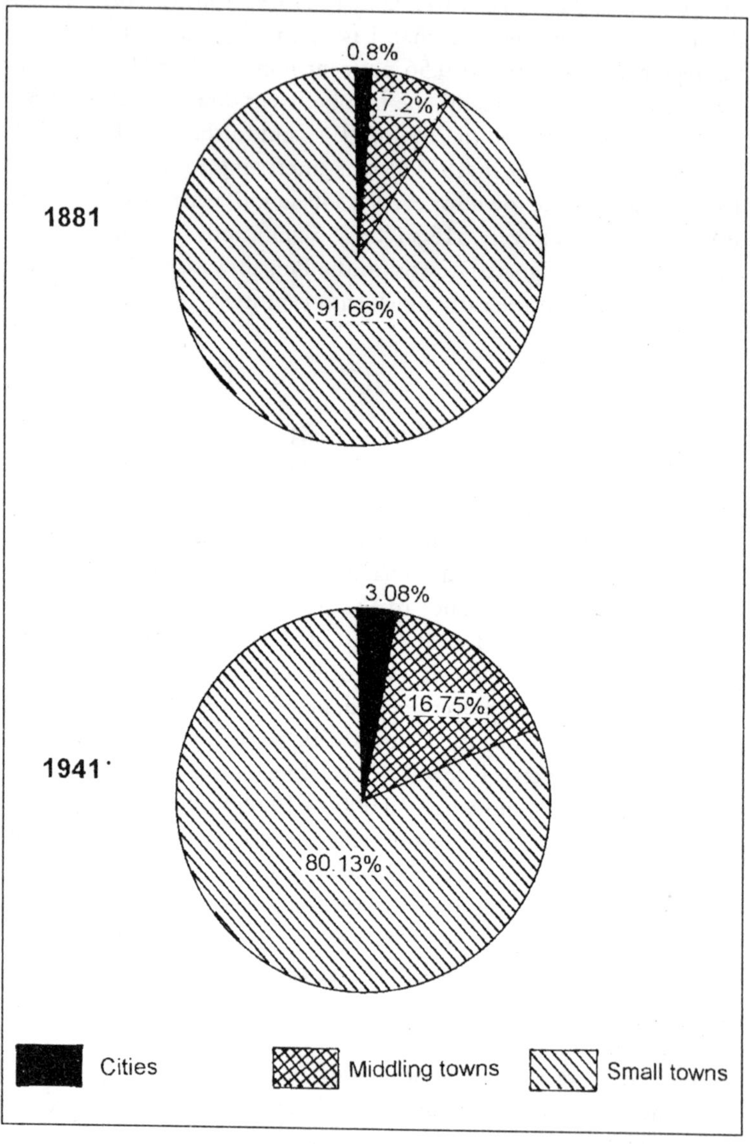

Figure 3.4: Proportion of Towns at Hierarchical Levels, 1881 and 1941

TABLE 3.1: NUMBER AND PROPORTION OF URBAN CENTRES, 1881–1941

Class	1881	1891	1901	1911	1921	1931	1941
Total Towns	240	220	238	208	203	249	292
I Number	2	2	2	2	2	6	9
% of Total	0.83	0.90	0.84	0.96	0.99	2.40	3.08
II Number	4	8	7	7	6	6	6
% of Total	1.66	3.63	2.94	3.36	2.96	2.40	2.05
III Number	14	15	15	17	23	27	43
% of Total	5.83	6.81	6.30	8.17	11.33	10.84	14.72
IV Number	35	34	37	34	30	47	61
% of Total	14.58	15.45	15.54	16.34	14.78	18.87	20.89
V Number	81	97	106	99	91	110	111
% of Total	33.75	44.09	44.53	47.59	44.83	44.17	38.01
VI Number	104	64	71	49	51	53	62
% of total	43.33	29.09	29.83	23.55	25.12	21.28	21.23

Source: Calculated from the actual number of towns listed in Table V of the Census Reports for 1881, 1891, 1901, 1911, 1921, 1931, and 1941.

Small towns formed over 91 per cent of the urban centres in 1881 and over 80 per cent in 1941 (Figure 3.5). Thus, there was an increase at the top of the urban scale in both cities and middling towns. Among the small centres class IV was a steady gainer, class V maintained an overall increase despite some fluctuations, but the proportion of class VI towns decreased from 43 per cent in 1881 to 21 per cent in 1941.

In absolute numbers, the first five categories of urban units showed an increase, but class I was the steadiest gainer, followed by Class III. The gain at these two levels was at the cost largely of classes II, V and VI. The towns of the smallest category came down from one hundred four to sixty-two, despite several additions over the period.

When seen at hierarchical levels, we find that the mountainous area had no cities or middling towns, with the exception of Kohat in the north-west since 1891, and Simla in the north-east in 1921 only.[17] High altitudes geographically restricted the presence of large urban settlements. It is noteworthy that inspite of its position as the summer capital of the empire and of the Punjab province, and as a resort and educational town for the Europeans, Simla could only attain class IV status under the British. The southern part of the region also had no cities, nor large towns, with the exception of Bahawalpur from 1931 onwards; but the area was dotted with small towns. The hill states had very few urban centres and that too of the smallest category. All other sub-regions had different sizes in their urban settlements.

III

In order to understand the pattern of urbanization in the Punjab under colonial rule it may be instructive to compare it with the other parts of British India (Table 3.2).

In 1881, in terms of the total urban settlements in British India,[18] Madras had over 27 per cent followed by United Provinces with over 20 per cent, Bengal over 17 per cent, and the Punjab slightly over 10 per cent of the total.[19] Assam and the Central Provinces had very few urban units, with 0.4 and 3.48 per cent, respectively. By 1941, the proportion in Assam exceeded 1 per cent and in the Central Provinces it exceeded four, the two still remaining the smallest. Bengal, Bombay and Madras lost the lead, having around 6, 7 and 15 per cent of the total units respectively. In 1941, the United Provinces came to have the

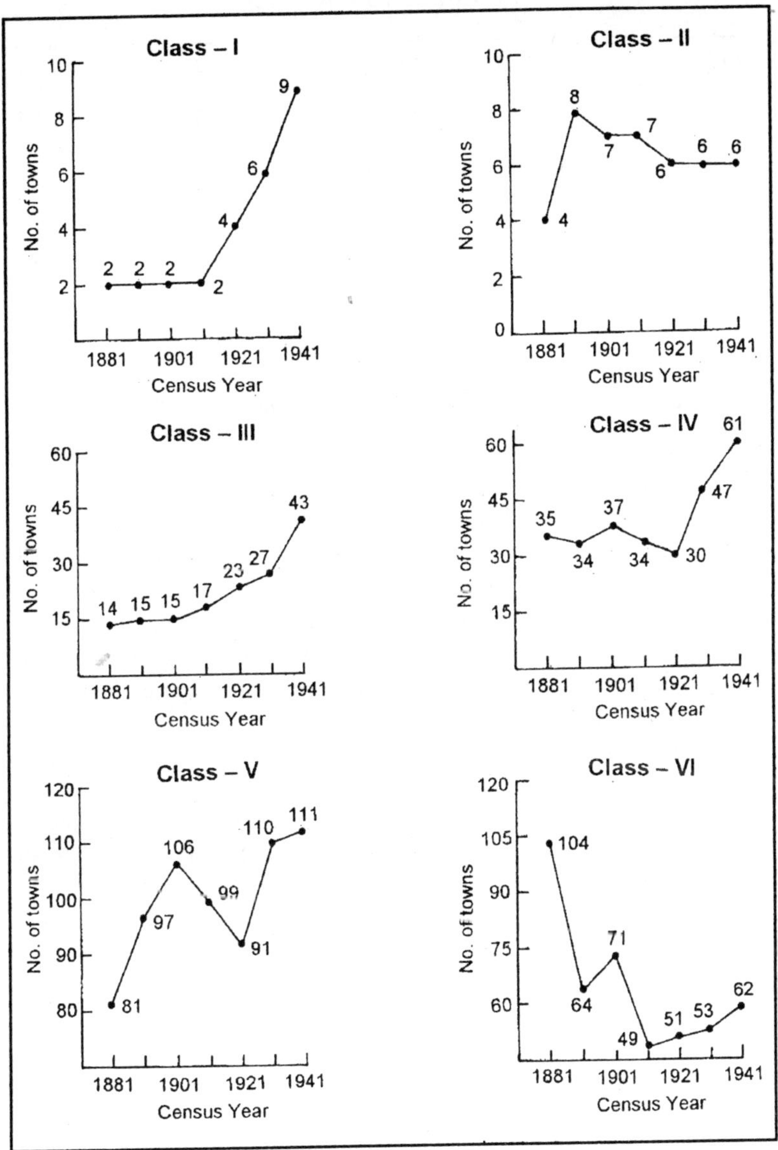

Figure 3.5: Class-wise Variations in Number of Towns, 1881–1941

TABLE 3.2: PERCENTAGE OF URBAN CENTRES IN VARIOUS PROVINCES

Province	1881	1891	1901	1911	1921	1931	1941
Assam	0.4	–	0.88	–	1.2	0.51	1.1
Bengal	17.4	–	8.47	–	5.6	13.7	5.5
Bombay	12.99	–	9.4	–	8.89	8.19	6.8
Central Provinces	3.48	–	2.7	–	4.8	2.8	4.4
Madras	27.4	–	10.8	–	13.6	26.3	15.05
United Provinces	20.8	–	21.08	–	18.7	7.7	16.4
Punjab	*10.04*	–	*11.2*	–	*8.8*	*9.32*	*10.9*

Source: *Census of the Punjab 1881,* Abstract 7, and the Census Reports of India from 1881 to 1941.

largest proportion of urban centres, with over 16 per cent. With nearly 11 per cent of the urban centres of the country, the Punjab registered minimum variation in its all-India position over the period. In terms of changes in the hierarchical level of the urban centres, only the United Provinces witnessed a change broadly similar to that in the Punjab, though decrease in the number of small towns was greater in the Punjab region (Table 3.3).

It may be interesting to note that because of its peculiar geography and size the pattern of urbanization in the Punjab region does not conform to the theoretical models of the number, size and spacing of urban centres, most notably the Central Place Theory and the Rank Size Rule.[20]

IV

For some additional angles to the pattern of urbanization in the Punjab, it may be worthwhile to have a closer look at the growing, declassified, and the new towns. To determine the level of growth,[21] four groups have been identified on the basis of the per cent variation over the entire period: extremely-high-growth towns, with over a 1,000 per cent increase; very-high-growth towns, with 400 to 800 per cent increase; high-growth towns registering 200 to 300 per cent growth; and average growth towns, with 100 to 200 per cent variation.[22]

TABLE 3.3: CLASS-WISE PERCENTAGE OF URBAN CENTRES IN THE PROVINCES

1881	I	II	III	IV	V–VI
Assam	–	–	–	30	70
Bengal	1.39	2.32	7.44	32	56
Bombay	1.5	1.8	5.9	28.9	61.6
Central Provinces	–	3.4	6.9	29.06	60.4
United Provinces	2.14	2.91	6.42	30.5	57.9
Madras	0.44	1.32	4.43	20.38	73.4
Punjab	*0.83*	*1.66*	*5.83*	*14.58*	*77.08*
1941	**I**	**II**	**III**	**IV**	**V–VI**
Assam	–	–	12	28	60
Bengal	0.55	1.95	6.56	14.94	75.97
Bombay	1.6	2.6	8.2	20.7	66.7
Central Provinces	1.56	3.9	11.7	27.3	55.4
United Provinces	3.05	3.05	11.9	21.6	60.27
Madras	6.59	2.07	5.6	12.6	79.05
Punjab	*3.08*	*2.05*	*14.72*	*20.89*	*59.24*

Source: Based on the Census Reports of India from 1881 to 1941.

The extremely-high-growth towns included Solan, Sheikhupura, Montgomery and Abohar.[23] The first is located in the submontane region; Sheikhupura is near Lahore in the Rachna Doab; Montgomery is in the Lower Rachna Doab; and Abohar is situated below the Sutlej. Of these, Solan grew as a cantonment, Montgomery and Sheikhupura as colony towns and district headquarters, and Abohar as a *mandi* or market town. Although, these towns did not fall in any one specific sub-region, they were in areas which were relatively less 'urbanized' at the beginning of the period.

Towns with a very-high-growth variation included Rawalpindi, Mianwali, Campbellpur, Lyallpur, Gojra, Muktsar and Ambala.[24] Two of these, Lyallpur and Gojra, were in the canal colony area; Mianwali, Campbellpur, Rawalpindi and Ambala grew as cantonments; and Muktsar grew as a *mandi*. Urban centres in this group were located mostly in the western plain.

Among the high-growth category were included Lahore, Kasur, Gujranwala, Sialkot, Rohtak, Ferozepore, Sargodha, Muzaffargarh and Khanewal.[25] Three of these were new towns—Sargodha and Khanewal being colony towns, and Rohtak a new district headquarters. Ferozepore developed primarily as a cantonment. The remaining were old urban centres which appear to have grown as a result of a combination of factors, particularly the administrative status, location on the railway, and factory industry. Again all these urban units were in the western plain or the southern parts of the Sutlej-Yamuna Divide.

Average growth in the Punjab ranged from 100 to 200 per cent and was noted in the case of the largest number of towns (see Appendix 3B). The urban centres in this category by and large included the previously existing ones. With a very few exceptions, they happened to be situated in the western part of the region and in the southern areas of the Sutlej-Yamuna Divide.

The rapidly growing towns were mostly located in the canal-irrigated western plain and in the area below the confluence of the Beas and the Sutlej. These included many new towns at different hierarchical levels, except the lowest.[26]

At the same time, several towns of different sizes located all over the region remained untouched by the cumulative effect of the various stimulants which accounted for the marked growth of the urban centres mentioned above. These surviving towns which had a much lower variation in population than the average for the region can be placed in four groups: the first had a range of 70 to 99 per cent variation; in the second it varied from 40 to 69 per cent; in the third from 20 to 39; and the fourth either recorded no growth or had less than 20 per cent variation during the entire period from 1881 to 1941 (see Appendix 3C). The surviving centres with over 70 per cent variation included Minchinabad, Banga, Kamalia, Sangrur, Hoshiarpur, Gujrat, Khudian, Karor, Mandi Gidderbaha, Kapurthala, Hazro, and Mandi in the Kangra hills. The second group, with variation between 40 and 69 per cent, included Wazirabad, Sirsa, Karnal, Dera Ghazi Khan, Kunja, Phagwara, Jagraon, Kaithal, Simla, Panipat, Talagang, Eminabad, and Dasuya. The third group, with variation between 20 and 39 per cent, had new towns as well as those at different hierarchical levels: Bahawalnagar, Toba Tek Singh, Hodal, Mandi Pattoki, Palwal, Jagadhri, Nabha, Patiala, Bhera, Fatehjang, Taunsa, Pasrur, and Una. The towns which barely survived with about 1 per cent growth were Beri, Gohana, Ropar, Nurmahal, and Pataudi. Some other urban units showing a negligible growth rate of up to 19 per cent were Payal, Thanesar, Sarhind, Ahmadpur Lamma, Isakhel, Bassi, Shahpur, and Ramdas.

Ironically, among these 'surviving' centres were included the imperial summer capital of Simla, some district and tahsil headquarters, state capitals and the *mandi* towns. In the case of Simla which had registered the highest and the second highest decadal growth in the Simla hill states during 1901–11 and 1911–21, the overall low rate of growth was due as much to its hilly location as to the exclusion of Jutogh cantonment in 1931. The remaining towns survived at a very low rate of growth apparently because of the relative distance from the main lines of communication and the near absence of modern industry. The state capitals were even worse off because of their economic backwardness. On the whole, the middling centres were relatively better survivors than the small towns, though there is no clear-cut pattern of surviving towns.

Not all towns, however, survived the period of colonial rule; they declined steadily to become village settlements. With a few exceptions like Rahon, Pind Dadan Khan, and Mohindergarh from class IV, the declining centres largely included towns of classes V and VI spread over the entire region (see Appendix 3D). Attock showed a decline of 62 per cent. A very minor decline of less than 2 per cent was evident in Hariana, Dera Baba Nanak, Chhachrauli, Murree, and Nurpur. Some new towns such as Sangla, Okara, and Chichawatni in the colony areas, and Dagshai, Sabathu, and Jutogh cantonments in the hills were also in this group of declining urban centres. Since the cantonments established by the British in the hills had no linkages with the villages around, they tended to decline with the movement of troops and services to other areas. The rest appear to have lost their population to the better situated urban centres in the neighbourhood.

Some urban units were even declassified in the census reports of the period (see Appendix 3E). Mostly of the small town category, such centres were not confined to any specific zone. In 1891, 39 such towns were declassified and in 1911, 62. In 1901, 1921, 1931, and 1941, respectively, 1, 10, 6 and 4 towns were declassified as they no longer met the requirements of being 'urban'. In 1911, several old towns in the hills were in a state of protracted decline, because of their location away from the new road and rail linkages, especially after the Kalka-Simla railway came into operation in 1903. The native states were losing their agricultural population to the hill stations to work as labourers and coolies, also losing in the process income from land and trade.[27] The capital towns continued to have less than 5,000 population, but they were reclassed because of their political status. Reclassification was carried out in other cases also. In 1901, five centres were reclassed as urban units, two in 1911, ten in 1921, ten again in the following decade and twenty-one in 1941 (see Appendix 3E). Uch, Sodhra, and Hafizabad and some other towns went through this process twice. On the whole, declassification and reclassification of towns was a limited process, affecting only some of the small towns in the region. It was left to the discretion of the census superintendent to include or exclude such borderline cases.

In all, one hundred and thirty-one new towns were added to the list of urban centres between the years 1881 and 1941 (see Appendix 3F). They belonged to all classes, though in class VI it was largely a revival of old settlements or inclusion of the large rural settlements which had existed at the beginning of the period; and which subsequently strengthened their manufactures, trade, and some other functions. The largest number was added in 1941, with forty-nine new centres. The year 1931 saw twenty-nine additions, seventeen were added in 1921, and eleven each in 1901 and 1911, and twenty-seven in 1891. Of this last twenty-seven, a large number were cantonment towns, like Dalhousie, Bakloh, Dharmsala, Kasauli, Jutogh, Sabathu, Dagshai, Naushehra, and Campbellpur which were established by the British in the Simla Hills and on the north-west frontier. Later on, Sanawar was developed as an educational centre for European children; Jogindernagar and Sunder-nagar as the loci of hydro-electric projects; and Kalka as an adjunct to the Simla Hills at the base of the mountains. Dhariwal in the Upper Bari Doab finally became a 'town' in 1941 because of the Egerton Woollen Mills established there in the 1880s. As early as 1852, the town of Gurdaspur was founded in this area as a district headquarters. The most notable among the newly founded towns in the plains were those in the canal colonies: Lyallpur, Montgomery, Gojra, Toba Tek Singh, Sargodha, Khanewal, Okara, and Arifwala, among others. In fact, the proportion of new towns in the western plain was 'staggering'; nearly two-thirds of the 82 small towns in 1941 happened to be new. Another group of small towns came up in Bahawalpur in 1941:

Chachran Sharif, Chishtian, Kot Sabzal, Khanqah Sharif, Rahim Yar Khan, Janpur, and Jhajja Abbasian. The remaining new urban centres were situated mostly along the lines of communication; they were *mandi* towns in the Lower Bari Doab as well as in the area below the confluence of the Beas and Sutlej rivers.

V

By the end of the colonial period, significant alterations in the urban pattern in the Punjab were evident. Nearly all classes were represented among the growing centres, with the units at the first five levels indicating an overall upward trend. There was a significant increase in size in the cities and middling towns. From the twin-city position of Lahore and Amritsar in 1881, the region came to have cities located at all corners, though they continued to be concentrated in the eastern plain. Simultaneously, several urban centres rose in the mountainous zone, Salt Range tract, and the western plain, though their overall proportion declined in the eastern plain and the submontane tract. The lower portions of the Chaj and Rachna Doab and the area below the Beas-Sutlej confluence were 'urbanized' for the first time. However, there was a wide divergence in the level of urbanization in the sub-regions, districts, urban classes, and also their political status. The towns in the princely states remained economically backward and even stagnant. In spite of the increase in the number of cities and middling towns, the broad hierarchical pattern of an urban pyramid with a larger number of small towns at the base continued. As a whole, the region does not appear to have experienced deurbanization. In their persistence through the period the pre-colonial urban centres showed a marked 'resilience and adaptability'.[28] The most important factor sustaining them was their position in the localized and sub-regional trade.

The new towns in the plains came up also as commercial centres to provide for the necessary facilities for trade in food grains and cash corps, the substantial chunk heading for overseas markets. The centres having processing and agro-based manufacturing in addition moved up in the urban scale, but their 'functional diversity' remained limited.[29] Urbanization based on agriculture accounted for the dispersal of small (occasionally also the middling) towns at regular intervals which were connected with metalled roads. Generally, the centres located on the railway and also enjoying an administrative status were high in the urban hierarchy. The migration of people to cities and large towns because of pressure on land, unremunerative traditional callings and poverty, and hopes of a better life brought about a substantial change in the demographic profile of the urban centres. Administrative centralization, new means of transportation and communication, and greater educational and economic opportunities also induced people to migrate to cities and towns in large numbers.[30] Changes in the pattern of urbanization thus brought about under colonial rule, were accompanied by changes also in the physical structure of urban centres.

NOTES

1. For a theoretical discussion of urban pattern, see R. Ramachandran, *Urbanization and Urban Systems in India*; 6th imp, New Delhi: OUP, 1997, pp. 120–50. Also, Louis K. Lowenstein, *Urban Studies*, New York: Free Press, 1971, pp. 5–14.
2. Reeta Grewal, 'Polity, Economy and Urbanization: Early 19th Century Punjab', *Journal of Regional History*, vol. IV, 1983, pp. 56–72.
3. It was in this area that most of the canals were constructed by the British from the 1880s onwards.
4. *Census of Punjab, 1881*, p. 7 and Abstract I, p. 6.
5. For the criteria for designating a settlement as a 'town' or a 'city' refer to Section II of the chapter.
6. Multan is categorized as a middling town here on the basis of its population. Its position as a 'city' in the early nineteenth century was based mainly on its importance as a primary centre of trade and manufactures.
7. Based on *Census of Punjab, 1881*, Appendix C, Supplementary Table K.
8. Calculated from figures of population of towns, *Census of Punjab, 1881*, Appendix C.
9. This uneven distribution of urban centres is called 'random' in the terminology of urban geographers. The pattern in the Punjab can be termed 'random' as the towns and cities were unevenly distributed over the region. See Harold Carter, *The Study of Urban Geography*, London: Arnold Heinemann, 1972, p. 119. A 'random' and 'aggregate' distribution of urban centres has also been studied for Pakistan: Qazi S. Ahmed, 'Distribution Pattern in Pakistan', *Pakistan Geographical Review*, vol. I, no. 22, 1967, p. 1.
10. Thanks to the new canal irrigation projects—Lower Chenab Canal, Triple Project, Upper Jhelum and Upper Chenab and the Lower Bari Doab

Canal—over 5 million acres were brought under cultivation. Malcolm Darling, *The Punjab Peasant in Prosperity and Debt*; rpt., New Delhi: Manohar, 1977, pp. 112–14.

11. Based on *Census of Punjab, 1941*, Table V, Population of Towns.
12. Based on *Census of Punjab, 1881*, and *Census of Punjab, 1941*, Table III, Population of Towns and Villages.
13. Based on *Census of Punjab, 1881* and *Census of India, 1941*, Table IV. Variation in numbers occurred largely due to the fact that the census superintendents had discretion regarding the inclusion of urban units at the lowest or class VI level.
14. Calculated from figures of area given in *Census of Punjab, 1881*, Table I, p. 6, and *Census of India, 1941*, p. 46.
15. This definition is consistent in all the Census Reports since 1901. In the Reports of 1881 and 1891 the headquarters of princely states were included despite their miniscule population.
16. In 1921, Rawalpindi and Peshawar were added to the two 'cities' in the region; they were joined by Multan and Sialkot in 1931, and by Jalandhar, Ludhiana and Ambala in 1941.
17. Places like Peshawar and Bannu are not included here as they are situated at much lower altitudes.
18. Calculated from Table I in *Census of India, 1921* and *Census of India, 1931*, and Abstract 7. Also *Census of Punjab, 1881*, p. 24.
19. The Punjab here refers to the area under study as specified in Chapter I. Though not given in Table 2, this proportion in the Punjab region was about 11 per cent in 1891 and about 9 per cent in 1911.
20. For a discussion of the Central Place Theory and the Rank Size Rule in relation to the Punjab, see the author's doctoral thesis entitled 'Urbanization in the Punjab, 1849–1947', GNDU, Amritsar 1988, pp. 65–70.
21. Levels of growth have been assigned by calculating the per cent variation of population in the census years 1881 and 1941. In the case of a new town this variation has been taken from the year it is designated as a town.
22. These groupings are made on the basis of the per cent variation of urban population as a whole in the region at this time which was about 150.
23. Based on population of towns listed in Table IV, *Census of Punjab 1881* and *Census of Punjab, 1941*. The per cent variation in the extremely-high-growth towns from 1881 to 1941 was:

Solan	3,311.47
Sheikhupura	2,102.96
Montgomery	1,106.57
Abohar	1,064.12

24. Ibid. The per cent increase in the very-high-growth group of towns was:

Mianwali	788.82	Muktsar	491.38
Campbellpur	854.26	Gojra	469.09
Rawalpindi	627.30	Tarn Taran	417.9
Lyallpur	662.51	Ambala	408.9
Hafizabad	596.82		

25. Ibid. The per cent variation in the high-growth-group was:

Bhatinda	388.4	Chiniot	220.9
Lahore	383.6	Rohtak	217.5
Fazilka	312.5	Gurdaspur	263.8
Sargodha	311.5	Khanewal	201.6
Sialkot	309.7	Faridkot	209.09
Ferozepore	295.3	Muzaffargarh	208.5
Gujranwala	282.4	Kasur	206.3
Kot Kapura	233.6		

26. G.S. Gosal, 'Agricultural Development and Urbanization, 1921–1981', in Indu Banga (ed.), *Five Punjabi Centuries*; rpt., New Delhi: Manohar, 2000, pp. 361–2.
27. Pamela Kanwar, *Essays on Urban Patterns in Nineteenth Century Himachal Pradesh*, Shimla: IIAS, 1999, pp. 114–37.
28. For a comparative statement of urban centres in the Mughal and British periods, see Kusum Chopra, Atiya Habeeb Kidwai and Subhash Marcus, 'Urbanization Process in the Undivided Punjab', in Reeta Grewal (ed.), *Five Thousand Years of Urbanization: The Punjab Region*, New Delhi: Manohar/Institute of Punjab Studies, 2005, Appendix I.
29. G.S. Gosal, 'Agricultural Development and Urbanization', p. 366.
30. For the factors promoting migration of artisans, peasants and the landless labourers from rural to urban areas of the region: Tom G. Kessinger, *Vilyatpur 1848–1968: Social and Economic Change in a North Indian Village*, 1st Indian edn., New Delhi: Young Asia Publications, 1979, pp. 175–6 and 183–96. Harish C. Sharma, *Artisans of the Punjab: A Study in Social Change in Historical Perspective* (*1849–1947*), New Delhi: Manohar, 1996, pp. 94–105.

APPENDIX 3A

Urban Centres Under Colonial Rule in 1881 and 1941*
(in alphabetical order in each class)

Year	Class I (1,00,000 and above)	Number
1881:	Amritsar and Lahore.	2
1941:	Ambala, Amritsar, Jalandhar, Lahore, Ludhiana, Multan, Peshawar, Rawalpindi, and Sialkot.	9
	Class II (50,000 to 99,999)	
1881:	Jalandhar, Multan, Patiala, and Peshawar.	4
1941:	Ferozepore, Gujranwala, Jhang-Maghiana, Kasur, Lyallpur, and Patiala.	6
	Class III (20,000 to 49,999)	
1881:	Ambala, Batala, Bhiwani, Ferozepore, Gujranwala, Hoshiarpur, Karnal, Ludhiana, Malerkotla, Narnaul, Panipat, Rawalpindi, Rewari, and Sialkot.	14
1941:	Abbottabad, Abohar, Bahawalpur, Bannu, Batala, Bhatinda, Bhera, Bhiwani, Chiniot, Dera Ghazi Khan, Dera Ismail Khan, Faridkot, Fazilka, Gujrat, Hansi, Hissar, Hoshiarpur, Jagraon, Jhelum, Kaithal, Kapurthala, Karnal, Kohat, Kot Kapura, Malerkotla, Mardan, Mianwali, Moga, Montgomery, Muktsar, Nabha, Narnaul, Nowshera, Panipat, Rewari, Rohtak, Sargodha, Sheikhupura, Sirsa and Wazirabad.	39
	Class IV (10,000 to 19,999)	
1881:	Bahawalpur, Basi, Bhera, Chiniot, Dera Ghazi Khan, Dera Ismail Khan, Gujrat, Hansi, Hissar, Jagadhari, Jagraon, Jalalpur, Jhajjar, Jhelum, Kaithal, Kapurthala, Kasur, Kohat, Maghiana, Mohindergarh, Nabha, Palwal, Phagwara, Pind Dadan Khan, Rahon, Rohtak, Ropar, Sadhaura, Shahabad, Simla, Sirsa, Sonepat, Sunam, Urmar Tanda, and Wazirabad.	35

*Based on Population of Towns, Table IV, *Census of Punjab, 1881* and *Census of India, 1941.*

1941: Ahmadpur, Barnala, Basi, Campbellpur, Chakwal, Chunian, Daska, Gojra, Gurdaspur, Hafizabad, Hazro, Jaito, Jalalpur, Jampur, Jandiala, Jind, Jhajjar, Kahror, Kamalia, Kamonki, Kartarpur, Khanewal, Khushab, Lala Musa, Leiah, Mandi Bahauddin, Mandi Pattoki, Mansa, Meham, Nakodar, Nankana Sahib, Narowal, Nawanshahar, Okara, Pak Pattan, Palwal, Pasrur, Pathankot, Patti, Phagwara, Pind Dadan Khan, Pindi Gheb, Raikot, Ropar, Samana, Sangrur, Shahabad, Simla, Sonepat, Sultanpur, Sunam, Tarn Taran, and Urmar Tanda. 53

Class V (5,000 to 9,999)

1881: Ahmadpur (Bahawalpur), Anandpur, Baffa, Bahadurgarh, Ballabhgarh, Banur, Barnala, Beri, Bhadaur, Buriya, Chachrauli, Chakwal, Chamba, Chunian, Dadri, Dajal, Daska, Dasuya, Dera Baba Nanak, Dhanaula, Dharmkot, Dinanagar, Dinga, Dujana, Eminabad, Faridkot, Faridabad, Farukhnagar, Fazilka, Firozepur Jhirka, Garhi Ikhtiar Khan, Gobindgarh, Gohana, Hadaya, Hariana, Hazro, Isakhel, Jandiala, Jhang, Jind, Kalabagh, Kamalia, Kangra, Kartarpur, Khanpur, Khem Karan, Khushab, Kot Kapura, Kulachi, Kunja, Leiah, Machhiwara, Mahatpur, Majitha, Mandi, Miani (Bist Doab), Miani (Chaj Doab), Nahan, Nakodar, Nalagarh, Nurmahal, Nurpur, Pak Pattan, Pasrur, Patti, Payal, Phillaur, Pindi Gheb, Raikot, Ramnagar, Sahiwal, Samana, Sanawar, Sangrur, Sarhind, Shahpur, Shujabad, Sujanpur, Sultanpur, Talagang, Thanesar, Uch, and Vairowal. 83

1941: Ahmadpur, Akalgarh, Arifwala, Bahadurgarh, Bahawalnagar, Ballabhgarh, Banga, Bawal, Beri, Bhadaur, Bhakkar, Bhalwal, Bhaun, Budhlada, Chhichawatni, Chishtian, Chuharkana, Dabwali, Dadri, Dajal, Dasuya, Dera Baba Nanak, Dera Bassi, Dhanaula, Dhariwal, Dharmkot, Dharmsala, Dhuri, Dinanagar, Dinga, Eminabad, Faridabad, Farukhnagar, Fatehjang, Firozepur Jhirka, Gakhar, Garhshankar, Gharaunda, Gohana, Hadali, Hariana, Hidayatpur, Hodal, Isakhel, Jalalpur Pirwala, Jand, Jaranwala, Jawarian, Kalabagh, Kalka, Khairpur, Khanna, Kharar, Khem Karan, Kot Adu, Kot Moman, Kunja, Lalian, Longowal, Mailsi, Majithia, Malakwal, Mandi, Mian Channu, Miani (Bist Doab), Miani (Chaj Doab), Mitha Tiwana, Mithankot, Mohindergarh, Morinda, Muzaffargarh, Nahan, Narwana, Nurmahal, Nurpur, Phillaur, Phul,

Phularwan, Pindi Bhattian, Rahim Yar Khan, Rahon, Raja Sansi, Rajanpur, Ramdas, Ramnagar, Safidon, Sahiwal, Sanaur, Sangla, Sharakpur, Shorkot, Shujabad, Sarhind, Sodhra, Sohna, Sultanwind, Talagang, Tulamba, Tandlianwala, Taunsa, Thanesar, Toba Tek Singh, Tohana, Una, and Zira. 111

Class VI (less than 5,000)

1881: Abbottabad, Adampur, Ahmadpur, Ahmadpur Lamma (Bahawalpur), Akalgarh, Alawalpur, Alipur, Attock, Bahlolpur, Bahrampur, Balanwali, Banga, Bawal, Bhakkar, Bilaspur, Bund, Dalha, Dalhousie, Darman, Dera Bassi, Dunyapur, Edwardesabad, Ellenabad, Fatehabad, Fatehgarh, Garhdiwala, Girot, Gurdaspur, Hadiabad, Hafizabad, Haripur (Hazara), Haripur (Kangra), Jalalpur, Jalalpur Pirwala, Jamke, Jampur, Jatoi, Jawalamukhi, Kahror (Dera Ismail Khan), Kalanaur, Kaliana, Karor (Multan), Khangarh, Khanna, Khairpur (Bahawalpur), Kharar, Kharkhauda, Khudian, Kila Didar Singh, Kila Sobha Singh, Kunjpura, Ladwa, Lakki, Loharu, Makhad, Makhu, Minchinabad, Mithankot, Mitranwali, Montogomery, Mukerian, Muktsar, Murree, Muzaffargarh, Nagar Bhojpur, Najafgarh, Nainakot, Narot, Narowal, Naushera, Nawanshahr, Paharpur, Pataudi, Pathankot, Pehowa, Phul, Pindi Bhattian, Pundri, Radaur, Rajanpur, Ramdas, Rampur-Bashahr, Rania, Rattia, Rori, Safidon, Sankhatra, Shakargarh, Shahar Sultan, Shahpur, Sharakpur, Sheikhupura, Sitpur, Sodhra, Sri Hargobindpur, Sujanpur (Kangra), Sukhochak, Tulamba, Tank, Taran Taran, Tohana, Una, Zafarwal, and Zira. 104

1941: Ahmadgarh, Ahmadpur Lamma, Allahabad (Bahawalpur), Alipur, Amloh, Attock, Bakloh, Balun, Bilaspur, Buria, Chachran Sharif, Chak Jhumra, Dagshai, Dalhousie, Dera Nawab Sahib, Dujana, Fort Abbas, Garhi Ikhtiar Khan, Goth Chani, Ghauspur, Harunabad, Hasilpur, Jhajja Abbasian, Janpur, Jogindernagar, Jutogh, Kallar Kot, Karor, Kasauli, Kasumpti, Khan Bela, Khangarh, Khanqah Sharif, Khudian, Kot Chhuta, Kot Sabzal, Loharu, Mandi Guru Hari Sahai, Mandi Sadiq, Minchinabad, Mubarakpur, Murree, Nalagarh, Pataudi, Payal, Qaimpur, Rajpura, Rampur-Bashahr, Rojhan, Sabathu, Sambrial, Sanawar, Sanjarpur, Shamsherpur, Sillanwali, Solan, Sot Samba, Sundernagar, Tajgarh, Tarrandah Mohammad Panah, Uch Sharif, and Vehoa. 62

APPENDIX 3B

Towns with Average Growth Rate (200–100 per cent), 1881–1941*

Pak Pattan 197.88, Bahawalpur 193.47, Pathankot 184.39, Jalalabad 174.91, Patti 174.62, Bakloh 174.57, Ahmadpur 167.23, Narowal 163.73, Phulerwan 161.16, Ludhiana 152.78, Tulamba 151.27, Hidayatpur 148.99, Multan 148.41, Daska 148.41, Jhang-Maghiana 141.37, Kahror 136.13, Jaito 134.19, Shorkot 133.49, Phul 126.97, Barnala 126.48, Leiah 121.85, Peshawar 120.88, Kila Didar Singh 117.11, Tohana 115.40, Jind 108.92, Nawanshahr 107.15, Chakwal 107.01, Dera Ismail Khan 105.16, Bhakar 104.63, Hissar 120.00, and Jampur 100.76.

* Based on Population of Towns, Table IV in the Census Reports of the Punjab, from 1881 to 1941. Appendices 3C–3E are also based on the same sources.

APPENDIX 3C

The Surviving Towns, 1881–1941

I (Towns with 99–70 per cent increase)

Banga 99.60, Jehlum 99.53, Khanna 99.12, Loharu 97.39, Moga 96.42, Minchinabad 91.49, Zira 90.68, Khushab 90.68, Alipur 89.00, Kamalia 88.24, Safidon 87.66, Sangrur 87.46, Kohat 85.93, Balun 83.37, Batala 83.09, Chichawatni 82.03, Okara 80.31, Mandi 79.58, Hansi 78.54, Sillianwala 78.04, Dhariwal 76.49, Jandiala 76.28, Mandi Gidderbaha 73.73, Gujrat 73.44, Karor 72.45, Hoshiarpur 71.76, Hazro 71.22, and Kapurthala 71.07.

II (Towns with 69–40 per cent increase)

Pindi Bhattian 69.86, Sirsa 68.54, Dera Ghazi Khan 68.41, Karnal 66.21, Wazirabad 64.45, Jalalpur Pirwala 62.70, Lalian 62.18, Jagraon 58.26, Mitha Tiwana 57.93, Mandi Guru Har Sahai 57.21, Samana 57.06, Kunja 53.00, Phagwara 52.35, Meham 52.35, Akalgarhf 51.80, Dalhousie 51.60, Kaithal 51.31, Raikot 49.44, Talagang 49.24, Simla 49.11, Majitha 48.75, Chawinda 48.45, Pindi Gheb 48.31, Panipat 47.50, Dasuya 47.34, Eminabad 47.34,

Sharakpur 47.20, Bhalwal 45.85, Khem Karan 45.44, Shahabad 44.30, Kalabagh 43.89, Kharar 42.36, Hasan Abdal 42.36, Malerkotla 42.19, Amloh 41.54, Kot Adu 41.31, and Nankana Sahib 41.24.

III (Towns with 39–20 per cent increase)

Mandi Pattoki 38.64, Kalka 38.62, Sodhra 38.08, Dharmkot 37.79, Sultanwind 36.00, Sonepat 35.97, Nahan 35.84, Palwal 35.58, Hodal 34.21, Jagadhri 33.51, Bhera 33.32, Ahmadgarh (Malerkotla) 33.04, Bahawalnagar 32.50, Toba Tek Singh 32.23, Nabha 32.18, Jhawarian 31.95, Dhanaula 31.60, Khairpur 31.27, Kartarpur 31.12, Garhshankar 30.52, Patiala 30.24, Bhiwani 30.09, Bhaon 30.07, Jalalpur Jattan 29.78, Nakodar 29.40, Tandlianwala 28.99, Khangarh 28.82, Rewari 27.95, Gharaunda 27.15, Shujabad 27.06, Phillaur 26.79, Chamba 26.42, Tohana 25.83, Pasrur 25.60, Rampur-Bashahr 25.52, Dinanagar 24.67, Ahmadpur (Bahawalpur) 24.37, Chunian 24.26, Jhajjar 23.81, Sultanpur 23.74, Urmar Tanda 23.69, Bahadurgarh 22.95, Una 22.89, and Fatehjang 22.06.

IV (Towns with less then 20 per cent increase)

Ramdas 19.98, Bawal 19.41, Isakhel 18.51, Rajanpur 17.49, Sunam 16.06, Narnaul 15.01, Bhadaur 13.74, Shahpur 12.45, Ahmadpur Lamma 12.34, Basi 11.66, Dadri 11.61, Thanesar 9.41, Sarhind 7.81, Dajal 3.93, Dera Bassi 3.32, Nurmahal 1.99, Pataudi 1.30, Beri 0.92, Ropar 0.51, and Gohana 0.44.

APENDIX 3D
The Declined Towns (negative per cent variation), 1881–1941

Garhi Ikhtiar Khan –73.00, Dagshai –71.25, Attock –62.61, Buria –47.95, Uch –46.07, Farukhnagar –41.38, Nalagarh –39.43, Sambrial –37.56, Budhlada –35.90, Jutogh –33.47, Pind Dadan Khan –31.56, Rahon –31.27, Firozpur Jhirka –24.80, Ramnagar –23.96, Sohna –22.70, Mithankot –20.07, Dujana –19.49, Sadhaura –18.33, Miani (Chaj Doab) –16.80, Khanpur –14.41, Ballabhgarh –12.24, Sangla –11.68, Sahiwal –8.89, Sanaur –7.69, Payal –7.36, Miani (Bist Doab) –6.89, Sabathu –6.35, Bilaspur –4.32, Murree –2.69, Nurpur –2.03, Dera Baba Nanak –1.41, Hariana –0.84 and, Chachrauli –0.27.

APPENDIX 3E

Declassified and Reclassified Towns*

Year		Number
1891:	*Declassed*: Ahmadpur, Balanwali, Bahlolpur, Bahrampur, Darman, Fatahabad, Girot, Hafizabad, Haripur, Jalalpur, Jatoi, Jwalamukhi, Kharar, Kunjpura, Mahatpur, Makhad, Mitranwali, Nainakot, Najafgarh, Narot, Naushera, Paharpur, Pehowa, Pindi Bhattian, Radaur, Ramdas, Rattia, Sankhatra, Shahpur, Shahr Sultan, Shakargarh, Sitpur, Sodhra, Sujanpur, Sukhochak, Talagang, Tank, Tohana, and Uch.	39
	Reclassed:	None
1901:	*Declassed*: Attock	1
	Reclassed: Balanwali, Hafizabad, Sohna, Tank, and Uch.	5
1911:	*Declassed*: Adampur, Alawalpur, Allahabad (Bahawalpur), Balanwali*, Bannu, Baroda, Bhaun, Bilaspur, Bund, Butana, Dalha, Dujana, Dunyapur, Ellenabad, Garhdiwala, Garhi Ikhtiar Khan, Hadiaya, Hadiabad, Hafizabad*, Hatin, Jalalpur Pirwala, Jamke, Jandiala, Kahnaur, Kalanaur, Kaliana, Kangra, Khairpur, Khanpur, Kharkhauda, Kila Didar Singh, Kila Sobha Singh, Ladwa, Machhiwara, Meham, Makhu, Minchinabad, Moga, Mudki, Mukerian, Nagar Bhojpur, Nalagarh, Narowal, Naushera (Bahawalpur), Nurpur, Pataudi, Payal, Pundri, Rampur, Rania, Rori, Safidon, Sodhra*, Solan, Sri Hargobindpur, Talamba, Uch*, Una, Vairowal, and Zafarwal.	62
	Reclassed: Attock and Talagang.	2
1921:	*Declassed*: Akalgarh, Anandpur, Chawinda, Dasuya, Farukhnagar, Garhshankar, Kalanaur, Khanna, Khudian, and Miani (Chaj Doab).	10
	Reclassed: Ahmadpur, Bhaun, Dujana, *Hafizabad, Meham, Moga, Nagar Bhojpur, Nurpur, Pataudi, and Safidon.	10

* All towns listed here belonged to classes V and VI. Towns marked with an asterisk were declassed and reclassed more than once.

1931:	*Declassed*: Ahmadpur Lamma, Dharmkot, Gurgaon, Madhopur, Nagar* Bhojpur, and Sujanpur.	6
	Reclassed: Akalgarh, Bilaspur, Chawinda, Garhshankar, Khanna, Miani (Chaj Doab), Narowal, Pindi Bhattian, Shahpur, and Solan.	10
1941:	*Declassed*: Baghbanpura, Ichhra, Jamalpur, and Shahdara.	4
	Reclassed: Ahmadpur Lamma, Allahabad (Bahawalpur), Dasuya, Dharmkot, Farukhnagar, Garhi Ikhtiar Khan, Jalalpur Pirwala, Kahror, Kangra, Khairpur, Kharar, Khudian, Kila Didar Singh, Minchinabad, Nalagarh, Payal, Ramdas, Rampur-Bashahr, Sodhra, Talamba, and Uch.	22

APPENDIX 3F

New Towns*

Year		Number
1891:	Bakloh, Baroda, *Bhaun, Butana, Campbellpur, Charsadda, Cherat, Dagshai, Dharmsala, Garhshankar*, Gurgaon, Hodal, Jamrud, Jandiala (Bist Doab), Jutogh, Kalanaur (Sutlej-Yamuna Divide), Kasauli, Meham, Mardan, Moga, Mudki, Naushera (Salt Range), Prang, and Sohna.	24
1901:	Allahabad (Bahawalpur), Chiral, Hatin, Kalka, Khanpur (Bist Doab), Lyallpur, Madhopur, Naushera (Bahawalpur), Parachinar, Solan, and Tank.	11
1911:	Abohar, Chawinda*, Gojra, Jaito, Jalalabad, Mianwali, Rojhan, Sambrial*, Sanawar, Sargodha, and Taunsa.	11
1921:	Amloh, Baghbanpura, Bhalwal, Ichhra, Jhawarian, Khanewal, Mitha* Tiwana, Phulerwan, Shahdara, Sheikhupura, Shorkot, Sillianwali, and Toba Tek Singh.	13
1931:	Ahmadgarh, Bahawalnagar, Balun, Budhlada, Chichawatni, Fatehjang*, Hasan Abdal*, Hidayatpur, Jamalpur, Jaranwala, Jogindernagar, Kasumpti, Kot Adu, Kot Chhuta, Lalian, Malakwal, Mandi Gidderbaha,	

* Added to the list of towns for the first time from the Census of 1891 onwards.

Mandi Guru Har Sahai, Mandi Pattoki, Nankana Sahib, Okara, Sangla, Shahpur, Shamsherpur, Sundernagar, Tandlianwala, and Vehowa. 27

1941: Arifwala, Burewala, Chachhran Sharif, Chak Jhumra, Chaklala, Chishtian, Dera Nawab Sahib, Dhariwal, Dhuri, Fort Abbas, Gakhar, Gharaunda, Ghaunspur, Got Chhani, Hadali, Harunabad, Hassilpur, Jajja Abbassian, Jand, Janpur, Kallur Kot, Kamonki, Khan Bela, Khanqah Sharif, Kot Moman, Kot Sabzal, Lala Musa, Longowal, Mailsi, Mandi Bahauddin, Mandi Chuharkana-Nokhar, Mandi Sadiq, Mansa, Mian Chhanu, Morinda, Mubarakpur, Nai Dabwali, Narwana, Qaimpur, Rahim Yar Khan, Raja Sansi, Sanjarpur, Sot Samba, Tajgah, and Tarandah Mohammad Panah. 45

4

New Urban Forms

Two basic urban forms can be identified to begin with: the walled town and the planned settlement. The new urban forms were either superimposed on the existing centres, or created as planned settlements away from the old town. The initial ground plans were irregular in the case of most walled towns, and regular, radial or grid patterned in the case of the planned centres.[1] Most urban centres in India, however, usually grew by a process of accretion and continuous restructuring superimposed on an irregular system. The heterogeneous structures that thus evolved combined certain essential features in different ways. Each had several focal points to meet the basic urban requirements of a main market, secondary markets, residential localities, religious and cultural institutions, seat of authority, and a hierarchy of roads connecting these different points and also providing links with the outside world.[2]

Town-planning has been known to the Punjab region since the third century BC. Archaeologists discovered the distinctiveness of the Harappan cities and towns which were followed, albeit after a gap, by fortified and planned structures elsewhere in the region from about the sixth century BC.[3] The literary and epigraphic sources of the later period point to the continued existence of urban centres of varying dimensions in the north-west during the early medieval period.[4] There is evidence also of thinking on city planning from Kautilya's *Arthashastra* and other texts. In fact, several types of town-plans existed, at least in theory, in ancient India.[5]

Essentially, on the ground, towns were generally walled, with two main streets dominating the otherwise irregular and narrow street system housing different localities, while the palace, fort, or the temple formed the core. Urban living was extended even beyond the walled area, with residences and gardens and other structures interspersed with the countryside. Class division was rigidly followed in residential areas, particularly within the walls.[6] The internal layout of the houses of the well-to-do at least was determined by regulations and specifications of buildings laid down by the *Silpa Sastras.*[7] This pattern continued to exist in the medieval period, with a notable contribution in the sphere of architecture and laying of gardens.[8] A marked difference, however, was brought about by the British when they entered the scene with the Western principles of town planning modified by colonial requirements of military dominance, political control and economic exploitation.[9]

The colonial Punjab was the only region in British India with four distinct urban forms,[10] three of which were created by the new rulers. In comparative terms, the 'indigenous' town underwent very little visible change, while the 'anglicized' town was that pre-colonial centre which acquired 'Western' extensions like the civil lines and the cantonment. By contrast, the 'colony town' in the canal-irrigated tract was entirely a new creation planned on Western lines. Another creation of the British—the 'hill station'—combined features of the last two urban forms with those of an English resort town, albeit moderated by the terrain.

I

Numerous indigenous centres dotted the entire region.[11] Most of them happened to be small and, despite additions to their structures, saw very little change in their basic form during the period. Both large and small urban centres were generally walled, like Lahore, Amritsar, Batala, Jalandhar, Phul, Nabha, Rewari, Farukhnagar, Kaithal, Shujabad, Jind, Dadri, and Sunam. The walled centres had gates: the towns had four to six gates, while the cities of Lahore and Amritsar and even Batala had twelve gates each. An average town was traversed by one, or sometimes two, main roads, the latter cutting across at right angles to each other. For instance, Kamalia, Rajanpur, Muktsar, Payal, Naushera, Kila Didar Singh, and Hafizabad had one main street, whereas Shujabad, Dadri, Jind, Dipalpur, Hodal, Zira, and Kaithal had two. These roads were wider than others and were usually paved, with open drains either in the centre or on both sides. At the intersection of these primary roads was the market centre or the *chowk.* The primary roads housed the main bazaar and had the closely built and better looking buildings of the town on them (Figure 4.1).

The streets other than the main roads were a worm-like system of

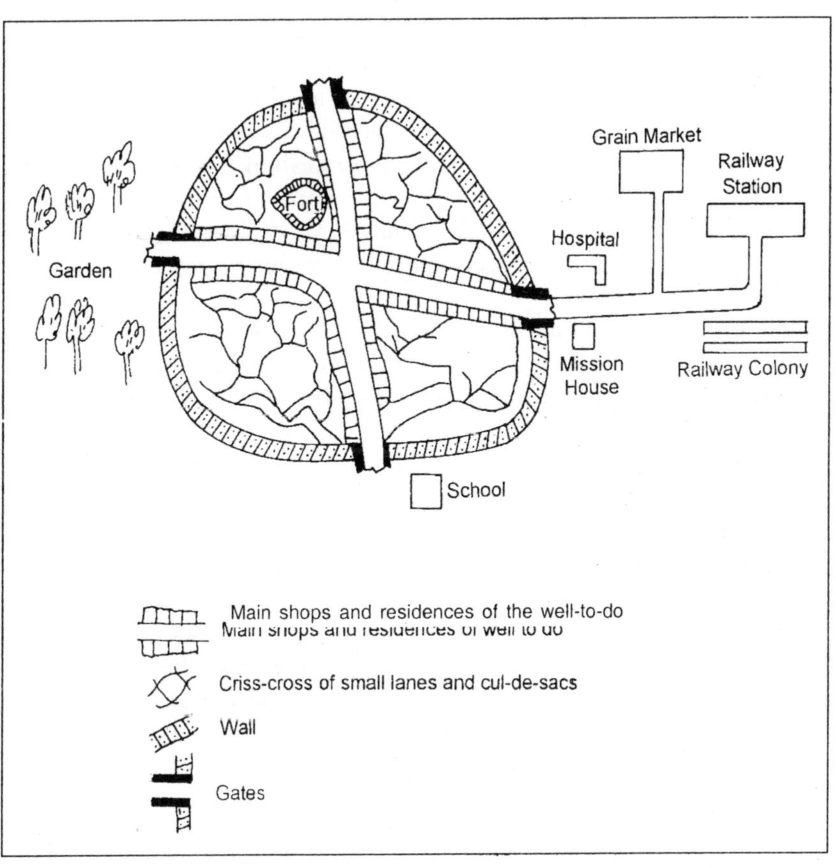

Figure 4.1: The Indigenous Town: Theoretical

narrow, tortuous lanes often ending in cul-de-sacs.[12] Here also drains ran through the centre or sides of the lanes which in many small towns were unpaved, though there were some with paved lanes—Sohna, Amritsar, Batala, Kasur, Pak Pattan, Gujranwala, Kila Sobha Singh, and Pasrur. The mohallas or residential localities were densely built and absorbed a large population. Different trades and crafts tended to concentrate in separate areas. The service-performing groups, particularly the outcastes, generally lived on the periphery and even outside the walled area in some cases. The mohallas mostly had their own shrines for worship. Most towns also had a bigger shrine and a Jami Masjid as the cultural focal points. Some towns had small suburbs or *bastis* close to the town, as in Jalandhar, Daska, Firozpur-Jhirka, Mithankot, and Safidon. Gardens were generally on the outskirts of the towns, for example in Zira, Bhera, Leiah, Kunjpura, Tank, Phul, Bawal, Dhanaula, and Batala. Sometimes gardens were located within the town as well, as in Amritsar and Kunja.

With the establishment of colonial rule, changes occurred in the physical form of some of the old centres.[13] In an effort to 'improve' the towns the British widened the roads and cut through the more congested areas to allocate building sites wherever space could be most easily found. Clock towers, statues and town halls were among the new structures added to the large indigenous centres as symbols of the metropolitan presence. A minor change in the existing form of such centres was made by adding a wide circular road around the town, as for instance in Amritsar, Batala, Jampur, Rohtak, Nabha, Rewari, Ferozepore, and Dera Ismail Khan. The coming of the railway added a new railway suburb to the towns it served. As the railway line could not penetrate the old centre it came as close as possible, and the railway colony was founded nearby for the employees. The bigger centres also had a railway workshop, as in Lahore, Amritsar and seven other places. To facilitate transporation of agricultural produce, the 'grain' *mandi* came to be located close to the railway station, as in Jalandhar, Bhatinda, and Pak Pattan. In themselves these railway suburbs remained small but they contributed to the altering of the indigenous pattern by determining the direction for further growth. Over time, additions like offices, schools, colleges, mission houses, and factories sprang up in the areas between the railway suburb and the old town, forming a linear extension to the urban centre (Figure 4.2).

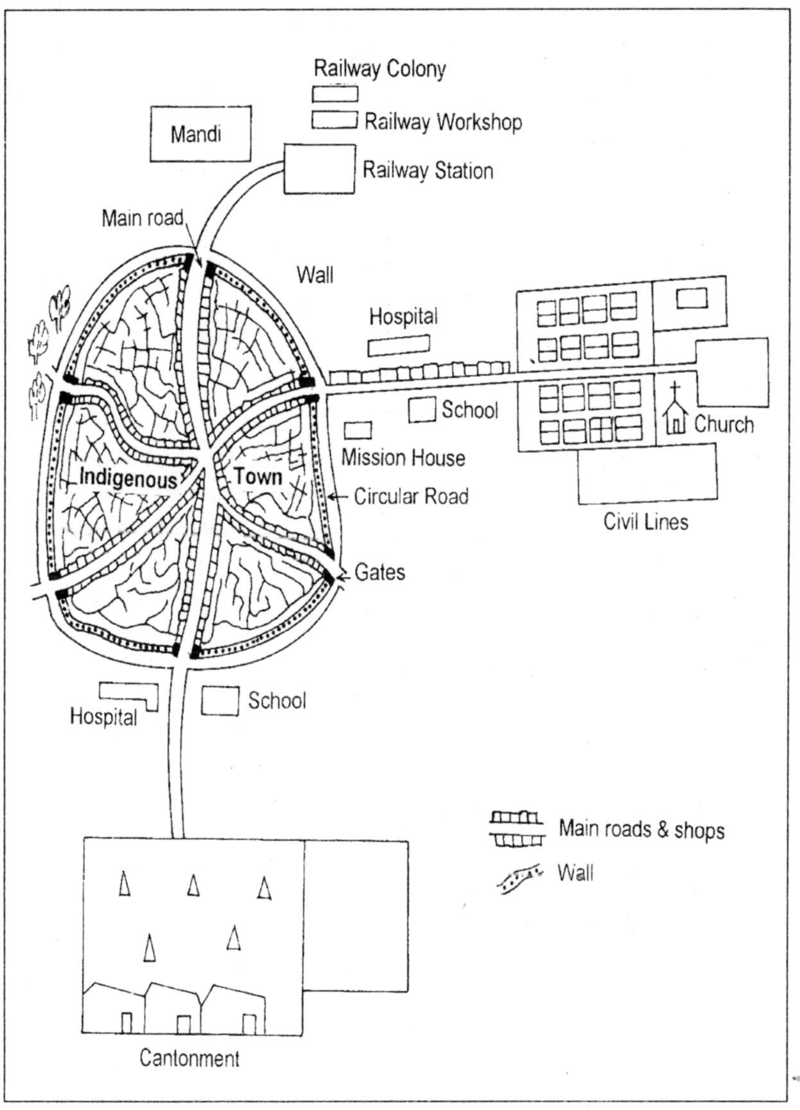

Figure 4.2: The Anglicized Town: Theoretical

The junctions of roads leading to the neighbouring urban centres also became the likely points of such additions. In Jalandhar, for example, several extensions and suburbs sprang up on the roads leading to Nakodar, Kapurthala, Tanda, and the Grand Trunk Road.[14] The 'anglicized' accretions and new suburbs thus at times encircled the old centre, becoming a distinct ring and yet remaining connected to it. Towards the end of colonial rule, residential suburbs such as Model Towns at Lahore and Amritsar and the Indian Station at Montgomery came up for the well-to-do and the professional people among Indians.[15] Such 'east-west' towns developed mainly in the district headquarters which became physically a 'collection of period pieces', with contrasting old and new areas.[16]

II

A distinctly 'anglicized' character was noticeable in the civil station which housed as well as represented the political and administrative authority. The British established separate colonies outside the towns and cities to serve as district headquarters. They found the indigenous centre 'unhealthy, noisy and distasteful',[17] and they needed to physically distance themselves from the ruled. This was the place where the head of the district administration and other representatives of colonial rule like the Deputy Commissioner, Superintendent of Police, Sessions Judge, Civil Surgeon, engineers, missionaries and the chaplain resided. The European businessmen, Anglo-Indians and sometimes the military officers also lived in the civil station, later called the civil lines.[18]

The planned settlement of civil lines stood in sharp contrast to the indigenous town.[19] Wide roads formed a gridiron and ran parallel to the central road, the Mall. The rectangles thus formed were further divided into regular plots of several acres housing the bungalows of officers. Gradually, the sites for building houses in the civil station began to be sold by the government to prominent persons, including the well-to-do Indians.[20] Offices were constructed between the residential area and the old town. Chapels, churches, cemeteries, schools, and some shops for Europeans followed. Recreation areas in the form of gymkhanas, clubs, and games courts were also added to the new settlement. Larger centres like Lahore, Amritsar and Jalandhar had race courses. The civil station covered an extensive area, yet had a low density of population (less than 20 persons per acre), and much less density of built-up area than the old city.[21] With its large residential plots, spacious one-storey houses, broad tree-lined roads, and generous provision of amenities, the civil station was comparable to 'an early twentieth century upper or middle class European suburb'.[22] In every way the new settlement was in marked contrast to the native town, separated from it by a green belt of gardens. However, the size of the settlement and the scale of its civic amenities varied according to the size of its European population. For example, six urban centres—Ambala, Lahore, Peshawar, Rawalpindi, Sialkot and Simla—which housed 73 per cent of the Europeans in the region in 1868 came to have relatively bigger civil stations and cantonment areas.[23]

Almost equidistant from both the civil station and the indigenous town was the cantonment or the permanent military station housing the armed forces distributed all over the subcontinent at strategically important locations. In the 1860s, there were some 114 'purpose-built' cantonments in the hills and plains of British India and some princely territories.[24] Over a fifth of the cantonments came to be located in the Punjab region, including the North-West Frontier Province.[25] For building a cantonment generally the best landscape in the vicinity of the indigenous town was chosen. An area of about two to five kilometres between the town and the new settlement was kept free of cultivation for security and health reasons. The town could thus provide the necessary services without impinging upon the military station. On an average, covering an area of about 18–20 sq km, a cantonment housed around 5,000 people.[26] It was laid out on the plan of a standing military camp. The structures were designed to meet the military and residential requirements of the officers, troops and ancillary personnel—both European and native.

The principle of racial segregation ran through nearly all the structures in the cantonment. There were barracks for the British troops, lines for the Indian sepoys, and bungalows for the British officers. There were separate parade grounds, exercise grounds, canteens, hospitals, churches, cemeteries, and shopping areas for the Europeans and natives. The regimental bazaar for the sepoys, called the Sadar Bazaar, was an adjunct to the cantonment. The houses of the people providing the necessary services, their burial and cremation grounds, 'in fact all essentials, excepting wells were placed rearward to European residences'.[27]

There were other widely dispersed structures in the cantonment to meet the needs of the garrison—shooting ranges, magazines, horse-lines, gunsheds, workshops and farms. In addition to a garrison church, there were some places of worship for the native troops, besides a soldiers' garden, generally called the Company Bagh. The visiting Europeans stayed in the Inspection Bungalow and the natives in the *sarai*. The Europeans could also stay in the club which had games courts and several other facilities. In addition, a large military station had a race course and some shops to cater exclusively for Europeans. With the passage of time, the cantonment came to have particularly good sanitary, conservancy and lighting arrangements, and a regular water supply. Since colonial rule depended ultimately on the armed forces, it was ensured that the cantonments had effective means of communication in metalled roads, rail links, post offices, telegraph lines, and telephone connections. The administration of the cantonment was overseen by a committee under the direction of the Commanding Officer of the area.[28]

The colonial urban form peculiar to the Punjab was the colony town. It was founded by the British as a planned 'model' settlement in the western plain inhabited mostly by the pastoralists, and brought under irrigation for the first time. Some notable towns in this category were Lyallpur, Montgomery, Okara, Chichawatni, Sargodha, Gojra, Toba Tek Singh, Sangla, and Arifwala. This group included small towns as well as those which developed into large urban centres over the period.

The colony town (Figure 4.3) was built at the specifically chosen market (*mandi*) site in the form of squares or rectangles. Broad metalled roads were laid out within these in a grid, with roads cutting across at right angles as in Sargodha, or radiating from a central chowk as in Lyallpur.[29] These primary roads formed a system of blocks for small industry and residential purposes. The *mandi* was a big square with shops on all sides. On the main roads were located the bazaars of the town. The government sold the sites for shops and houses by auction. Link roads connected the blocks to the main roads and were at times unmetalled. The main bazaars were also residential, and the additional residences were located on the roads parallel to and behind the main streets. Residential blocks had two entrances and enclosed a spacious square with a wide lane around, containing two rows of houses. The caste or religious groupings were adhered to in these blocks as in the

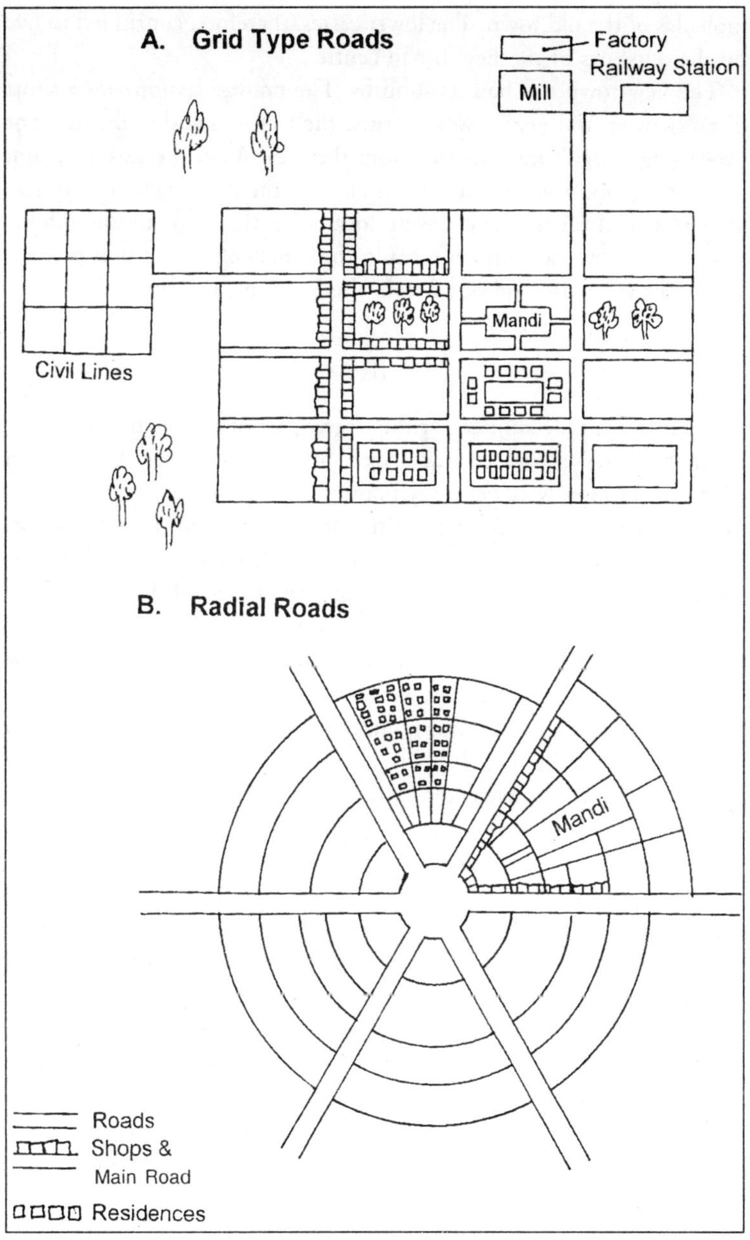

Figure 4.3: The Colony Town: Theoretical

mohallas of the old town. The lower castes, therefore, continued to live on the outskirts of the new urban centre.

The new town too had its suburbs. The railway station was a short distance away and near it were located the factories and mills, using or processing agricultural produce from the area. As in the eastern plain, the civil station was a separate unit close to the new town. The offices as well as official residences were located in the civil station. There, however, was no cantonment area in the canal colony. Various gardens and parks were also laid out within the limits of the town.

III

Residential units accounted for the largest part of an urban centre. The indigenous town was characterized by closely spaced housing in mohallas. Houses were generally built of brick or stone, and the houses of the well-to-do were of two or three storeys. In an average house, the most used part was the *dalan* or *verah* (an open space), enclosed by rooms which were used more for living by members of the joint family than for specific functions. The entrance opening into a vestibule was known as the *deorhi.* The houses of the rich also had a *taikhana* (basement) for summer. Toilets were mostly on the roof; and bathrooms, wherever provided, were on the ground floor. Town houses were generally dingy with little light and fresh air, and often with no provision for water. The houses constructed in the new localities outside the walled area were more open and airy, and with more basic amenities. The general pattern in these new houses was of a well proportioned block of two or three storeys, commonly called *kothi.* Among the new features were a deep verandah, a colonnaded portico and, at places, a small garden compound—all of these features were borrowed from the bungalow.[30]

The bungalow-compound complex was the residential form typical of the colonial period; it represented 'one of the most striking aspects of "Westernisation" in the Indian urban system'.[31] As a house type belonging to the colonial community, the bungalow reflected the cultural distinctiveness and political dominance of the Sahibs. Etymologically, from '*bangala*' for a single-room thatched dwelling in rural Bengal, the bungalow as a residential unit catered for one nuclear family. Space was functionally divided into high-ceilinged rooms for sitting, dining, working, sleeping, bathing, and dressing. A deep verandah, a colonnaded porch and a driveway were features in the front, while the store, shed for horses and ponies, and quarters for the staff were at the back at some distance. Sometimes Graeco-Roman or Gothic features were superimposed to elevate the external appearance, but this was more common in non-government structures. Before the introduction of regular water supply a bungalow also had two wells—for use by servants and Sahibs. This dwelling unit was set in a compound or enclosed garden space which became a means of maintaining individual identity and privacy as well as distance from the natives. The bungalow-compound remained the standard dwelling unit of the Europeans in the civil lines and cantonments. Its size and features could vary according to the official position of the occupant.[32] In due course, the bungalow was 'adopted as the universal form of colonial housing throughout the Empire'.[33]

IV

As a special feature of colonial urban development, the hill station deserves discussion at some length. The interest of the British in the hill settlements goes back to 1815 when, after the Anglo-Nepalese war, they occupied Simla and Mussourie primarily as defence outposts. Between 1815 and 1947 the British created over 80 hill stations on the lower ranges between about 1,200 m and 2,450 m. The most important of these new settlements were located in different regions of the subcontinent: Darjeeling and Shillong in the east; Poona and Mahabaleshwar in the west; Ootacamund, Coonoor and Kodaikanal in the south; and Simla, Mussourie, Nainital, Dalhousie and several others in the north. The northern ranges of the Himalayas in fact came to have the largest number of hill stations.[34]

Several considerations went into the development of hill stations. All the Europeans serving in the tropical climate of India could not go home to Britain for holidays and recuperation. They found the answer in the cooler and, presumably, healthier environment of the hills. Moreover, out of an estimated number of about 126,000 Europeans in India in the early 1860s, around 85,000 happened to be troops, and the British could scarcely afford their falling sick.[35] Housed in the cantonments in the high altitudes in the Himalayas, the troops would remain within easy reach of the Punjab plains. They could also be kept away from the natives: close contact with them was likely to create social and health problems, it was feared. Thus, even before the Punjab plains were conquered, the cantonments of Sabathu (1840), Kasauli (1842), Jutogh (1843) and Dagshai (1847) came up in the Simla hills. The site of Dalhousie was acquired from Chamba in 1853. Several hill stations came to have the sanitaria, becoming something like convalescent points for Europeans.[36] Another factor which appears to have carried some weight with the British chastened by the uprising of 1857–8, was that they found the local people in the Simla hills to be 'simple-minded' and 'submissive to authority'.[37] Simla was finally chosen to be the summer capital of the Government of India at the insistence of John Lawrence who, as the Governor-General (1864–9), regarded its proximity to the relatively docile Punjab, with its dependable 'war like races', a special advantage. He also argued that the government would do 'more work in Simla in one day than in five down in Calcutta'.[38]

Moving offices to the hills in hot weather became as necessary as administering India. In 1864 the Army Headquarters and several ancillary departments were shifted permanently from Calcutta to Simla.[39] In 1876 the summer headquarters of the Punjab Government were shifted from Murree to Simla. Murree continued to serve as the summer headquarters of the British Indian army stationed in the north. The divisional and district officers in different parts of the Punjab and the North-West Frontier Province spent the hot weather in the nearby stations like Murree, Dalhousie, Kasauli, Hazara Gali, Sakesar (Salt Range), and Shekhbuddin (Sulaiman Range).[40] In due course, Simla and stations like Murree, Dalhousie and Kasauli acquired the characteristics of an 'English provincial resort' where the British annually repaired for rest, recreation and, above all, relief from the plains, officialdom and natives.[41] The Englishwomen stayed in the hills for longer duration and their children went to schools there.

The construction of hill stations would not have been possible without the special advantages that the British came to enjoy during the nineteenth century. Their political dominance facilitated the selection of sites and mobilization of men and resources for construction. Their command of industrial technology and knowledge of cartography enabled them to build roads and bridges.[42] In the 1850s construction of the Hindustan-Tibet Road was taken up, and a 270-m long tunnel through solid rock was constructed in 1851–2. 'Some 10,000 prisoners and over 8,000 free labourers' were reported to be employed in its execution.[43] The Cart Road between Kalka and Simla was completed in 1856.[44] By the time John Lawrence recommended the use of Simla as the summer capital of the empire on strategic grounds, the Great Hindustan-Tibet Road had been built and the railway introduced in the subcontinent. Yet, to 'consider seriously the idea of ruling one-fifth of mankind from a remote Himalayan village whose only connection with the outside world was one tortuous and precipitous road', was 'an indication of the extraordinary confidence that pervaded the Raj' at the peak of the Industrial Revolution.[45] In 1891, that is in less than three decades, the railway link between Kalka and Simla became operational for goods traffic, and was opened for passenger traffic in 1903.[46]

The hill stations were mostly created on the ridges commanding the valleys and overlooking the Punjab plains. The only deviations were the cantonments of Dharmsala and Murree and, later Yol, which were developed on the spurs. The hill top location was in marked contrast to the indigenous hill towns which, excepting Nahan, happened to be located in the valleys.[47] In laying the settlement the British had to carry out extensive modifications of the terrain. Spaces were levelled for roads, military barracks, parade grounds, horse racing, polo, golf, cricket, and tennis. Each residential plot was a private space created by digging into the hill side. The houses, often called 'cottages', had several rooms, glazed verandahs and some open spaces, but compared to the bungalows in the plains, these houses had much smaller area. The 'cottages' or 'Swiss-chalet bungalows' were connected to one another by narrow pedestrian and equestrian roads which also led to the Mall, the main thoroughfare and the only artery of the station. The Mall gave access to the church, principal hotel, European stores, library, post office, and the club. All hill stations had cemeteries, and some also had a church for natives and a school for European children.[48] As mentioned before, an entire township, Sanawar, was developed around a school for European children, called Lawrence Military School.

The information regarding the civic amenities in Simla is quite suggestive of what existed in other hill stations on a smaller scale. Water supply to Simla was ensured by constructing huge reservoirs in catchment areas and by installing powerful pumping engines to lift up water. The material and service requirements of Europeans were met by the out of sight and congested native bazaar located at a lower elevation. Its haphazard growth, closely built structures, and high density were in absolute contrast to the meticulous planning, spaciousness, and civic amenities of the European area. There was hardly any provision for accommodation for the clerks, peons, porters, and rickshaw pullers who were required to move up every summer. Furthermore, the average water requirement of a European in Simla was estimated by its municipality to be five times more than that of a native. Finally, as may be expected *a priori*, the access to European areas was regulated, and even the Indian princes were directly or indirectly restrained from purchasing property in the European areas.[49]

V

The functional zones of the urban centres were interlinked with their morphology and reflected a distinct pattern of land use. While the old indigenous towns had an overlapping land use, the new areas, namely the civil stations, cantonments, colony towns, and hill stations, showed a specific land use.

The old city had its commercial centre in the chowk or the intersection of the main roads. The bazaars were extended along the main roads and also served as residential areas for the well-to-do shopkeepers. Other residential localities based on caste groups formed separate mohallas which were located between the main crossroads. The mohalla also served as a centre of small-scale manufacture pursued by the residing occupational caste. By the beginning of the twentieth century, in many cases, industry and even trade came to be located near the railway station, as in Bhatinda (Bathinda at present) Amritsar, Jalandhar, and Sangrur. Administrative offices were at times housed in the old fort, as at Bawal, Nakodar, Nabha, and Jind; or in the *sarai* as was the case at Nurmahal and Talamba; or sometimes in the old palace as at Shujabad and Farukhnagar. The fort often housed the school and the post office and, sometimes, the police station as well. Open spaces and gardens were not given much area within the town and were located mostly on the periphery as at Zira, Phul, Dhanaula, Kunjpura, Safidon, and Haripur. Kunja and Basi had gardens within the town but this was not common. In Amritsar, however, the old ponds (*dhabs*) were filled up and utilized as parks and green spaces within the walled area.[50]

The main business area was thus delimited by the main roads. Residential localities filled up the whole town, though the well-to-do generally lived at the centre and the poor, including the outcastes, on the periphery. Manufacturing units were scattered all over the town, and factories came to be located in the suburbs towards the railway station. Other new structures such as offices, schools, hospitals, dispensaries, clubs, and reading rooms were distributed in the old and new areas of the town. In other words, though a main business area can be delimited, most of the old urban centres combined all functions and had a multiple land use pattern.[51]

In the 'anglicized' areas the business district extended along the Mall in the civil lines and the Sadar Bazaar in the cantonment (Figure 4.4). The indigenous towns also remained important commercially. In many places, such as Gujrat and Amritsar, shops catering for the Europeans were located inside one of the gates of the walled town. The residential areas in the civil lines and cantonments were free of commercial or administrative pockets. In fact, offices and residences were clearly demarcated and there was no industrial zone in the civil lines and cantonments. Schools, mission houses, dispensaries, and hospitals had branches in the new localities outside the old town; at times, lager establishments were built in the 'anglicized' section as space was available. As a whole, zones of residences and offices were clearly demarcated in the British settlements. Linear extensions from the old town towards the 'anglicized' areas were also noticeable in some centres.

In the colony towns (Figure 4.5) the business district followed the main roads again, and this also had the residences of shopkeepers. The blocks housing inhabitants by and large remained their work place as well, though big industrial establishments were located at the new sites near the railway lines or away from the town. An industrial zone was demarcated, whereas businesses and residences shared the same areas of the town. Compared to the indigenous centres, more open spaces were provided for in the colony towns. Functionally, thus the colony towns synthesized the features of the indigenous and colonial urban forms.

The land use in the hill stations was closer to that in the civil stations and cantonments. However, as dictated by the terrain, the functional areas of the towns were located at several levels of the hills. As noted before, the highest and the widest road, the Mall, gave access to the European necessities and residences scattered over hill tops and hill

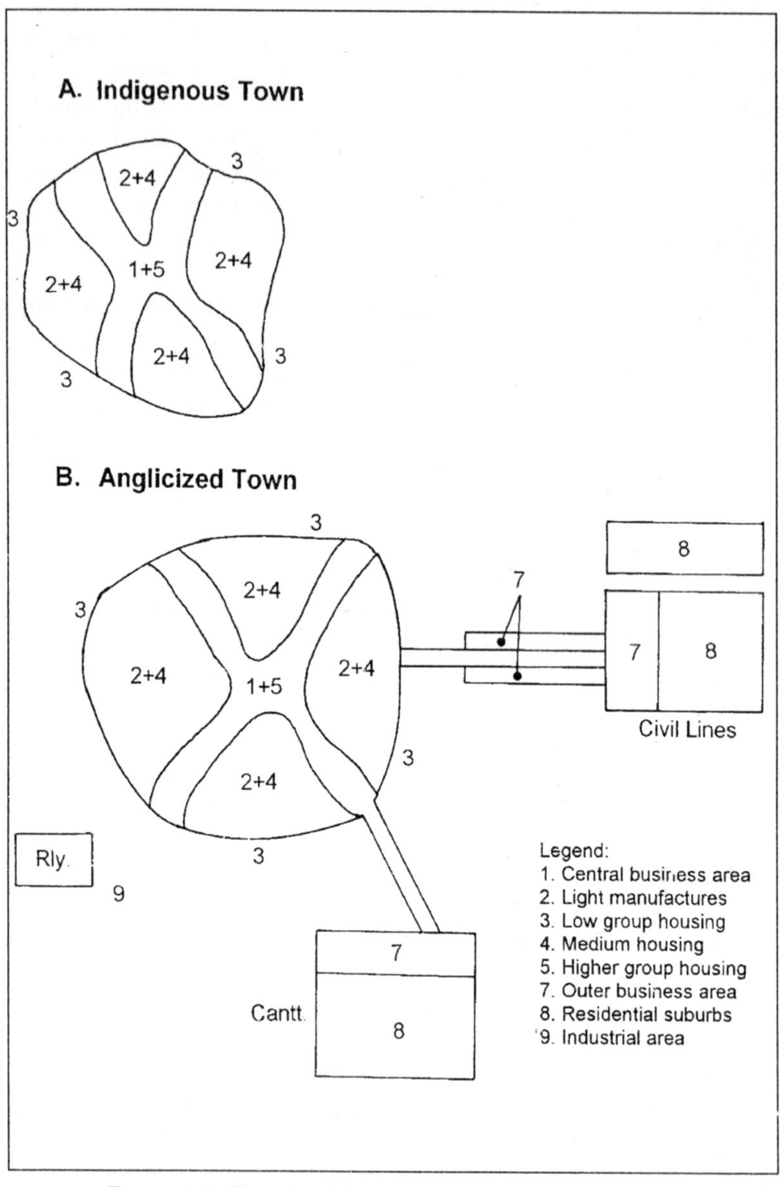

Figure 4.4: Functional Zones in the Towns of the Punjab

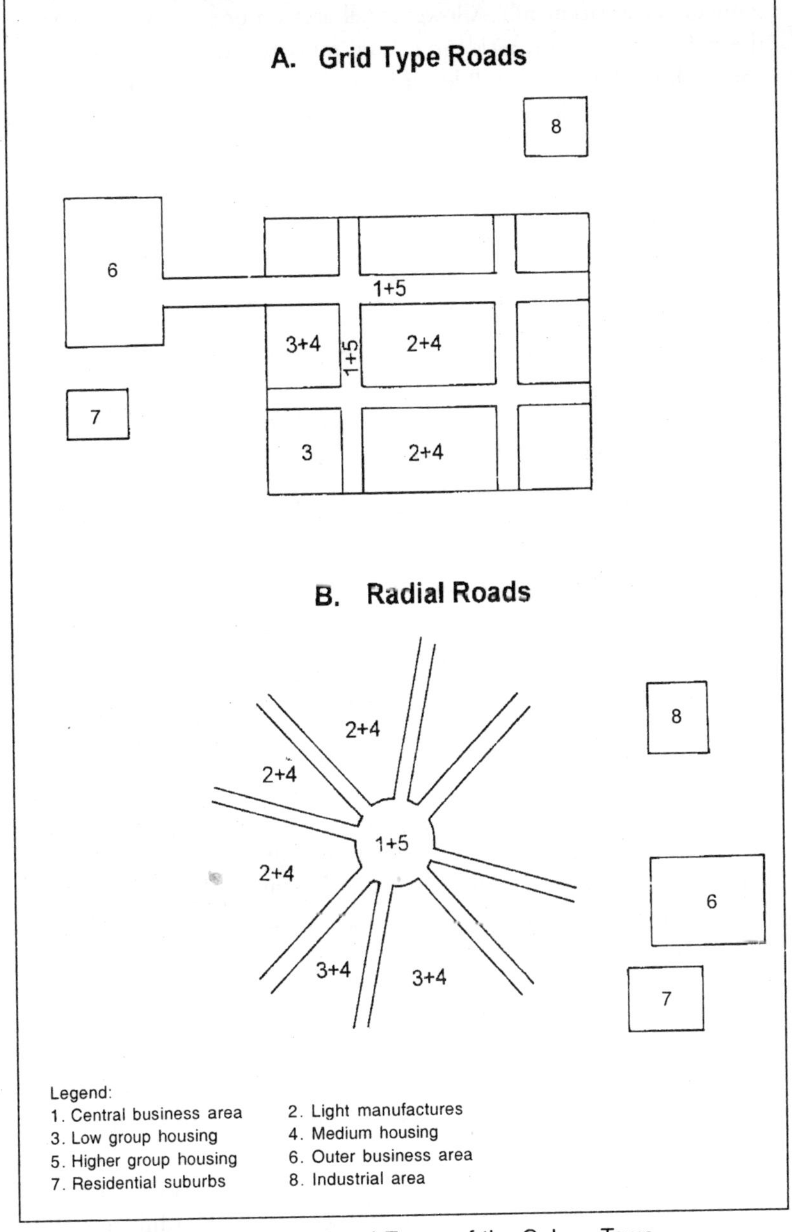

Figure 4.5: Functional Zones of the Colony Town

sides. The needs of the army were met by levelling large areas on the same or the adjacent hill. A lower small area on one side was given to the native bazaar and residences. The railway station and the main approach road were at a still lower height. The water reservoirs serving a hill station were located at the lowest level.

VI

In conclusion, some generalizations about the internal spatial patterns in the urban centres of colonial Punjab may be in order. The small centres—the indigenous as well as the colony towns—tended to have a business area along the main streets. With the growth of the urban centre, smaller secondary clusters sprang up at intersections or along transportation lines, as noticed in the 'anglicized' towns. Factories in these towns tended to develop on the periphery of the centre and near the railway station to be close to the line of transportation. The residential areas largely grew as clusters based on socio-economic, cultural or racial identities broadly similar to those in the indigenous towns. Some composite colonies of the new middle class also came up. For the British administrators and higher income groups the colony towns developed residential suburbs away from the business area.

The general picture which emerges is that of a combination of the east-west urban forms in the towns and cities of the Punjab. The indigenous town underwent only a few changes and remained the 'traditional Indian city', with a small suburb of colonial 'necessity'. In the 'anglicized' town, the old city and the new Western suburbs remained distinct but functionally integrated in one urban form. The principles of Western urban planning were most clearly evident in the colony towns which were wholly the product of colonial rule in their physical form, though not in social structure. Yet, the Western concepts, which were most visible in these new towns and in the new areas of the old towns, did not appreciably modify the features of the indigenous centres, particularly their social division of space. It was not even intended. The outcome was a duality characteristic of colonial rule. It may be pertinent to mention that the physical features of the urban centres during this period did not conform to any of the models of structure and growth developed by urban geographers and sociologists. The closest approximation, however, was to the multiple nuclei pattern according to which land use in an urban centre developed around not one but several nuclei.[52]

Finally, the new nuclei were created largely to meet the administrative, military, economic, and cultural needs of the colonial state. There were considerable differences between the European and native areas. In addition to overt expressions of racialism, the areas inhabited by Europeans were characterized by a generous use of space, low density of population, and high quality of civic amenities. While large open spaces were left around the civil and military stations, the old towns were allowed expansion only in certain directions. Suffering was built into the urban development of the period. To obtain space for the colonial necessities, a number of flourishing villages in the vicinity of the old centres were totally relocated or even dislocated.[53]

Moreover, in the process of building hill stations, hills were depleted of woods, and people living in the valley were deprived of their sources of water which was diverted to meet the needs of the station. The hill people were obliged to provide thousands of low-paid porters for the Sahibs every year. The hill rulers were required to send *begaris* (forced or underpaid labour) for roads and other construction work which was generally at the cost of agricultural production. Reordering of roads and the building of the railway spelt decline of trade and population for the indigenous hill towns which had been in existence for hundreds of years. Lastly, there were no provisions even of a basic nature for the white collar and other workers who were so essential for the efficiency and physical comfort of the Sahibs. The native service providers even in the summer capital of British India remained confined to hovels in the congested bazaars and lower areas.[54] In short, the quality of life sought for themselves by the British was made possible only by consigning the supporting native population to an existence which could be termed sub-human by comparison.

NOTES

1. Arthur B. Gallion and Simon Eisner, *The Urban Pattern*, first Indian edn., New Delhi: CBS Publishers, 1984, pp. 11–16. Harold Carter, *The Study of Urban Geography*, London: Arnold Heinemann, 1972, p. 144.

   The distinct political and cultural identity of the towns in the ancient world was expressed generally through the thickness of their boundary wall and the central shrine. J.N. Postgate, *Early Mesopotamia: Society and Economy at the Dawn of History*, London: Routledge, 1992, p. 75.

2. Cf. R. Ramachandran, *Urbanization and Urban Systems in India*; rpt., New Delhi: OUP, 1997, pp. 5–6.
3. Dilip Chakrabarti, *The Archaeology of Ancient Indian Cities*, New Delhi: OUP, 1997, pp. 242–4 and 249–55. The important among the planned centres excavated in the region were Taxila and Sakal (later Sialkot). See also, Brajadulal Chattopadhyaya, *The Making of Early Medieval India*; rpt., New Delhi: OUP, 1999, p. 158 and n. 7.
4. Renu Thakur, 'Urban Centres in the North-West (*c.* AD 600–1200)', in Reeta Grewal (ed.), *Five Thousand Years of Urbanization: The Punjab Region*, New Delhi: Manohar, 2005, pp. 79–89.
5. K.S. Ramegowda, *Urban and Regional Planning*, Mysore: University of Mysore, 1972, pp. 3–8. Among the different types of town-plans were *dandaka* where the male deities were in the north and the female deities outside; *saroathobhadra* in which the temple dominated the centre; *nandyavarta* were square or circular sites with the deity in the centre; and *padmaka* resembled a lotus in shape. Some other town-plans were *sivastika, prastara, karmukha,* and *chaturmukha*. See also, Chakrabarti, *Archaeology of Ancient Indian Cities*, pp. 255–8; A. Ghosh, *The City in Early Historical India*; rpt., Shimla: IIAS, 1990, pp. 43–50.
6. Ramachandran, *Urbanization and Urban Systems*, pp. 28–50. This description by and large applies to both north and south India in the pre-Turkish period. For example: Chattopadhyaya, *Making of Early Medieval India*, pp. 155-82. Ghosh, *City in Early Historical India*, pp. 51-2. Cf. D.C. Sircar, 'Foundation of Early Indian Cities and Towns', in Vijay Kumar Thakur (ed.), *Towns in Pre-Modern India*, Patna: Janaki Prakashan, 1994, pp. 90–104.

   Regional and local variations notwithstanding, urban forms in south India too shared most of these features. R. Champakalakshmi, *Trade, Ideology and Urbanization: South India, 300 BC to AD 1300*, New Delhi: OUP, 1996, pp. 63, 67–70, 127, 380–1. James Heitzman, 'Urbanization and Political Economy in Early South India during the Cola Period', in Kenneth W. Hall (ed.), *Structure and Society in Early South India*, New Delhi: OUP, 2001, pp. 126–8.
7. Ramegowda, *Urban and Regional Planning*, pp. 8–10.
8. Ibid., p. 12. For an average town like Batala in medieval Punjab, J.S. Grewal, *In the By-Lanes of History: Some Persian Documents from a Punjab Town*, Shimla: IIAS, 1975, pp. 10–24. For the architecture and gardens of Lahore, Syed Muhammad Latif, *Lahore—Its History, Architectural Remains and Antiquities*, Lahore, n.p., 1892, pp. 102–230 and 246–50.

For imperial cities, Stephen P. Blake, *Shahjahanabad: The Sovereign City in Mughal India, 1639–1739*; 1st Indian edn., New Delhi: Foundation Books, 1993, pp. 26–82. Cf. S. Ali Nadeem Rezavi, 'Uniqueness of the Eastern "Imperial City"? Testing the Model with Fathpur Sikri', in Krishna Mohan Shrimali (ed.), *Reason and Archaeology*, Delhi: Association for the Study of History and Archaeology, 1998, pp. 103–17. See also Reeta Grewal, 'Urbanization in Medieval India', in the *State and Society in Medieval India*, History of Indian Science, Philosophy and Culture, vol. VII, pt. 1, New Delhi: OUP, 2005, p. 420.

9. Ramachandran, *Urbanization and Urban Systems*, pp. 62–9.
10. Cf. Sudha Saxena, *Trends of Urbanization in Uttar Pradesh*, Agra: Satish Book Enterprise, 1970, p. 160. Saxena notices only three urban forms in Uttar Pradesh: indigenous, anglicized, and modern. In another study only the indigenous and the anglicized towns are noted. A.E. Smailes, 'The Indian City: A Descriptive Model', *Geographic Zeit Schrift*, vol. 57, 1969, pp. 179–80.
11. This understanding is based on the different series of the District Gazetteers (prefixed hereafter as *DG*) published by the British in 1884, 1890s, 1900s, and 1910s. For a theoretical reconstruction of the indigenous town see Figure 4.1. See also, Gerald Breese, *Urbanization in Newly Developing Countries*, New Delhi: Prentice Hall, 1978, p. 64.
12. Based on the DG series of 1884. For some field studies: Grewal, *In the By-Lanes of History*, p. 18, for Batala; K.D. Sharma, *Urban Development in Metropolitan Shadow*, New Delhi: Inter India, 1985, pp. 57 and 74–8, for Rohtak; and Anand Gauba, *Amritsar: A Study in Urban History (1840–1947)*, Jalandhar: ABS, 1988, pp. 11–12 for Amritsar.
13. Based on DG series of 1884, 1897, and 1904.
14. Kanchan Jyoti, 'Jullundur 1846-1947: An Urban History', Ph.D. thesis, GNDU, Amritsar, 1988, pp. 87–95.
15. A building cooperative society was established by the retired government officials at Lahore. Prakash Tandon, *Punjabi Saga (1857–2000)*; rpt., New Delhi: Rupa & Co., 2003, pp. 212–18.
16. Emrys Jones, *Towns and Cities*, London: OUP, 1966, p. 43.
17. Jacqueline Tyrwhitt, *Patrick Geddes in India*, London: Lund Humphries, 1947, p. 19.
18. Anthony D. King, *Colonial Urban Development: Culture, Social Power and Environment*, London: Routledge & Kegan Paul, 1976, pp. 82–3.
19. Based on DG series of 1884, 1890s, and 1900s. See also, Breese, *Urbanization in Newly Developing Countries*, pp. 65–6; Sharma, *Urban Development in Metropolitan Shadow*, pp. 61, 80–5 and 95–8.
20. *DG Montgomery*, 1933, p. 72. It may be of some interest to know that around 1930, the price of land in Montgomery and Lyallpur was Rs. 50

per acre. This, however, was about one-fifth of the average price of 'all types of land', including urban lands, in the Punjab in 1938–9. Karunamoy Mukerji, 'Land Prices in Punjab', in M.K. Chaudhuri (ed.), *Trends of Socio-Economic Change in India, 1871–1961,* Simla: IIAS, 1969, p. 534.

21. Breese, *Urbanization in Newly Developing Countries,* pp. 65-6.
22. King, *Colonial Urban Development,* p. 33.
23. The numbers of Europeans at these six places ranged from 1195 to 3375 persons in 1868. By contrast, Amritsar, the largest city till 1881, had just over 600 Europeans, and a small civil station and cantonment area to house them. At this time, the Europeans in Lahore numbered around 3300, and the civil lines, cantonments and the railway colony housing them 'resulted in a dual city' in Lahore. Ian J. Kerr, 'Urbanization and Colonial Rule in 19th-Century India: Lahore and Amritsar, 1849–81', *Panjab Past and Present,* vol. XIV, pt. 1, 1980, pp. 214–24.
24. King, *Colonial Urban Development,* p. 98. See also, Vijaya Kumar Vashishtha, 'Cantonments and Emergence of Towns in Rajasthan During British Paramountcy', in Makrand Mehta (ed.), *Urbanization in Western India: Historical Perspective,* Ahmedabad: Gujarat University, 1988, pp. 245–77.
25. James Douie, *The Panjab North-West Frontier Province and Kashmir* (cited hereafter as *Panjab, NWFP*); rpt., Delhi: Low Price Publications, 1994, pp. 347–56.
26. King, *Colonial Urban Development,* p. 98.
27. Quoted in ibid., p. 111.
28. Ibid., pp. 100–22, supplemented by Professor Indu Banga's field studies of the cantonments of Ambala, Jalandhar and Amritsar, so kindly lent to the author.
29. For the layout of the colony towns: *DG Montgomery,* 1933, pt. A, pp. 76–87. *Gazetteer of the Chenab Colony,* 1904, pp. 151–3. Tandon, *Punjabi Saga,* pp. 145–47. See also, Reeta Grewal and J.S. Grewal, 'Urbanization in Colonial Punjab', in Reeta Grewal (ed.), *Five Thousand Years of Urbanization: The Punjab Region,* pp. 156–9.
30. For detail, Tandon, *Punjabi Saga,* pp. 87–9 and 213–14; Gauba, *Amritsar,* pp. 53–6.
31. King, *Colonial Urban Development,* p. 91.
32. Ibid., pp. 89–92 and 123–55. Also, Philip Davies, *Splendours of the Raj: British Architecture in India, 1660 to 1947,* New Delhi: Dass Media, 1985, pp. 104–11.
33. Davies, *Splendours of the Raj,* p. 105.
34. Ibid., pp. 111–13.
35. King, *Colonial Urban Development,* p. 159. This estimate was given by the

Royal Commission on the Sanitary State of the Army in India (1863). *Parliamentary Papers*, vol. XIX, p. 1. For the 1830s, their numbers were estimated by a contemporary observer at 37,000 troops out of about 41,000 Europeans.

36. Douie, *Panjab, NWFP*, p. 355.
37. Vipin Pubby, *Shimla Then & Now*, 2nd edn., New Delhi: Indus, 1996, p. 19.
38. Quoted in ibid., pp. 33-4.
39. Ibid., p. 36. In 1884, the offices of the Criminal Investigation Department, Meteorological Department, and the Sanitary Department also were shifted to Simla.
40. Douie, *Panjab, NWFP*, pp. 350, 352 and 356. The Deputy Commissioner of Ambala used Kasauli and that of Hoshiarpur repaired to Bharwain on the nearby Chintpurni range of hills. Pamela Kanwar, *Essays on Urban Patterns in Nineteenth Century Himachal Pradesh*, Shimla: IIAS, 1999, p. 132.
41. Davies, *Splendours of the Raj*, p. 111.
42. King, *Colonial Urban Development*, pp. 157 and 165.
43. Edward J, Buck, *Simla Past and Present*, Calcutta: Thacker Spink, 1904, p. 182.
44. Pubby, *Simla Then & Now*, p. 44.
45. Davies, *Splendours of the Raj*, p. 116.
46. Pubby, *Simla Then & Now*, p. 45. The laying of about 96-km long railway line involved the construction of 103 tunnels, aggregating about 8 km.
47. Douie, *Panjab, NWFP*, p. 352. For further detail, see Surya Kant, 'Urbanization in Himachal Pradesh: Analysis of Patterns and Trends (1901-2001)', in Reeta Grewal (ed.), *Five Thousand Years of Urbanization: The Punjab Region*, New Delhi: Manohar/Institute of Punjab Studies, 2005, pp. 212 and 214–15.
48. King, *Colonial Urban Development*, pp. 175–9. This is also substantiated by the author's personal observation.
49. Pubby, *Simla Then & Now*, pp. 47–58 and 74–85. The lower location of the properties actually owned by the princes in Shimla also points to this.
50. *DG Amritsar*, 1892–3, p. 160. See also, Gauba, *Amritsar*, p. 52. The Nichol Park in Amritsar was one such filled pond.
51. A multiple land use pattern is also seen in the studies respectively of Madras and Serampore. Susan M. Neild, 'Colonial Urbanism: The Development of Madras City in the 18th and 19th Centuries', *Modern Asian Studies*, vol. 13, no. 2, 1979, pp. 217-46. Pranabranjan Ray, 'Urbanization in Colonial Situation: Serampore', in M.S.A. Rao (ed.), *Urban Sociology in India*, New Delhi: Orient Longman, 1974, pp. 119–50.
52. For a discussion, see Appendix 4A.

53. Ramachandran, *Urbanization and Urban Systems*, p. 294.
54. Kanwar, *Essays on Urban Patterns*, pp. 12–14, 107–12 and 124–30. A British administrator feeling uncomfortable about the system of *begar* and actually doing something to curb it was rather exceptional. Idem, *Imperial Simla: The Political Culture of the Raj*, New Delhi: OUP, 1990, pp. 29–30.

APPENDIX 4A

Models of Urban Land-use*

To determine how far the zonal distribution of land use in different categories of towns in the Punjab region is comparable to models of land use, reference may be made to three 'ideal' patterns of city structure, namely, the concentric zone theory, the sector theory, and the multiple-nuclei pattern.

At the beginning of the twentieth century, Richard Hurd observed that cities tended to expand in concentric circles and in axial spokes along the main transportation lines. At that time little attention was paid to this aspect. In 1923, Earnest Burgess propounded what is referred to as the concentric zone theory. He conceptualized the city developing as five concentric rings around a central business core area. Outside this ring was a transition zone of the low income group houses and extension of the business core. Zone three was the medium group housing, surrounded by a ring of higher income group residences. The outer zone was of commuters and was along the transportation lines; this zone also had elite residences and specific suburbs, interspersed with cultivated areas. These radiating centres moving outwards from the central business core were the result of the struggle over time between competing functions.

However, the morphological pattern in the Punjab region did not conform to the concentric zone hypothesis on several counts. In the first place, the core area was not necessarily a ring but often extended radially along the major routes as seen in the indigenous towns of colonial Punjab. Secondly, development of the sub centres of business was noticed also in the Sadar Bazaar and the Mall of the 'anglicized' towns. Thirdly, industry was located not only within but also outside the zones close to the towns as, for instance, near the railway suburb. Lastly, residential areas were not fixed but sprang up at any convenient location.

Homer Hoyt visualized the structure and physical growth of the town in terms of sectoral development 'along transport lines and paths of least resistance'. Different functional sectors were assumed to emerge around a core

* This understanding of the models of land use is based on the following studies: Gerald Breese, *Urbanization in Newly Developing Countries*, Delhi: Prentice Hall, 1978, pp. 104–5. V.L.S. Prakasa Rao, *Urbanization in India: Spatial Dimensions*, Delhi: Concept, 1983, p. 173. Jugendra Sahai, *Urban Complex of an Industrial City*, Allahabad: Chugh, 1980, pp. 50–1. Chauncy Harris and Edward Ullman, 'The Nature of Cities', in Harold Meyer and Clyde F. Kohn (eds.), *Readings in Urban Geography*, South Asian edn., Allahabad: Central Book Depot, 1967, pp. 282–5. John E. Brush, 'The Morphology of Indian Cities', in Roy Turner (ed.), *India's Urban Future*, Berkeley: University of California Press, 1962, pp. 224–36.

business area with the residences arranging themselves like wedges along radial lines from the centre to the fringes. In this pattern low grade houses lay close to the core, followed by medium income housing. This model too does not encompass the growth of the suburbs around the town, nor the existence of small industrial pockets within the residential areas, or even combined with them.

In the mid-1940s, Chauncy Harris and Edward Ullman theorized that land use pattern in a city developed around not one but several nuclei. These nuclei either existed previously near the town or were specifically developed for special land use. The multiple nuclei pattern thus consists of a core area as well as several suburbs. The core business area is surrounded by the small manufacturing units and low income housing on one side, and medium income housing on the other. Residences of higher income groups are located in the outer zone and have an adjoining business area as well. Heavy industry, according to this theory, also has a separate nucleus (Figure 4.6).

Yet another model of the colonial city given by T.G. McGee describes it as 'dual', structured with its bazaar-peasant economy juxtaposed with firm capitalist economy. However, one fails to identify a 'firm capitalist type' of economy in any of the towns in the Punjab. McGee also admits to an over-simplification and the possibility of 'intermediate' economy bases.

The towns and cities of the Punjab do not strictly follow any of these models of functional layout. In a way, the indigenous towns were close to Gideon Sjoberg's characterization of pre-industrial cities of a 'rich centre and poor periphery', but in terms which is an over-simplification and which does not take into account growth over time. In fact, the indigenous towns had a linear core area. John Brush's assumption that a dominant central business district was 'scarcely existent' in India may be valid only for the contemporary times. The towns of colonial Punjab at all levels had a recognizable core which can be legitimately referred to as the central or main business area.

This core combining the main business and high-grade housing was surrounded by areas of light manufacture and medium housing in the town, adjoining which was the poor-grade residential area. Over time these towns developed industrial, commercial and residential suburbs, thus coming close to the multi-nuclei pattern.

The 'anglicized' towns were also close to the multiple nuclei pattern, though the core was different. Here too the central business area combined higher-income group residences, surrounded by small manufactures and medium-grade housing. Low-income groups remained on the periphery. With the establishment of the civil lines, a high-grade residential suburb was added along with an outer business area and other residential localities. On another side of the urban unit sprang up an industrial suburb.

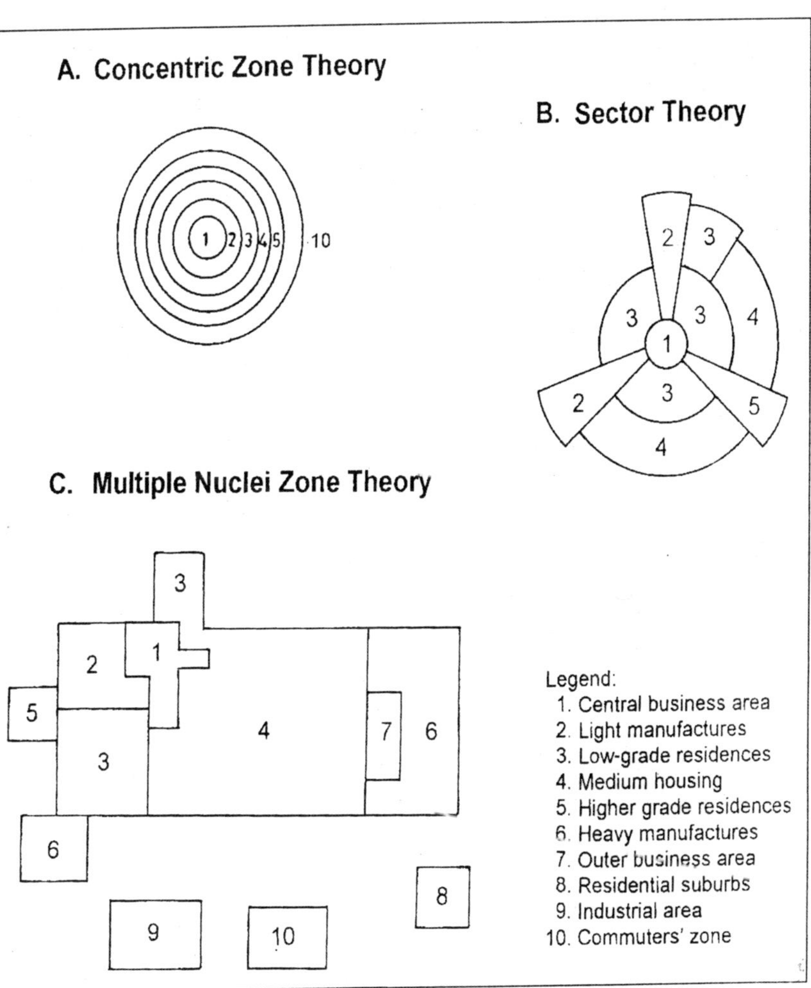

Figure 4.6: Models of Urban Land-use

The colony towns too shared some similarities with the multiple nuclei pattern. The central business area and higher-income group residences were surrounded by the light manufacturing units and the middle-group housing areas. Low- grade housing was on the outer zones of the town. With the passage of time residential suburbs of the higher-income groups as well as an industrial suburb were added to the new towns.

In short, the urban centres of the Punjab plains were by and large close to the multiple nuclei pattern, though their business zones were distinct from the business-cum-higher income group residential zone. The industrial zone too differed in the sense that it was also a trading and commercial area for grain and cotton, in addition to being the location of various mills and factories.

5

Changing Structure of Urban Population

Migration of people from rural to urban areas and from small towns to cities and larger urban centres is the 'basic mechanism of urbanization'.[1] From 1881 to 1941, population in the cities of the region increased by over 600 per cent; in the middling centres by over 1400 per cent; and in the small towns by about 10 per cent. The increase in the small towns alone broadly corresponded to the rate of natural increase; at the two higher levels it was overwhelmingly due to migration. In itself a major indicator of spatial mobility, this growth entailed several parameters of social mobility and social change resulting from developments under colonial rule. This chapter analyses the growth, structure and composition of urban population in the Punjab in the wider context of British India.

I

Urban population in the Punjab region increased from 9.8 per cent in 1881 to 13.9 per cent in 1941.[2] Its analysis at the intercensal level, however, shows that the pattern of growth was more an erratic one than a steady increase over the period. From 1881 to 1911, the increase was small, rising only up to 10.57 per cent. Moreover, there was a slight dip in 1901. In 1921, the urban population fell to a surprising 9 per cent, the lowest proportion recorded. Thereafter, figures shot up to 11.7 per cent in 1931, and to 13.9 per cent in 1941. There were thus two main phases of growth in the region's urban population. The first from 1881 to 1911 with a slight variation, and the second from 1921 onwards, showing a substantial rise in the number of urban people and consequent increase in the size of urban centres (Figure 5.1).[3]

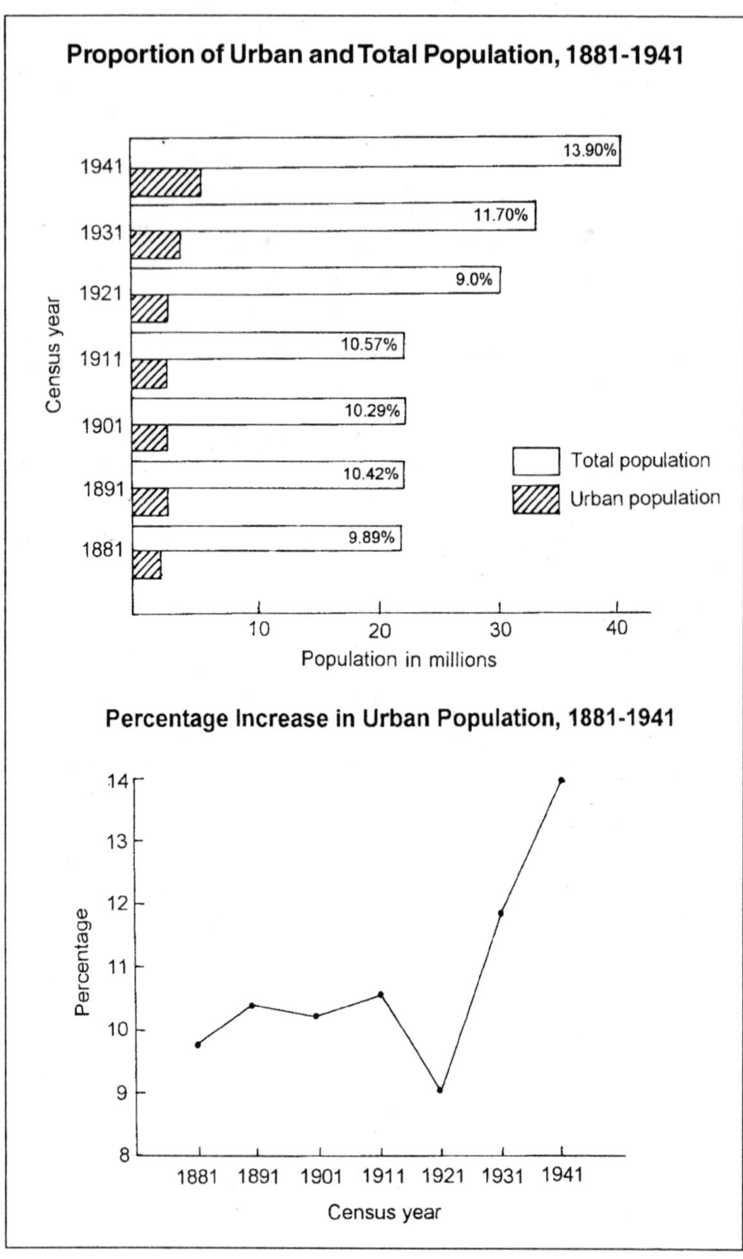

Figure 5.1: Urban Population in the Punjab, 1881–1941

These two broad phases appear to have been influenced by two altogether different sets of circumstances. The fluctuations in urban population may be explained largely in terms of the effects of the epidemics, droughts and famines, and migration to canal colonies. From the 1860s to the 1890s there were six major outbreaks of cholera and two of smallpox. The plague erupted several times from 1897 to the 1920s. After the outbreak of the influenza epidemic in 1918, the Punjab was relatively free from any major epidemics, though 'fever' intermittently affected its population throughout the period.[4] The period of the worst famines in the Punjab was also confined to the later half of the nineteenth century, reaching its peak in the late 1890s. In fact, famines and epidemics were mutually sustaining.

The 'new trend' evident in 1921–31 may also be attributed to the setting in motion of 'the wheels of economic and social development' by this time.[5] To recapitulate briefly, by this time, the network of railways and metalled roads had reached most towns and villages, and some of the sub-regions had been brought under irrigation for the first time. Private enterprise in lorry service began to supplement the railway. The post-War reorientations in the industrial policy of the Government of India encouraged investments in industry. The number of factories coming under the purview of the Factory Act nearly doubled by 1928, and between 1921 and 1931, their number rose from 297 to 647. The hydro-electric schemes at Jogindernagar and Sundernagar were also undertaken in this phase. These developments, coupled with the relative absence of major natural calamities and improvement in public health measures in urban areas, initiated a process of steady urban growth in the region. [6]

Significantly, the growth of urban population in the Punjab was the closest to the all-India average for the census years 1881 and 1941. In 1881, 9.3 per cent people lived in the towns and cities of India. By 1941 this proportion had risen to 13.8 per cent. With the exception of a slight decrease recorded in 1911, there was 'a slow but steady upward trend'.[7] In the various provinces of British India too, an overall increase is noted, though with marked divergence. From 1881 to 1941, urban population in Bengal rose from 5.2 per cent to 9.84 per cent; in the Central Provinces from 6 to 11.2 per cent; in Madras from 9.7 to 15.93 per cent; from 11.5 to 17 per cent in Berar; and from 17.4 to 25.95 per cent in Bombay. On the other hand, Assam reached only 2.74 per cent from 1.4 per cent, while Orissa recorded a small increase, from 3.0 in 1881 to 3.87 in 1941. In Bihar no change is recorded in urban population, the proportion remaining 5.3 per cent in both the census years (Table 5.1).

In terms of urban hierarchy in the Punjab in 1881, the largest proportion of urban people were at the class V level, followed respectively, by classes IV, III, VI and I. Class II towns at this time had the smallest population. By 1941, it was the class I cities which together housed the largest proportion of urban people, followed respectively by classes III, IV, V and II. As a category, class VI towns had the smallest number of people. From a heavy base at the beginning of the period, the urban population in the 1940s came to be concentrated at the top, while the middling rung came second in both cases (Table 5.2).

In 1881, the two cities of the region housed 12.88 per cent of the urban population; by 1941 its nine cities accounted for 36.29 per cent of the urban people.[8] This increase was largely at the cost of class II towns; their share in the population decreased from about 10 per cent to 7.28 per cent. The population of class III towns rose from 15.32 per cent in 1881 to 22.47 per cent in 1941. The remaining three classes registered decrease over the period, respectively from 21.30, 24.98 and 15.37 per cent in 1881 to 16.03, 14.94 and 2.94 per cent by the end of the period.

TABLE 5.1: PERCENTAGE OF URBAN POPULATION IN BRITISH INDIA

Province	1881	1941
India	9.3	13.8
Bengal	5.2	9.84
Central Provinces	6.0	11.2
Madras	9.7	15.93
Bombay	17.4	25.95
Berar	11.5	17.0
Assam	1.4	2.74
Orissa	3.0	3.87
Bihar	5.3	5.3
Punjab	9.8	13.9

Source: Tables on Urban Population in the *Census of India*, 1881 and 1941.

TABLE 5.2: URBAN CLASSES AND URBAN POPULATION IN THE PUNJAB, 1881–1941

Census Year	% of Urban Population in Total Populaiton	% of Urban Population in Classes of Towns					
		I	II	III	IV	V	VI
1881	9.89	12.88	9.92	15.32	21.30	24.98	15.57
1891	10.42	11.97	20.56	15.38	18.04	26.16	7.8
1901	10.29	13.20	19.08	15.98	18.29	24.91	8.5
1911	10.57	13.88	19.96	17.63	17.52	24.74	6.24
1921	9.00	23.85	15.06	22.16	15.41	16.88	6.61
1931	11.70	29.70	10.83	18.49	15.72	21.22	4.00
1941	13.90	36.29	7.28	22.47	16.03	14.94	2.94
% of increase/decrease between 1881 and 1941	+4.01	+23.41	-2.64	+7.17	-5.27	-10.04	-12.63

Source: Tables on 'Towns Classified by Population', *Census of the Punjab* for 1881, 1891, 1901, 1911, 1921, 1931 and 1941.

The increase or decrease in the different classes of towns and cities in the Punjab at the intercensal level was not steady in all cases.[9] After an initial dip in 1891, the cities remained at more or less the same level up to 1911, after which the proportion shot up in the next three decades. Class II towns exhibited a substantial increase in population in 1891, a slight decline in 1901, with a small rise in the following decade, and then a sharp decline after 1911, to slide even lower than their initial proportion in 1881. Simultaneously, however, the larger ones among class II centres were gaining in population and entering the class I category. The proportion of urban people in class III towns remained more or less the same up to 1901, increasing steadily in the next two decades to dip somewhat in 1931 and again rise by 1941. Class IV towns were declining slowly after 1881, with only a slight increase in 1941. The proportion of people in class V towns rose slightly in 1891 but slipped back to the initial position in the next two decades. Population at this level declined in the next two censuses, rose in 1931, and finally registered a sharp decrease in 1941. The class VI towns recorded a sharp decline in 1891, a minor rise in the succeeding decade, followed by a steady decline.

To compare urban hierarchy in the Punjab region with the hierarchical levels in British India in the 1870s, it may be noted that the largest proportion of urban people were living in classes III and IV towns, each having over 24 per cent population. Classes V and VI came next, with about 15 per cent each. Class II centres had 12.4 per cent of the urban population, while, with 7.6 per cent, class I cities had the smallest proportion of urban people.[10] By 1931, however, their largest proportion, that is 27.4 per cent, was living in cities, followed respectively by classes IV, III and V, with 19, 18.8 and 17.3 per cent of urban population. Class II towns registered a small decrease since the 1870s, at 11.9 per cent of the population, but the class VI towns came to have the smallest proportion at 5.6 per cent in 1931.[11] The general pattern of the country and the region, thus, was similar with respect to changes in urban population at different levels of the urban hierarchy.

II

Natural increase in population as a component of urban growth is determined by fertility and mortality.[12] The birth and death rates of urban population in India in 1881, at 45.3 and 39.2 per thousand (mille) respectively, seem to be both higher and lower than the rates for the Punjab as a whole.[13] In 1881, with the exception of the town of Gujrat which had a birth rate equal to that of the Punjab, Ferozepore, Wazirabad and Gujranwala, among others, had a lower birth rate, at 18.1, 35.4 and 39.5 per thousand, respectively. Jalandhar had a higher birth rate at 49.3. The death rates in these towns varied from 19.9 to 39.2, being generally lower than the rate for the province.[14]

A comparison of the birth rates of 1901 and 1911 shows the absence of a pattern. The birth rate had decreased in the towns of Dera Ismail Khan, Kohat, Gujrat, Gujranwala, Eminabad, Kasur, Kapurthala, Dhanaula, Phul, Jind, and Sangrur, among others. At the same time, an increase is noted in some other urban centres, for example, in Lahore, Sialkot, Wazirabad, Ramnagar, Daska, Pasrur, Jalalpur, Patti, Montgomery, Kamalia, Pak Pattan, Chiniot, Hoshiarpur, Sultanpur, Anandpur, Ropar, Ambala, and Nabha.[15] From nearly all levels of the urban hierarchy in both eastern and western plains, these centres included the district and tahsil headquarters, cantonments and the capitals of native states. There is, thus, no relation necessarily between the size and character of an urban centre and its birth rate, nor between the birth rates of urban and rural areas, there being exceptions in both situations. In the decade 1911–21 also, towns had birth rates both higher and lower than the average birth rate of 38.3 for the province.[16]

The overall death rate in the urban centres in 1911, interestingly, does not seem to be more than the previous census year, despite the severity of the plague epidemic in the 1900s. In the case of Lahore, Kasur, Patti, Gujrat, Wazirabad, Ramnagar, Sialkot, Jalalpur, Phagwara, Kapurthala, Jind, Sangrur, Nabha, Montgomery, Kamalia, Pak Pattan, Dera Ismail Khan, and Kohat, among others, the death rate was even lower than that of the 1901 and 1911 average of the province at 33.45. The rate had, however, risen in Phul, Dhanaula, Hoshiarpur, Anandpur, Ambala, Ropar, Sultanpur, Chiniot, Gujranwala, Eminabad, Daska and Pasrur, and possibly in some other centres as well.[17] This was perhaps because the plague hit the small towns in the agriculturally developed areas more severely. Then there could be local variations in the intensity of the plague and in the attempts to combat it according to variations in humidity conditions, public health measures, awareness of the towns people, and alacrity of the local administration. On the whole, the cantonments and district headquarters were better provided in terms of health facilities.[18] Thus, size in itself does not seem to be related to these variations as both large and small towns experienced increase and decrease in death rates.

III

In terms of religious affiliation, more than 50 per cent people of the Punjab in the 1880s were Muslim, about 40 per cent Hindu, while Sikhs constituted over 7 per cent, and Christians about 2 per cent of the total inhabitants.[19] Furthermore, the Muslims dominated the western parts of the region, while the Hindus lived largely in the eastern areas. The Sikhs lived in all parts of the region but the majority of them were concentrated in the central districts. Jains had a strong base in Phagwara, but were conspicuous by their absence from the Chaj and Sindh Sagar Doabs and the trans-Indus areas. The relative proportions in 1941 were broadly similar, with a small decrease of Hindus, to about 37 per cent, and Christians to less than 2 per cent, and a compensating increase in the proportion of Sikhs to more than 13 per cent.[20]

The distribution of urban people with respect to their religious affiliation seems to follow the general pattern of the region. There is, however, a variation over time in the relative proportions of the major communities within urban centres. In 1881, Hindus dominated in a number of small and large towns in all parts of the Punjab. For instance, in Rewari, Farukhnagar, Jind, Gurgaon, Patiala, Phagwara, Gurdaspur, Dunyapur, and Bannu they formed half or more of the population. By and large, Hindus ranged from 15 to over 50 per cent of the population in urban centres. Muslims were dominant in the cities of Lahore and Amritsar and in towns like Dera Ghazi Khan, Kohat, Chiniot, Jalandhar, Gujranwala, Pasrur, Kasur, Tarn Taran, Dera Baba Nanak, Zira, and Montgomery where they formed 30 to 80 per cent of the towns people. Tarn Taran and Dera Baba Nanak had a large proportion of Sikhs, over 30 per cent, while centres such as Dunyapur had no Sikh population. In other places, they varied from less than 1 to about 15 per cent. Jains formed a much lower proportion, from less than 1 to 2 per cent, though Farukhnagar and Pasrur had a relatively larger proportion of Jains—over 4 per cent. Christians also did not form a major segment in any town at this time. The small number of Jains in the province tended to live in towns, though the Christians were scattered in the countryside too.[21]

By 1941, the relative position of the major communities within the urban centres of the region had changed.[22] The previously Muslim majority towns, such as Chiniot and Montgomery, now had Hindus as the major community, though they were not in a much larger proportion than before. The Muslims in these towns had declined drastically in number, coming to about 7 and 6 per cent from over 66 and over 53 per cent, respectively. Hindus appear to have come to these towns as traders, commission agents, and moneylenders.

This change in the communal proportions still seems to be exceptional. Hindus also increased in Jind, Zira, Patiala, Tarn Taran, Phagwara and Dera Baba Nanak where Muslims had declined in relative proportions. In some places, however, it was the proportion of Hindus which had decreased as in Lahore, Amritsar, Dera Ghazi Khan, Gurdaspur, Gujranwala, Jalandhar, Pasrur, and Farukhnagar. In most of these places where Hindus decreased in number, Muslims increased in proportion through migration from the neighbouring countryside.

There was substantial change in the proportion of Sikhs in urban areas. In 1881, Sikhs had been in large numbers in Dera Baba Nanak, about 34 per cent, but came down to a mere 4 per cent in 1941. Apparently, they migrated to the bigger centres. In Tarn Taran, the Sikhs remained the second major community though their proportion was the same in both census years. In most towns, however, the number of Sikhs had increased in relation to their own proportions due to in-migration. In each town they had increased manifold though in comparison to others they were still a minority group. For example, they rose from about 4 to 14 per cent in Phagwara, 13 to 23 per cent in Patiala, 5 to 13 per cent in Gujranwala and 3 to over 10 per cent in Gurdaspur. This increase in the number of Sikhs could also be attributed to the fact that, availing the choice of returning one's religion given to the people at the time of the census of 1911, a number of Sehajdharis, who did not follow the Khalsa way of life, had returned themselves as Sikhs; they had been enumerated as Hindus earlier.[23]

Among the smaller groups, the Jains increased at some places such as Jind, Gurdaspur, and Amritsar, though very slightly. In Gujranwala, Jalandhar, Pasrur, Rewari, Farukhnagar, and Patiala they decreased by slight margins. By 1941, they were no longer residing in Phagwara, among others, while they took up residence in Tarn Taran where they had been absent in 1881. The Christians too, who had not been counted as a group previously, were present in almost all towns where, in addition to the European officials, there were a large number of missionaries and also Indian converts to Christianity. The only exceptions were Zira and Patiala. As a whole, their proportion was rather negligible in the urban areas, being less than 1 or just about 1 per cent in most cases. Lahore and Gurdaspur, however, had 8 and 4 per cent Christians, respectively.

IV

The occupational structure and workforce of urban centres in a region serve as sensitive indices of its economy and stage of development. A 'worker' may be broadly defined as a person 'whose main activity is participation in an economically productive work by his physical or mental activity'.[24] In 1881 the occupational structure of the urban population was dominated by textile workers who accounted for over 20 per cent of the working men and over 40 per cent of the occupied women.[25] The second major category, with about 13 to 15 per cent people, was of those engaged in agriculture, dairying, and the production of food and drink. The latter also employed over 19 per cent of the women. Over 11 per cent men worked with minerals, over 8 as labourers, and about 6 per cent in entertainment and 'personal offices'. Government officials, including defence personnel, formed about 10 per cent of the urban people. Nearly 5 per cent were professional men: teachers, doctors, journalists and others. Only 3 per cent followed 'arts and mechanical work' as their occupation, with the same proportion in transport. About 6 per cent of the working population was engaged in miscellaneous pursuits. Significantly, in 1881, the urban employed in the subcontinent were mainly males, forming over 80 per cent of the workforce.

Unfortunately, because of the absence of data, the occupational pattern of the urban population for the later decades cannot be discerned. Comparison, however, can be made among the major cities of the region for which figures are available at different points of time.

At the inception of colonial rule, about 52 per cent of the males in the city of Lahore were reported to be employed.[26] About 11 per cent were engaged in crafts; over 6 in textiles; about 21 per cent in trade; only 1 per cent in transportation, while over 11 per cent provided other services. By the end of the nineteenth century, about 32 per cent were recorded as manufacturers of some kind; about 13 per cent as traders and transporters; and nearly 16 per cent as domestic servants. Government servants formed 10 per cent of the urban people, while agriculturists and labourers had a proportion of over 7 per cent each. More than 6 per cent were professionals.[27] In the first 50 years of British rule, thus, the proportion of people engaged in manufacturing and crafts in the city had increased substantially. Compared to the general occupational structure of the urban centres of the region in 1901, the categories of textile workers and agriculturists were much smaller in Lahore; government employees and labourers were relatively at the same proportion; professionals, understandably were a notch above the average for the region; and industry engaged a considerably larger proportion of the workforce in the city.

By 1921, the occupational structure of Lahore had undergone some changes.[28] Persons employed in traditional textiles had decreased from over 6 per cent in the 1840s to a mere 1 per cent in 1921. Groups which increased substantially were engaged in modern industry and transport. Compared to 1881, those engaged in industry rose from about 11 to over 18 per cent, though their percentage had declined in relation to 1901. Within this category, textile workers were over 1 per cent; wood workers over 2. Around 1 per cent were workers in metal, food, and building, while over 4 per cent worked in apparel making. Those engaged in transportation increased from 1 to over 7 per cent by this time, reflecting the extensive network of rail and road communications and the growing mobility of the people. The proportion of domestic labour at 12 per cent was higher by 4 per cent when compared to the general pattern in 1881. Miscellaneous services now employed over 25 per cent people against about 11 per cent in 1881. Learned professionals and government officials, when compared to the region's urban averages in 1881, were at the same proportion, that is, at 5 and 10 per cent respectively. In 1921 the proportion of traders fell to 13 per cent from 21 in 1881. Unproductive people formed about 4 per cent of the population in 1921.

A decade later, the proportion of workers in agriculture, domestic work and additional services had decreased in Lahore.[29] On the other hand, industrial workers had increased to almost 23 per cent and traders to over 15 per cent. Government servants increased from about 10 to over 18 per cent. Within the broad category of industry, workers in textiles, wood and metal, besides apparel makers, had a slightly larger proportion over that in 1921; the proportions of those employed in food and construction work had somewhat declined in 1931.[30] Transporters were at the same level as were professionals. Unproductive people had decreased in proportion by this time. On the whole, the manufacturing group was on the rise in Lahore, with a corresponding increase of traders and transporters. The proportion of officials had also grown over time, and so also of domestic labour.

In the city of Amritsar in 1901, the largest segment of the workforce was that of manufacturers, at about 53 per cent.[31] This was larger that that of Lahore at that time. Traders and transporters followed with nearly 19 per cent, again higher than Lahore. Government servants, labourers and agriculturists were over 3.5 per cent each; domestics constituted over 8 per cent; and professionals accounted for about 4.5 per cent of the population of the city. In short, Amritsar had fewer government officials and agriculturists than Lahore, but more people were engaged in trade and manufactures.

In 1931 too the largest segment of urban people in Amrtisar was employed in industry, that is over 31 per cent.[32] Within this segment about 7 per cent were engaged in textiles; 3 each in wood and metal manufactures; over 2 per cent in foods; 8 per cent in apparel; while 1 per cent of urban workers earned their livelihood by construction work. Amritsar had retained its lead over Lahore in this sphere. Transporters, however, were smaller in proportion in Amritsar than in Lahore, being only 5 per cent. By 1931, traders had increased to more than 26 per cent of the population of the city. Over 4 per cent workers were professionals and more than 8 per cent were domestic labourers, being at the same level as before. Miscellaneous services were carried out by over 20 per cent people. Government officials constituted about 8 per cent, which was much more than the previous decade, though still considerably less than in Lahore. With a little over 1 per cent, the unproductive segment in Amritsar remained less than in Lahore.

Thus, around 1931, the two cities had a large proportion of workers in manufactures, trade, transport, and miscellaneous services. Agriculture and related work engaged relatively smaller proportion of people. In comparison with the average of towns for 1881, there were about the same proportion of government personnel in Amritsar, though their percentage had almost doubled in Lahore. There was no change in the relative proportions of labour and professional groups. The statistics for the province as a whole, however, suggest that in the early twentieth century, the largest occupational group was that of agriculturists, accounting for 54.8 per cent of the working male population in 1911, and 63.5 per cent in 1951.[33] This was in sharp contrast to the position of the cities of Lahore and Amristar where agriculturists had declined while manufacturers, transporters and other service groups had become larger over time. When viewed at the primary, secondary and tertiary levels of occupations, the cities of Lahore and Amritsar had less than 10 per cent in the primary sector, between 20 to 30 per cent in secondary occupations, and the rest were absorbed in the tertiary sector.[34]

V

Literacy stands for ability to read and write a simple letter with understanding. A certain minimum level of literacy is 'a basic requirement for people to get out of ignorance and backwardness'.[35] As a qualitative attribute of population, literacy is 'a fairly reliable index of the socio-economic development of an area.[36] The literacy figures from 1881 to 1931 point to fluctuations in the region as a whole.[37] The percentage of literates in the region was 6.2 in 1881 which rose to 7.3 in 1891. Thereafter, for two successive decades there was a decline to 6.7 per cent in 1901, and 6.8 per cent in 1911. A slight improvement, at 7.2 per cent was recorded in 1921, but the percentage remained lower than the 1891 figure. With 9.4 per cent literates in 1931, however, there was a definite increase in the general rate of literacy for both rural and urban areas.

A much larger rate of literacy was noted in the cities. In Lahore and Amritsar, for instance, over 13 per cent people were literate in 1901.[38] Among males, over 20 per cent of the total were literate, while their percentage among females was 3 per cent. By 1921, the proportion of literate people had increased in the major towns and cities, ranging from about 8 to 19 per cent (Table 5.3).

In 1921, Lahore, Ambala, and Ferozepore had the highest proportion of literate population, while Multan had the least proportion. More than 80 per cent of the literate people continued to be males, though in Amritsar their proportion was over 90 per cent. The proportion of literate males in the total population ranged from 11 to 27 per cent,

TABLE 5.3: PERCENTAGE OF MALE AND FEMALE LITERATES IN LARGE URBAN CENTRES, 1921

Urban Centre	Literates %	Males among Litertes %	Literate Males in Population (%)	Literate Females in Population (%)
Lahore	19.06	81.66	24.43	9.67
Amritsar	10.14	92.74	15.84	1.80
Multan	7.78	83.03	11.30	3.05
Rawalpindi	16.45	83.74	19.86	8.70
Ambala	19.00	86.95	27.54	6.19
Jalandhar	15.42	82.54	22.26	6.28
Sialkot	16.06	84.48	23.36	5.94
Ferozepore	18.04	82.77	24.83	7.79

Source: *Census of Punjab and Delhi, 1921*, vol. II, pt. C, pp.127–30, Table VII: 'Education'.

with Ambala, Ferozepore, Lahore, and Sialkot having the largest proportions. Obviously, the status of these centres as divisional and district headquarters and cantonments accounted for the high rate of male literacy which was a condition for employment. Females were far behind in literacy in 1921, their proportions ranging from nearly 2 per cent in Amristar to over 9 per cent in Lahore which had more facilities for female education than other centres. In fact, in comparison with 1901, the city of Lahore had increased its literacy rate substantially, while Amritsar registered a decrease.[39]

In 1931, the percentage of literate people in the major towns and cities increased from about 12 to nearly 34 per cent.[40] Among these, Sialkot had the least proportion of literates while Lyallpur had the highest, as it was a new colony town with a large proportion of officers and traders adding to the educated segment. The proportion of males among literates in the canal colony areas ranged from 73 to over 90 per cent, the first figure being for Sargodha and the second for Lyallpur. By now, Rawalpindi and Multan also had a high proportion of males among the literate people. The proportion of literate males in the total population ranged from 18 per cent in Sialkot to over 40 per cent in Lyallpur. Lyallpur also had the largest proportion of literate females, while Sialkot had the smallest. Sargodha too had a higher proportion of literate females.

In comparison with 1921, Sialkot and Ambala, among the major towns and cities, registered decrease in the relative proportion of literates, while the other large centres registered an increase. The percentage of males who could read and write had decreased in Lahore and Ambala where the labour force had increased over the years. For female literacy the relative proportions declined in Lahore, Rawalpindi and Sialkot. Jalandhar retained the same proportions for both literate males and females in 1921 and 1931.

Thus, there apparently was no relation of size with literacy.[41] The largest city in the region, Lahore, initially had a high literacy rate as well. However, by 1931, Lyallpur and Sargodha, both new colony towns, had higher proportions of people who could read and write. As categories, cantonments and new colony towns had a relatively larger literate body, formed mainly by military personnel, government employees and those engaged in trade. In fact, throughout the period, towns and cities had a larger proportion of literates than the region as a whole. As may be expected, this difference was substantial in the class I and II centres, but does not appear to be so marked at the small-town level.[42]

VI

The age structure as an indicator of the socio-economic character of population and also of the urban centres in the region can be studied only for the later decades of colonial rule, because detailed information is not available for the earlier period. In 1931, in the British districts the largest proportion of people, about 35 per cent, were in the 20 to 40 age group.[43] The percentage in the 40–60 age group and infants was over 13 per cent, while children in the 5–15 age group constituted over 11 per cent of the population. Significantly, the segment of 60 years and above was the smallest, with less that 4 per cent. The regional proportions, however, did not conform to the age structure in the urban areas (Table 5.4).

In some of these large towns and cities, the proportion of the under-15 age group was much smaller, as at Rawalpindi, Ferozepore and Ambala, all of which were military centres. Rawalpindi as the headquarters of the Northern Military Command had the maximum proportion of the 20–40 age group. It was followed by Lahore and the cantonments of Ferozepore and Ambala. Correspondingly, the 60-plus

TABLE 5.4: AGE STRUCTURE IN LARGE URBAN CENTRES, 1921–31

Urban Centre	Census Year	Age Group and Percentage						
		0–5	5–10	10–15	15–20	20–40	40–60	60+
Lahore	1921	11.86	9.33	8.65	9.85	38.63	16.54	5.4
	1931	12.73	10.14	9.92	12.12	39.91	12.33	9.2
Amritsar	1921	11.3	11.77	9.96	8.69	35.81	17.12	5.32
	1931	13.15	11.69	11.22	10.51	35.26	14.18	3.9
Multan	1921	11.30	12.42	11.10	9.34	34.3	15.82	5.56
	1931	12.98	11.56	11.05	10.67	35.51	14.32	3.88
Rawalpindi	1921	8.54	8.49	8.12	10.31	46.59	14.43	3.49
	1931	12.71	10,24	9,78	11.27	41.10	12.33	2.54
Jalandhar	1921	11.81	12.53	10.85	9.62	32.13	16.19	6.84
	1931	13.94	11.86	11.26	10.59	32.96	14.31	5.04
Ambala	1921	10.51	11.58	9.90	8.93	37.11	16.30	5.65
	1931	12.67	10.90	11.29	11.02	36.38	14.28	3.99
Sialkot	1921	12.39	12.79	11.15	9.96	33.56	14.57	5.54
	1931	14.82	11.87	11.10	11.10	35.16	12.23	3.68
Ferozepore	1921	10.65	11.45	10.43	9.59	37.38	15.76	4.71
	1931	12.73	10.74	10.42	11.32	37.59	13.66	3.51

Source: *Census of Punjab and Delhi 1921*, pt. II, pt. C, pp. 91–8, Table VII: 'Age, Sex and Civil Condition for Selected Towns'. *Census of India 1931*, pt. II, pt. C, Table VII, pp.123–44: 'Age, Sex and Civil Condition—Details for Cities and Selected Towns'.

group also was small in the cantonments. The provincial capital with better health facilities and larger number of retirees and professional people accounted for their highest proportion at 9.2 per cent. As a whole, however, compared to the average for the region at 3.80 per cent, the proportion of the 60-plus group was higher in the large urban centres. In the 40–60 age group, the proportions were both higher and lower than the average for the region, with Amritsar having their maximum percentage, at 17.12 per cent.

Some variations in different age groups occurred in these towns and cities from 1921 to 1931. The proportion of children in the 5–10 years category decreased at Amritsar, Multan, Jalandhar, and Ambala, while it increased in the remaining four centres. The 10–15 age group declined only at Multan. The 20–40 category decreased only at Amritsar, Ambala, and Rawalpindi. The 40–60 segment increased only at Lahore as did the 60 plus group.

The basic pattern noticeable in all these urban centres is that of a large component of the 20–40 age group consisting of the working population, followed by the 40–60 age group, almost at par with that of the children, with the older people forming the smallest proportion. This age structure was generally applicable to the small and medium centres in 1931, with some exceptions. A smaller proportion of children was recorded in Bakloh and Ḍagshai, both being hill cantonments. On the other hand, a relatively higher percentage was noticed in Daska and Gidderbaha, both functioning as *mandis* or grain markets. In the working age group of 20-40 years, cantonments and the colony towns exhibited a higher proportion than the regional average, while in the remaining towns of different categories, like Daska, Khushab, Ludhiana, and Mandi Gidderbaha, the proportions of the 20–40 age group were lower (Table 5.5).

The variation in age structure may be explained in terms of the dominant character of an urban centre, like the presence of military personnel in cantonments and of immigrants in the new towns of Mandi Pattoki and Lyallpur. For the same reason, a lower proportion of the 60-plus people were recorded in the colony towns, cantonments and *mandis*. On the other hand, a higher proportion of the older group was present in the older centres of Khushab, Daska, and Kasur and also in Ludhiana. A smaller proportion of children was due as much to the high incidence of infant mortality as to the large presence of a working

TABLE 5.5: AGE STRUCTURE IN DIFFERENT CATEGORIES OF URBAN CENTRES, 1931

Urban Centre	Age Group and Percentage						
	0–5	5–10	10–15	15–20	20–40	40–60	60+
City							
Lahore	12.73	10.14	09.92	12.12	39.91	12.32	9.2
Large Town							
Ludhiana	13.11	11.73	11.62	11.04	33.62	14.25	4.61
Medium Town							
Kasur	12.42	11.42	11.15	10.83	34.79	13.93	4.44
Small Towns							
Hissar	12.62	10.98	11.57	11.86	36.00	14.38	2.56
Daska	16.36	13.76	12.29	9.95	29.94	13.38	4.28
Khushab	14.54	12.49	11.00	10.01	33.92	14.00	4.05
Colony Towns							
Lyallpur	12.91	10.68	10.54	12.34	39.29	12.07	2.16
Sargodha	14.81	11.83	11.19	10.99	37.29	12.46	2.02
Sangla	13.83	11.39	11.03	10.38	36.64	13.61	3.08
Mandi Towns							
Mandi Pattoki	13.43	10.57	09.88	9.73	40.36	13.19	2.80
Mandi	15.78	14.68	13.83	12.89	29.53	10.72	2.53
Gidderbaha							
Cantonments							
Dagshai	11.77	10,48	9.66	10.82	38.12	15.25	3.88
Bakloh	14.04	7.93	7.68	15.77	45.19	07.31	2.03

Source: *Census of the Punjab, 1931*, pt. III, pp. 26–31, Table VII-D: 'Age and Sex of British Districts'.

population. The number of old persons was small because of the low life expectancy.

The urban centres in the Punjab had a larger proportion of unmarried men than women as evident from the figures of the 'civil' condition of the towns people in 1921 and 1931.[44] Women dominated the 'married' category, except in Multan and Sialkot in 1931, while Lyallpur had an equal proportion of married males and females. This pattern was different from that for the Punjab as a whole. Though the proportion of unmarried men remained larger in the region in 1921, the proportion of men and women was equal in the married group, while the difference in the proportion of widows and widowers was rather small (Table 5.6). By and large, towns and cities had a smaller proportion of married men and widowers than the province as a whole.[45]

Variations from the general pattern can be seen over the decade 1921–31. In the cities and towns selected here the number of unmarried males increased with time, except in Multan, while that of unmarried females increased in all cases. On the other hand, the proportion of married men relatively decreased in Lahore, Amritsar, Rawalpindi, and Ambala, whereas the number of married females increased only in Lahore. In the case of widows, their proportion decreased over the decade, except in Sialkot where it remained the same. In Sialkot and Jalandhar the proportion of widowers also remained the same, though it had decreased in other centres. In the 1920s, thus, the number of married and widowed people decreased while the proportion of the unmarried rose. The 'civil' condition during the decade appears to register and reflect several trends in the socio-economic life in the region: migration to cities and large centres in search of employment; growth of modern industry; spread of girls' education; increase in the age of marriage; and, in some cases, remarriage of widows. In comparison with the widowed men, however, the proportion of the widowed women was much higher. Their relative constraints and disadvantages also were greater.

VII

It is not surprising that the proportion of females to per thousand males in the urban centres, or the urban sex ratio, was lower than the ratio for the region (Figure 5.2).

TABLE 5.6: CIVIL CONDITION IN SELECT TOWNS, 1921–31

Urban Centre	Census Year	Unmarried		Married		Widowed	
		% Men	Women	% Men	Women	% Men	Women
Lahore	1921	49.28	40.36	43.19	46.98	7.52	12.65
	1931	52.98	43.00	41.67	47.63	5.33	9.29
Amritsar	1921	50.44	37.43	41.20	47.73	8.34	14.82
	1931	54.40	44.46	39.44	44.71	6.15	10.76
Multan	1921	54.07	40.83	37.65	45.40	8.26	13.76
	1931	53.50	48.50	39.97	38.70	6.51	12.78
Rawalpindi	1921	48.63	35.88	44.79	51.42	6.58	12.69
	1931	52.10	42.14	42.58	46.57	5.31	11.26
Jalandhar	1921	50.30	39.63	40.53	46.30	9.16	14.05
	1931	53.08	46.13	38.35	42.42	9.53	11.57
Ambala	1921	46.53	35.85	44.02	50.53	9.43	13.60
	1931	47.75	39.09	43.26	49.48	9.98	11.47
Sialkot	1921	53.51	40.32	39.79	47.99	6.68	11.67
	1931	64.69	46.23	46.37	43.94	6.60	11.78
Ferozepore	1921	49.37	37.55	41.97	47.82	8.64	14.61
	1931	50.63	41.25	42.05	46.82	7.30	11.91
Ludhiana	1931	52.19	44.45	37.92	44.82	8.32	10.71
Lyallpur	1931	49.51	46.00	46.55	46.85	3.93	7.40
Sargodha	1931	52.27	46.11	42.82	45.41	4.85	9.44

Source: *Census of Punjab and Delhi, 1921*, vol. II, pp. 91–8, Table VII. *Census of India, 1931*, vol. II, pp. 123–44, Table VII.

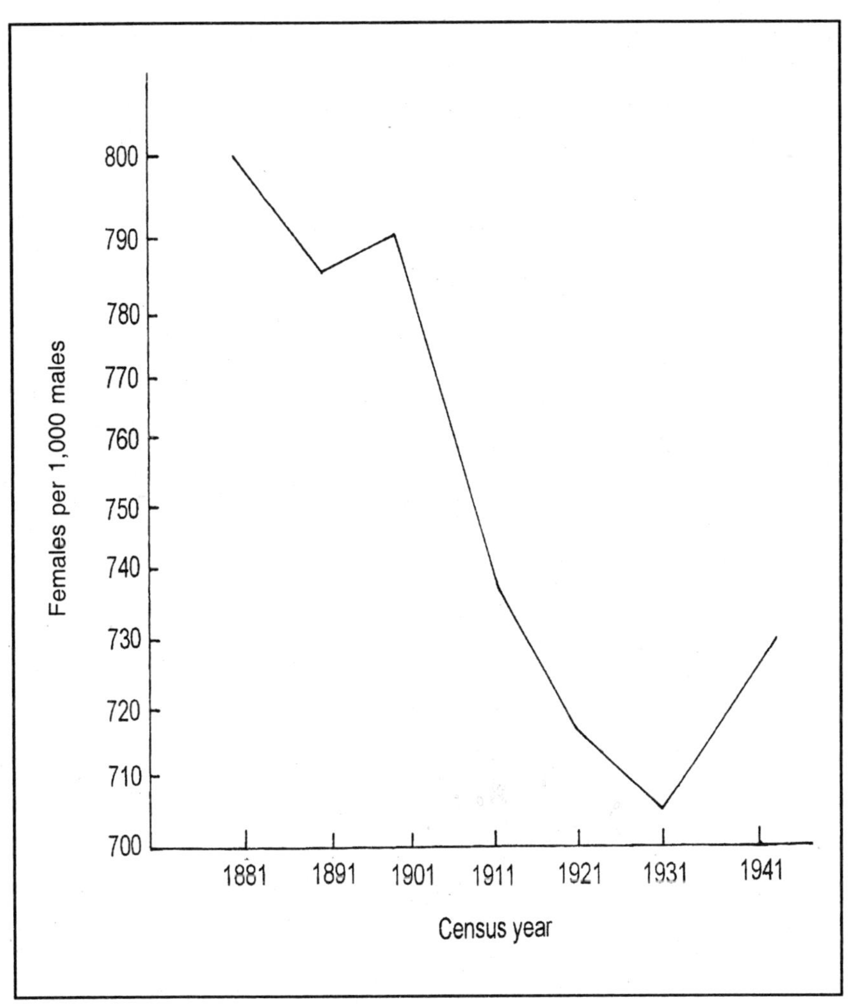

Figure 5.2: The Punjab: Changing Sex Ratio, 1881–1941

In 1881 the regional ratio was 817 against the urban ratio of 800 females to a 1,000 males.[46] In the next census, the urban sex ratio decreased to 784. There was a slight rise in 1901, to 790, but it came down in the succeeding censuses—740 in 1911, 717 in 1921, and 705 in 1931. The 1941 census registered some increase, at 731, but it remained far below the regional average of 846 (Table 5.7).

Significantly, the regional and urban ratios of the Punjab remained lower than the proportions for India as a whole. The sex ratio for towns and cities of the country ranged from 831 to 910 and that for the territory of British India from 945 to 972.[47] Taking up the figures for particular provinces, for instance, the ratios in Bengal, Bihar and Orissa in 1881 were 821, 1021 and 958, respectively.[48] In 1931, in addition to these three, Madras, Bombay, Central Provinces, United Provinces, and Rajputana had higher urban sex ratios than the Punjab region. With 577 females to 1000 males, Assam alone had a lower ratio at this time than the Punjab.[49] The rather low sex ratio in the Punjab reflects societal preference for male children and the generally poor health and nutrition of females of all ages, in addition to the practice of female infanticide, particularly noticed in the region by the British administrators.[50]

It may be possible to identify certain sub-groups in the Punjab having similar characteristics in urban sex ratio despite variations from place to place. In 1881, the sex ratio in the two cities of the region—Lahore and Amritsar—respectively at 705 and 751, was lower than

TABLE 5.7: REGIONAL AND URBAN SEX RATIO, 1901–41

Census Year	Regional Sex Ratio	Urban Sex Ratio
1901	854	790
1911	817	740
1921	828	717
1931	828	717
1931	831	705
1941	846	731

Source: Table IV, *Census of the Punjab* for the years 1901, 1911, 1921, 1931, and Table V, *Census of the Punjab, 1941*. B.S. Saini, *Social and Economic History of India, 1901–39*, Delhi: Ess Ess Publications, 1975, p. 24.

800, the average of the region.[51] Class II or large towns of Peshawar, Multan, Jalandhar, Sialkot, and Ambala also exhibited a lower sex ratio at this time.[52] There was a wide divergence in urban sex ratios in the remaining categories of towns. For example, among the Class III towns, the ratio was 789 in Ludhiana, 844 in Hoshiarpur, 843 in Gujranwala, 982 in Batala, 1012 in Panipat, and 1027 in Rewari. Class IV towns of Kohat and Kasur respectively had 481 and 954 females per 1000 males. A similar divergence is noticed in the other categories as well, though most of the small towns, particularly the non-administrative centres, show smaller difference of sexes.[53]

The sex ratio in the cities and larger towns was low because most of the immigrants who swelled the population of these centres were males. They were either working—or came in search of work—in the various government offices, military establishments and institutions, as well as in the markets and industries located in these places. The diversification in urban functions and services served as a magnet for the rural and small town migrants who, facilitated by the new means of communication, thronged the cities. Such migrants rarely brought their families with them and, therefore, there remained a preponderance of males in the cities. The smaller centres, in which these pull factors were less developed or even absent, tended to show very little difference of sexes.

Some kind of pattern may be discerned in relation to very high and very low sex ratios. The towns with very high sex ratio, with a few exceptions, were located close to the city of Delhi: Panipat, Rewari, Bahadurgarh, Maham, Palwal, Shahabad, Sonepat, and Jhajjar; their sex ratio ranged from 1002 to 1068. Migration of males to the city of Delhi in search of work from these less developed centres may explain this phenomenon. Other urban places with a thousand plus ratio were Khushab, Eminabad, and Dunyapur, located in the eastern and western plains.[54] Perhaps, the males migrated to the nearby cantonments and district headquarters in search of employment.

Urban settlements such as cantonments or towns with large cantonment areas also exhibited a very low sex ratio. In 1881, for instance, Simla had 359 females per 1,000 males, Naushera 259, Dagshai 303, Campbellpur 492, Abbotabad 290, and Bannu had 320 females. The substantial presence of military personnel accounted for a rather low sex ratio in Rawalpindi, Peshawar, Kohat and Jhelum, with 472, 589, 481 and 410 females, respectively.[55]

The pattern remained very much similar in 1941. Though the individual urban centres may have gone up or down on the scale of sex ratio, the change was not considerable. The difference over time is most visible in the cities as most of them show a lower sex ratio. In Lahore, for example, it decreased from 705 in 1881 to 596 in 1941.[56] The other class I centres of Ambala, Jalandhar, and Ludhiana also show lower sex ratios.[57] Except in the case of Multan, which continued to have a relatively large proporation of females, all the cities had a lower ratio than the average of the region.[58] There apparently was an inverse relationship between the high sex ratio and low development of industry. Among the class II towns, Patiala and Ferozepore had 706 and 612 females respectively, which was lower than the urban ratio for the region, but it was higher in Gujranwala, with 791 females. In the remaining categories of towns, the urban sex ratio varied from very low to very high in each class, though most of them showed little difference of sexes due to the near absence of pull factors.[59]

The cantonments exhibited a very low sex ratio in 1941 also. Only a small proportion of the army personnel had been provided accommodation for families over the period. Dalhousie, for instance, had 373 females per 1,000 males; Bakloh had 380; while Balun had 504. Rawalpindi, which became a class I centre in 1921, had a considerable cantonment with a sex ratio of 551 females per 1,000 males. The new towns in the canal colonies also had a lower ratio but not as low as in the cantonments. Lyallpur had 633 females; and their numbers were 667 in Montgomery; 637 in Okara; 561 in Arifwala; 541 in Burewala; and 503 in Khanewal. Of these, the last two developed as railway junctions, with a high work force of males.

By 1941, very few urban places had a very high sex ratio, and these were no longer concentrated in any geographical area. Farukhnagar and Faridabad in the Sutlej-Yamuna Divide had a ratio of 1,010 and 1,030 respectively, while Bhaun in the Salt Range tract showed a proportion of 1,004. No other town with very high sex ratio is identified. This is probably because by the 1930s, spatial mobility had increased consi-derably, and migrants to urban centres had settled down and brought their families, thereby reducing the gap in the sex ratio.

In short, the urban sex ratio had a wide range in the towns and cities of the region and no particular pattern can be identified with respect to their location or size. On the whole, urban centres with a high military and service component generally had a very low proportion of females, and so did the new towns.[60]

VIII

To sum up, during 1881–1941, there was an absolute increase in the urban population of the region as well as an increase in the percentage of population, particularly after 1921. The cities of the Punjab grew at the expense of the small towns. This growth in urban population was less due to natural increase and more due to migration. This is reflected also in the sex ratio in the urban centres which was generally much lower than in the province, the difference being most marked in the cities, cantonments and the new colony towns, though the gap tended to decrease over time. The overall birth and death rates were both higher and lower than the average for the region. As a rule, however, the large urban centres had a lower death rate. The age structure was similar to the pattern in the region, with a large 20–40 years group and an almost equal proportion of children and 40–60-years old persons. The older people, however, formed a very small component of the urban population. In the cantonments, the number of children was still less, while the older people here, as also in the colony towns, formed a smaller segment than in other towns. There was some increase in the proportion of working population over time, and some changes in their relative proportions in different occupations.

The 'civil' condition of urban people was marked by a male-dominated unmarried group, and a larger proportion of females in the married group. There was a very small proportion of widowed persons, the women outnumbering men in this category. Most of the literates in the towns were males, and the proportion of literate people in urban areas was much higher than in the province as a whole. Initially, the cities and towns with cantonments had the largest proportion of literates, but over time, the colony towns emerged with a higher rate of literacy. There was now a sizeable proportion of the professional people in service and self-employment based on education and special training. In response to new economic opportunities and technological advancement, people tended to move from petty trading and traditional crafts to factory industry as well as to external trade and transportation. Diversification in economic activities and spread of educational opportunities meant diversification and reorientations in urban functions.

NOTES

1. R. Ramachandran, *Urbanization and Urban Systems in India,* Delhi: OUP, 1997, p. 91. See also, Ashish Bose, *Studies in India's Urbanization 1901–71,* New Delhi: Tata McGraw Hill, 1973, p. 3.
2. All calculations are based on tables giving details of population in each town in each census year. The total urban population by this method is higher than the consolidated figures given in the Census Reports, except for the years 1881 and 1911.
3. Broadly similar trends are evident in the recent historical studies of Amritsar and Jalandhar. Anand Gauba, *Amritsar: A Study in Urban History (1840–1947),* Jalandhar: ABS Publications, 1988, pp. 220–43. Kanchan Jyoti, 'The City of Jullundur: A Study in Urban History (1846–1947)', Ph.D. thesis, GNDU, Amritsar, 1988, pp. 99–115.
4. Sasha, 'The State, Society and Epidemics in Colonial Punjab, 1849–1947', Ph.D. thesis, Panjab University, Chandigarh, 2003, pp. 33–49. See also, Ashok Mitra, *India's Population: Aspects of Quality and Control,* vol. II, Delhi: Abhinav Publications, 1975, pp. 766–8 and 789–99. For detail on famines, Navtej Singh, 'Famines in the Punjab, 1858–1901, Ph.D. thesis, Panjab University, Chandigarh, 1986, pp. 65–6, 116, 165–6, 187–8 and 392–499.
5. Gurdev Singh Gosal, 'Agricultural Development and Urbanization, 1921–81', in Indu Bangal (ed.), *Five Punjabi Centuries: Polity, Economy, Society and Culture*; rpt., New Delhi: Manohar, 2000, p. 361.
6. These developments have been taken up in some detail in Chapters 2, 6 and 7.
7. Ramachandran, *Urbanization and Urban Systems,* p. 9.
8. Based on *Census of the Punjab, 1881,* Appendix C, Supplementary Table K, and *Census of Punjab, 1941,* Table V.
9. Based on Table IV in *Census of the Punjab,* for the years 1881, 1891, 1901, 1911, 1921, 1931 and 1941, and Table V in the case of 1941 only.
10. Ian J. Kerr, 'Urbanization and Colonial Rule in 19th-Century India: Lahore and Amritsar, 1849-1881', *The Panjab Past and Present,* vol. XIV, pt. I, 1981, p. 213. It may be pointed out that Kerr's data pertains to the 'district headquarter towns in British India', available in the 1872 Census of India.
11. R.P. Misra, 'Million Cities and World Urbanization', in R.P. Misra (ed.), *Million Cities of India,* New Delhi: Vikas, 1978, p. 34, Table 9.
12. Ashish Bose, *Bibliography on Urbanization in India, 1947–76,* New Delhi: Tata-McGraw Hill, 1976, p. xxvi.
13. Mitra, *India's Population,* vol. II, p. 11.

14. Based on urban population statistics in the *District Gazetteer* series of 1883–4.
15. Based on Table 13: 'Births and Deaths in Towns', in *District Gazetteer* series of the 1900s and 1910s.
16. *Census of India, 1921*, vol. I, p. 60.
17. Calculated from Subsidiary Table V, *Census of India, 1911*, vol. I, p. 60. Statistics for later years are not available for individual towns.
18. Sasha, 'Social History of the Plague with Special Reference to the Medieval and Modern Punjab', M.Phil. dissertation, Panjab University, Chandigarh, 1999, pp. 49 and 93-116.
19. Based on *Census of the Punjab, 1891*, pt. II, Table VI.
20. Calculated from figures available in Table IV of *Census of the Punjab, 1941*. During 1911–31, there was a 42.85 per cent increase recorded in the number of Sikhs. For factors contributing towards this substantial increase, see Joginder Singh, 'The Sikh Community: Demography and Occupational Change,1881–1931', in Indu Banga (ed.), *Five Punjabi Centuries*, pp. 470–5 and 488, Table 1. For detail, idem, *The Sikh Resurgence*, Delhi: National Book Organization, 1997, pp. 29–48.
21. Based on the Population Tables in the *District Gazetteers*. For calculating the proportion of the religious communities, the following urban centres from all classes, and spread all over the region, have been randomly selected: Lahore, Amritsar, Dera Ghazi Khan, Chiniot, Bannu, Montgomery, Dunyapur, Gujranwala, Jind, Jalandhar, Kasur, Pasrur, Rewari, Farukh-nagar, Zira, Patiala, Kohat, Tarn Taran, Alawalpur, Gurgaon, Phagwara, Dera Baba Nanak, and Gurdaspur.
22. *Census of the Punjab, 1941*, pp. 30–9, Table V.
23. Joginder Singh, 'The Sikh Community', pp. 474–5. A Sehajdhari Sikh was not baptized as a Khalsa, or the follower of Guru Gobind Singh, and did not follow the Khalsa code of discipline (*rehat*). Idem., *The Sikh Resurgence*, pp. 32–3.
24. *Census of India, 1971*, Census Centenary Monograph No. 1, New Delhi: Registrar General, India, 1972, p. 169. See also, Bose, *Studies in India's Urbanization*, p. 96. For a comparative discussion. Lynn Smith, *Fundamentals of Population Study*, Chicago: J.B. Lippincott Company, 1960, pp. 230–50.
25. Based on *Census of the Punjab, 1881*, Table XII: 'Distribution of Occupations'.
26. These figures for Lahore are from the first census of the city taken in 1847. Tom G. Kessinger, 'Regional Economy (1757–1857): North India', in Dharma Kumar (ed.), *The Cambridge Economic History of India*, vol. 2: *c.1757–1970*, Hyderabad: Orient Longman, 1982, p. 244, Table 3.1.

27. Based on *Census of the Punjab, 1901,* Table XV: 'Means of Occupation'.
28. Based on *Census of India, 1921,* pp. 344–51, Table XVII: 'Occupations or Means of Livelihood'.
29. Based on *Census of India, 1931,* pt. III: 'Cities', pp. 400–11, Table X: 'Occupations or Means of Livelihood'.
30. Ibid. The textile and metal workers constituted over 2 per cent; wood workers nearly 3; apparel makers about 5; those employed in food were over 1 per cent; and those engaged in building were less that 1 per cent.
31. Based on *Census of the Punjab, 1901,* Table XV: 'Occupations'. There is no information available on the occupations or means of livelihood in Amritsar for the 1880s.
32. Based on *Census of India, 1931,* pt. III: 'Cities', pp. 400-11, Table X: 'Occupations or Means of Livelihood'.
33. This is based on the 'Retabulated Census Data for India and Pakistan', quoted in J. Krishnamurty, 'The Occupational Structure', in Dharma Kumar (ed.), *The Cambridge Economic History of India,* vol. 2, Table 6.7, p. 543.
34. Cf. K. Prabha, *Towns: A Structural Analysis: A Case Study of Punjab,* Delhi: Inter India, 1979, p. 79.
35. R.C. Chandana and Manjit S. Sidhu, *Introduction to Population Geography,* New Delhi: Kalyani Publishers, 1980, p. 96.
36. Gurdev Singh Gosal, 'Spatial Perspective on Literacy in India', *Population* Geography, vols. 1 and 2, 1979, p. 41.
37. *Census of the Punjab, 1931,* vol. II, p. 267, Subsidiary Table VI: 'Progress of Literacy since 1881'.
38. Calculated from *Census of the Punjab, 1901,* Table VIII: 'Education-III, Cities'. Figures for particular towns for the earlier decades are not available.
39. 'Comparing between 1901 and 1921, the proportions at Lahore had increased from 20.79 to 24.43 per cent for males and from 3.7 to 9.6 per cent for females, whereas at Amritsar the proportions fell to 15.8 in the case of males and to 1.8 for females, respectively from 20.9 and 2.5. *Census of the Punjab, 1901,* Table VIII: 'Education', and *Census of the Punjab and Delhi, 1921,* vol. II, pt. C, Table VII: 'Education', pp. 127–30.
40. *Based on Census of India, 1931,* pt. III, Table XIII: 'Literacy by Religion and Age', pp. 444–7, and *Census of the Punjab 1931,* pt. I, 'Report', p. 251. At no time did the proportion of literate persons exceed 50 per cent. Cf. Prabha, *Towns: A Structural Analysis,* p. 46.
41. Cf. Prabha, *Towns: A Structural Analysis,* p. 49.
42. The exact proportion of literates in small towns cannot be ascertained because of non-availability of data.
43. Calculated from *Census of the Punjab, 1931,* pt. III, Table VIID: 'Age and Sex of British Districts', pp. 26–7.

44. The term 'civil' condition is used in the Census Reports.
45. Based on *Census of India, 1921*, part I, p. 57.
    The relative percentages in the Punjab as a whole in 1921 were:

Unmarried	Males	29.51	Females	18.56
Married	Males	20.36	Females	20.79
Widowed	Males	4.72	Females	5.98

    Significantly, the widowed persons also included children below 15 years who constituted 3.2 per cent of the married minors in 1921. Vijay Lakshmi, 'Children in the Colonial Punjab: A Social History', M.Phil. dissertation, Panjab University, Chandigarh 2001, p. 41.
46. Male and Female proportions for 1881 and the successive decades are based on Table IV, *Census of the Punjab* for the years 1891, 1901, 1911, 1921 and 1931, and Table V, *Census of the Punjab, 1941*. The urban sex ratio is not directly available in the Census Report of 1881.
47. Ashish Bose, *India's Urbanization 1901-2001*; rev. edn, New Delhi: Tata McGraw Hill/Institute of Economic Growth, 1978, Table 13, p. 348. See also, M.K. Premi et al., *An Introduction to Social Demography*, Delhi: Vikas, 1983, p. 41.
48. Based on female population of urban areas recorded in *Census of India, 1881*.
49. *Census of India, 1931*, 'Report', p. 47.
50. Janaki Nair, *Women and Law in Colonial India: A Social History*, New Delhi: Kali for Women, 1996, pp. 84–9.
    Direct or indirect violence against women in both urban and rural areas has persisted even after Independence. Rainuka Dagar, 'Patriarchal Structure and Violence against Women', in J.S. Grewal and Indu Banga (eds.), *Punjab in Prosperity and Violence: Administration, Politics and Social Change, 1947–97*, New Delhi: K.K. Publishers/Institute of Punjab Studies, 1998, pp. 187–206. Idem, *Identifying and Controlling Female Foeticide and Infanticide in Punjab*, Chandigarh: Institute for Development and Communication, 2002, pp. 1–15.
51. *Census of the Punjab, 1891*, Table IV. Cf. Prabha, *Towns: A Structural Analysis*, p. 44.
52. The sex ratio of these urban centres was: Peshawar 589, Multan 712, Ambala 715, Sialkot 775, and Jalandhar 799. *Census of the Punjab, 1891*, Table IV.
53. Cf. Prabha, *Towns: A Structural Analysis*, pp. 44 and 63.
54. The sex ratio in the thousand plus towns was: Dunyapur 1,182, Maham 1,068, Bahadurgarh 1,065, Jhajjar 1,046, Sonepat, Rewari and Khushab, 1,027, Panipat 1,012, Eminabad 1,010, Shahabad 1,007, and Palwal 1,002.

55. Based on *Census of the Punjab, 1891*, Table IV. Cf. Prabha, *Towns: A Structural Analysis*, p. 61.
56. Based on *Census of the Punjab, 1941*, pp. 32-9, Table V.
57. The sex ratio in these cities over the period was:

City	1941	1881
Ambala	646	715
Jalandhar	696	799
Ludhiana	715	789

58. The urban sex ratio in Multan was 799 against the regional average of 731 for urban areas in 1941.
59. Prabha, *Towns: A Structural Analysis*, p. 64.
60. Cf. Ibid., p. 61. These towns with a large proportion of males are comparable to the project towns of the post-Independence period.

6

Reorientations in Urban Functions

The traditional urban functions as centres of trade and manufactures, and as loci of learning, medical practice, and religious activity, especially of the institutional kind, continued to be performed by the cities and towns under colonial rule.[1] However, the priorities of the new regime, the vast area under its domination, and the technology at its disposal brought about substantial reorientations in the urban functions. The rail and road connections and the links with the overseas markets changed the pattern of urban linkages both within and outside the region. The impact of the new administrative and cultural functions assumed by the colonial state too was felt more in cities and towns though, as may be expected a priori, these new developments would not leave the countryside unaffected. This chapter focuses on reorientations in what may be regarded as the basic urban functions like collection, distribution, and production of goods, particularly in terms of scale and specialization, the nature and availability of health care, and generation and dissemination of knowledge. Urban centres also functioned as centres of religion, recreation, and information, and as articulators of will in the public domain.

I

The predominant economic activity in the urban centres of the landlocked Punjab region before and during the colonial period remained mercantile, providing links with the countryside and the outside markets. At the inception of colonial rule a small urban centre served as the focal point of a number of villages, and of the system of exports and imports.[2] Such centres collected local produce like wheat, rice, cereals, ghee, gur, sugar, and cotton from the surrounding villages, to be passed on to the medium size town or other nearby centres for redistribution, or to be forwarded to the cities which sent them to other parts of the region and beyond. For instance, the small town of Jalalpur in the upper Rachna Doab collected grain and ghee from the villages around and sent these to the medium size town of Sialkot which also received rice and tobacco from Kangra in the north, and redistributed these commodities through the nearby middling towns of Jhelum and Pind Dadan Khan as well as through the cities of Lahore and Amritsar. In return, Sialkot received tea from the city of Amritsar and salt from Pind Dadan Khan which were distributed to the small towns and villages in the neighbourhood.[3] Similarly, the middling town of Gujranwala collected wheat and ghee from the nearby small town of Ramnagar and the medium town of Gujrat and exported these commodities to the city of Multan for distribution beyond the region.[4] Conversely, com-modities like iron, wood, dry fruits and piece goods from Europe and Central Asia came first to the cities of the region and through them reached the larger towns, to be further distributed to the small urban centres. Silk and wool of Bokhara, for example, reached Amritsar via Multan, and filtered down to the small towns of Gurdaspur, Sujanpur and Sri Hargobindpur. Villagers came to the towns for these finer items as well as for fine tools and implements and gold and silver ornaments.[5]

By the beginning of the twentieth century, the trading network had changed substantially as a result mainly of the extension of railways. 'Nearly all towns in the plain areas came to be directly or indirectly connected with Karachi' which became 'the "natural port" for the immense grain production in the canal-irrigated tracts in the region'.[6] Commercialization of agriculture and colonization of large areas led to manifold increase in agricultural produce. In 1935, about 30 per cent of the total wheat acreage in India was in the Punjab region.[7] With 'modern' transportation facilities, trade began to be diverted to new urban centres. For example, Kasur, which used to send wheat and oilseeds to the nearby city of Lahore became the largest exporter of these items to Multan and Karachi after the opening of the railway.[8] Lahore was bypassed also in favour of the small towns of Shahdara and Raiwind on the railway line. Ferozepore and Peshawar became convenient points of trade for local produce due to their rail connections.[9] Urban centres of the newly colonized lower Bari Doab— Okara, Montgomery and Chichawatni—sent cotton and grain directly to Karachi, bypassing the city of Multan.[10] This re-alignment of trade in agricultural produce was intensified in the early decades of the twentieth century.

In the 1920s, even points of lorry haltage on arterial roads became primary markets where producers directly disposed of their goods without the agency of intermediaries.[11] Such centres as well as those on the railway gradually grew into *mandis*, or the permanent points for daily transaction of wholesale distribution. By the end of colonial period, the Punjab came to have 157 wholesale markets, each serving villages within a radius of around 55 km. In fact, 44 per cent of the produce was brought from a radius of about 16 km. In the canal colonies the *mandis* served areas within the radius of 24 to 32 km.[12] *Mandis* were especially established for this purpose.[13]

To facilitate export of agricultural produce to Britain, and to safeguard the interests of the agriculturists *vis-à-vis* the grain traders, in 1939 the provincial government (dominated by the Unionist Party) set up regulated markets in towns like Ludhiana, Fazilka, Sargodha, Okara, Khanewal, Montgomery, and Lyallpur. Transactions in these markets were conducted under the rules framed by market committees. By 1944, there were 130 such markets in the region, covering 80 per cent of the *mandis*.[14] The *arhtias* or commission agents based in the wholesale markets played a key role in moving commodities from producers to the exporting centres and in arranging for storage. They also acted as agents of European exporting firms and buyers located in other regions of the subcontinent. In 1937, the number of *arhtias* in the big grain markets like Lyallpur, Okara and Amritsar was reported to be 97, 100, and 159, respectively.[15]

The wheat market at Amritsar was the biggest centre of 'futures' or speculative trading in India. Speculation in grain became a feature of other *mandis* too.[16] There was a sophisticated market mechanism for wheat in the colony towns, with Lyallpur and Okara having 'a thriving futures market' in this commodity. Even in the smaller *mandi* towns in the canal colonies the latest information was readily available on the prices of wheat prevailing not only in the major markets and export centres in the country, but also in the important places of import overseas.[17]

Finance for export trade came from a variety of sources. The *arhtias*, individual moneylenders, and the traditional banking firms continued to provide the major part of credit. The enterprising firms of hereditary traders and moneylenders, who had come from the central districts, were flourishing in the colony towns of Lyallpur, Gojra, Toba Tek Singh, Shahpur and Jhang. At a more modest level, by the 1940s, the money-lenders in *mandis* and even in large villages extended substantial amounts of credit to agriculturists.[18] Simultaneously, new financing institutions like grain exchanges financed the purchase and storage of grain by their members in Amritsar and Jalandhar. The joint stock and co-operatives banks coming up in the early decades of the twentieth century constituted yet another source of credit for wheat traders.[19] For their transactions, foreign firms generally depended on foreign exchange banks.[20] Most of these agencies, particularly traders in specific articles, financed import trade, among others, in cotton, silk and woollen piece goods.[21]

Trade in locally manufactured goods too was reoriented during the period. At the inception of colonial rule, Sialkot sent its famed paper and brassware to the nearby medium and small towns as well as to the cities of Lahore and Amritsar for consumption and redistribution within and outside the region.[22] Multan exported silks to the countries in the West and to the cities of Lahore and Amritsar for further distribution to the medium towns like Gujrat and the nearby small towns.[23] Within half a century, however, these cities were no longer functioning as centres of trade in paper or silk. Paper was imported largely from the United Provinces and Bengal because local supply was 'deficient', and Multan dealt mainly with European piece goods which it sent inland.[24] However, Multan's location on the rail route to Karachi enabled it to retain its pre-colonial economic importance as a centre of trade.[25] Sialkot continued to export its brass and copperware to the nearby town of Gujranwala and the cities of Lahore and Amritsar.[26] At the same time, the extension of communications added a number of small urban centres like Rewari, Jagadhari, Panipat, and Karnal to the ranks of brass exporters.[27]

At the same time, a substantial part of the wholesale and retail trade of an urban centre catered to its internal requirements. The large centres and some colony towns served as terminal markets for the agricultural produce needed by the local mills and factories. The farmers came to towns for purchasing seeds of the improved and new varieties, and the finer and lighter agricultural implements and also for their repairs. The

Agricultural College and Experimental Farm established at Lyallpur in 1909 was a major centre for better variety of crops, new seeds and implements. Gurdaspur, Hansi, Sirsa, Multan, Montgomery, Rawalpindi and Jalandhar also had extension experimental farms.[28]

The presence of Europeans in towns and cities induced some changes in vegetable gardening and retail trade. The Agri-Horticultural Society, founded in Lahore in 1851, was instrumental in the introduction of potato and several other new crops and varieties.[29] Some enterprising Khatri traders responded to the new situation by opening retail stores in Lahore catering specifically to Europeans and stocking imported items including wines and liquors. This indeed required some change in the social attitudes, for wine trade was traditionally regarded as a low-caste occupation.[30] In due course, such stores would come up in district headquarters and cantonments. For example, some of the new consumer items that appeared in the shops in Jalandhar over the period were baked breads, biscuits, pastries, tea, coffee, ice, soda, refined sugar, vegetable ghee, cigarettes, soaps, celluloid toys, Western clothes, hosiery articles, leather boots, boot polish, wrist watches, spectacles, sunglasses, sports goods, allopathic medicines, photographic materials, English books and stationery, crockery, bicycles, sewing machines, electrical appliances, and radios.[31] While the educated professionals and other well-to-do people in cities and large towns increasingly took to the use of these articles, their penetration in the countryside appears to have been slow and limited.

On the whole, urban centres under colonial rule continued to function as focal points for the exchange of locally produced goods. The wider the sphere of trading activity, the larger was the size of the urban unit. Notwithstanding their role in the export trade, the towns that remained small had a small sphere of trade, often confined to the surrounding villages. Even when the medium size centres had a larger share of the external trade, they generally served their own neighbourhood, besides that of the nearby small towns. The cities of the region had the widest range of trade network, covering the entire region and some places beyond. The volume of Punjab's exports remained much larger than its imports. Its exports consisted of agricultural produce, salt and hides and skins—all non-urban products. Imports, on the other hand, targetted both urban and rural areas, and consisted mainly of cotton piece goods, iron and steel, sugar, woollens, gunny bags, cloth, dyes, electric fans, agricultural implements, hardware, machinery, wines and liquors, and petroleum products.[32] The extensive trade links of Jalandhar can give a fair idea of the variety and extent of the exports and imports of an average urban centre in the colonial period.[33] Obviously, the imports had an inverse relationship with manufacturing activity in the region.

II

In the period immediately preceding annexation, most of the urban centres manufactured goods of one kind or the other—in cotton, silk, wool, metal, wood, leather, stone, and pottery. In all probability, in the basic kinds of manufactures the small urban centres and large villages within a sub-region were not much different; they probably shared manpower and skills as well. In most cases, the raw material was available in the vicinity or it came through the larger centres in the region. All centres produced goods for local consumption and some specialized in certain items.[34] Within half a century of colonial rule, some traditional manufactures declined and others tried to readjust by adopting new techniques and new designs and by using imported raw materials. In some other cases, the introduction of modern factories replaced the traditional manufactures. These changes affected not only the urban and rural patterns of consumption but also the organization of production and financing which was essentially pre-industrial in character. There is enough evidence to suggest that the rural artisans were probably more affected by the developments under colonial rule than their urban counterparts.[35]

Throughout the nineteenth century, that is before and after annexation, cotton cloth of several fine varieties, such as *ghati, dotahi, bulbul chashm,* and *jajam,* besides *lungi* and white damask continued to be woven in urban centres of different sizes in nearly all parts of the region.[36] Cotton cloth was exported on a large scale and the produce of Multan and Rahon was particularly well known. By the beginning of the next century, the fine-weave fabrics were replaced by English cloth, imitations of the striped *susi,* and products of Bombay. In addition to the imitations of European fabrics on a small scale, some towns continued to produce coarse cotton cloth for local consumption.[37]

Silks of the famed varieties like *gulbadan, daryai, dhupchhaon, susi,* and *shuja* were among the major products of Multan at the beginning of colonial rule. The cities of Lahore and Amritsar and the middling towns of Jalandhar and Batala also produced silk textiles. In a few decades, the silk industry of Lahore and Amritsar declined considerably due to decreased demand and inferior quality of products.[38] By about 1900, the silk manufactures even of Multan, Jalandhar, Batala, Ludhiana, Sialkot, and Khushab were substantially reduced and confined to making *daryais* and turbans of a much inferior quality. The craftsmen at these centres also turned to using artificial silk yarn.[39]

Woollen cloth, shawls and blankets were produced at the beginning of colonial rule in the city of Amritsar, the medium towns of Ludhiana, Jalandhar and Gujrat, and in the small towns of Bilga, Sujanpur, Nurpur, Dinanagar, and Dera Baba Nanak.[40] In half a century, the produce of Bilga, Nurpur, Dinanagar and Sujanpur, which was of an inferior kind, suffered decline. So did the fine pashmina shawls made at Amritsar.[41] By this time, the Egerton Woollen Mills at Dhariwal, founded in 1882, began to meet the needs of the British Indian army and the provincial police.[42] In the second decade of the twentieth century, Panipat also emerged as a manufacturer of blankets.[43]

The hosiery industry made a beginning with the introduction of knitting machines in 1890. Hosiery items like socks and gloves began to be manufactured in cotton, wool and silk at Lahore, Ludhiana and Rawalpindi. The use of power and imported yarns in hosiery production saw the industry turn out quality goods fit to compete with the imported items. Ludhiana took to woollen hosiery and by 1935 increased its produce twofold, valued at Rs. 4,000,000. By 1941, the city had more than a hundred hosiery factories.[44]

Some other related industries like carpet weaving, printing and dyeing also underwent change. At the time of annexation, carpets in cotton, silk and wool were manufactured in the cities of Multan and Amritsar and the middling centres of Gujrat, Sialkot, and Batala.[45] This activity declined by the end of the nineteenth century due to reduction in demand and the monopolistic introduction of carpet making in the jails of Lahore, Amritsar, Multan, and Montgomery. Cotton printing carried out at Bahrampur and Kamalia in the first half of the colonial period virtually disappeared by the turn of the century.[46] Already, in the 1880s, dyers of cotton, silk and wool in Lahore, Amritsar and Multan had switched over to the use of imported synthetic dyes.[47]

At the inception of British rule, small-scale manufactures in brass, copper, iron, gold and silver existed in places like Amritsar, Jalandhar, Batala, Sialkot, Bhera, Daska, Narowal, Rewari, and Jagadhari.[48] The items manufactured included vessels, swords, razors, locks, boxes, knives, stirrups, armour, shields, arrows, wire or *kandla-kashi*, and jewellery. Sialkot was famous for its ornamental damascened work on sword hilts, knife handles, shields, and boxes. By about 1900, some of these traditional arts declined, especially wire and tinsel work, as there was no demand for them, while others adjusted to newer models copied from European items. New items like cutlery and screws also began to be produced. A major change came with the establishment of iron foundries which made agricultural implements like ploughs, chaff cutters, sugarcane crushers, belt pulleys, and husking machines. By 1939, Batala emerged as a centre of foundry industry, having 29 out of 46 foundries in the Punjab.[49] Some of the towns produced electrical appliances, printing presses, bicycles, and knitting and sewing machines, albeit on a limited scale; most places dealt in repairs and spare parts.[50] Jalandhar emerged as a centre for the production of most of these items in its 25 (out of 40) factories in the 1940s.[51]

Wooden articles were manufactured at several places in the region in the 1850s. Pak Pattan, Sahiwal, Chiniot, and Hoshiarpur specialized in lacquered toys, carved articles and boxes. Amritsar, Lahore, Sialkot, Gujranwala, Jalandhar, Kartarpur, and Batala made several items of household use; Jandiala made carts and wheels; and Wazirabad, Jhelum, and Kalabagh specialized in boat building.[52] As may be expected, the extension of roads and railways in the next half a century led to a considerable decline in the demand for boats.[53] The demand for lacquered toys also was much reduced.[54] The foremost among the new wooden items was European-style furniture. The 'Gujrat chair' was very popular and so were the cabinets made at Jalandhar, Kartarpur, and Gujrat.[55] Sawmills with new electrical appliances were set up at Lahore, Amritsar, Rawalpindi, and Sialkot some time in the first decade of the twentieth century.[56] In the 1930s, Montgomery and Arifwala were constructing bodies of lorries which had been introduced after World War I.[57] Sports goods manufactures, like racquets for tennis and badminton and cricketing equipment, began at Sialkot towards the end of the nineteenth century, and soon caught on.[58]

At the time of annexation, traditional items in leather such as shoes, *hukkas, kuppas*, harnesses, saddlery, and drums were manufactured at urban centres of all sizes—in the city of Lahore, the medium towns of Kasur, Gujrat, Sialkot, and Rawalpindi, and in the small towns of Jhang, Dinanagar, and Pathankot, among others.[59] By the beginning of the twentieth century, European-style shoes and belts—earlier the products of local urban units—were superseded by goods from Kanpur and Meerut and also from outside India. The decrease of horse-drawn traffic and the introduction of tins for oil drastically reduced the demand for leather items.[60] To support the sagging leather industry, the government introduced tanneries at Rawalpindi, Jalandhar, Sialkot, and Wazirabad in the 1920s, but it did not have much effect due to local rivalries and lack of trained instructors.[61] The growing import of dressed leather affected the urban middlemen as well as the tanners operating from the countryside. A village tanning demonstration party formed in 1928 to acquaint the rural leather workers with new and improved techniques remained ineffective in bringing about any appreciable change.[62]

The glazed and enamelled pottery articles like bowls, vessels, cups, teapots, and inkpots, traditionally manufactured at Multan, Sialkot, Gujrat, Gujranwala, Pasrur, and Batala, could not withstand competition from the European goods which flooded the market within a few decades of annexation.[63] Consequently, the production of these items was substantially curtailed to meet only the local demand.[64] The Lahore Porcelain Works, a modern undertaking established in the second decade of the twentieth century, failed to take off due to lack of capital.[65]

Many varieties of paper produced in the region were hit by the new developments. From over a thousand workers in paper manufacture in Sialkot alone in 1881–2, only 400 were recorded in the 1890s, while the number of manufactories at Jalalpur Pirwala in Multan district decreased from about 50 in the 1880s to 5 in less than three decades.[66] Apart from the flooding of the market with paper from modern mills in other provinces, this decline was due to the grant of monopoly to produce paper to jails at Lahore, Multan, Ludhiana, Gujranwala, Jhang, and Montgomery in the 1870s.[67]

At the same time, some traditional manufactures of an ancillary kind continued on a smaller scale throughout the period. Among these was the making of ropes and twine at Lahore, Amritsar, Panipat, Rewari, Hissar, and Rawalpindi. Ivory carving continued to be done at Lahore, Amritsar, Multan, Sahiwal, and Hoshiarpur, among others. Glass bangles were made at Multan, Jhelum, and Hoshiarpur.[68] Kaithal, Hissar, and

Panipat produced refined alum and *naushadar* or salammoniac.[69] Under the European influence some changes in the scale and techniques of production were introduced in these ancillary industries. For instance, modern glass works were set up at Ambala and Panipat; saltpetre refineries were started at Jind, Hissar, Gurgaon, Karnal, Panipat, and Kaithal; Jagadhri made lead oxide and had a borax refinery; Lahore and Amritsar came to have chemical works for producing sulphuric acid.[70]

Among the new developments of a positive significance was the establishment of a number of modern mills and factories in the urban centres of the agriculturally well developed areas. Among these were cotton ginning, pressing and baling mills in the cities of Lahore and Amritsar, the large towns of Kasur, Sialkot, Gujranwala, Lyallpur, and Ferozepore, and the small towns of Montgomery, Dipalpur, Okara, Chunian, Raiwind, Gojra, Sangla, and Fazilka, among others. Flour mills and rice husking factories were set up at Lahore, Amritsar, Sialkot, Gujranwala, Ferozepore, Dera Ghazi Khan, and Akalgarh. Modern oil presses came up at Lahore, Amritsar, Gujranwala, and Dera Ghazi Khan. Iron foundries were established at Lahore, Multan, Jalandhar, Ambala, Ludhiana, Rawalpindi, Rewari, and Ropar, in addition to Batala, as noted already. Ice factories came up at places like Jalandhar, Dipalpur, Okara, Pak Pattan, and Arifwala. Breweries and distilleries, which were started much earlier, came to be located at Amritsar, Jalandhar, Gurdaspur, Sujanpur, Dera Ismail Khan, Nakodar, and Nawanshahar.[71] With the government's emphasis clearly on consumer industries, virtually no heavy or large-scale chemical industry was set up in the region.[72]

On the whole, traditional urban manufactures in the Punjab underwent a decline in some centres—as in the case of paper and metal industry—while in others, the scale of activity was considerably diminished, like in cotton, silk and woollen textiles, pottery-making, leatherwork, and woodcarving. The weavers, metalworkers, woodworkers and shoemakers in many urban centres felt obliged to modify their techniques and designs to meet the demands of the new situation. Limited in scale, these manufactures now came to be formally labelled as the cottage or small-scale industry, in contradistinction to the factory or large-scale industry using power and working with 20 or more operatives.[73] Yet, compared to the 'small-scale industry', the 'large-scale industry' had only half of the turnover and one-twelfth of the workers. According to one estimate, the number of factories in the Punjab in 1943 was 1191, employing 132,480 workers.[74] The largest single employer with a 'truly industrial type of employment', was the Railway Workshop at Lahore. Founded in the early 1860s, it came to have nearly 10,000 workers by 1918.[75]

However, unlike several other parts of British India, the urban artisans and craftsmen in the Punjab did not have to fall back on the villages. Rather, the new means of communication and the new industrial ventures attracted rural artisans to towns. For example, in the nine railway workshops in the Punjab in 1925, over 30 per cent workmen happened to be traditional carpenters (Tarkhans), blacksmiths (Lohars) and leather workers (Chamars). They were employed in large numbers in other industries also. Among the unskilled labourers in factories, the number of Kumhars (potters), Chamars and Mochis (Hindu and Muslim leather workers, respectively) was substantial.[76] Over 80 per cent of the factory labour either belonged to the district of employment or came from the adjacent areas within the province.[77]

The traditional complementarity of agriculture and village manufactures was disrupted as a result of the increasing inflow of the factory-made goods into the rural areas. Breakdown of the traditional patron-client relationship (*sepidari* system) obliged many of the skilled artisans (*sepidars*) in rural areas to either abandon their hereditary occupations or readjust with the market forces. The weavers in particular became dependent on the urban middlemen for loans for purchasing raw materials and selling the handloom products. Since the market and the modern industry could not absorb all the disadvantaged rural artisans, they turned to other occupations offered by the urban areas. Some of them took to service and managed to educate their sons who obtained white collar and supervisory jobs in government offices and factories during the early decades of the twentieth century.[78]

III

The colonial rule stood for a conception of governance that enveloped matters hitherto outside the purview of the state. To enhance its legitimacy and authority, and to function more effectively and efficiently, the state made provision for Western medicine and Western education, causing thus substantial reorientations in the traditional urban functions.

Significant changes in the sphere of medicine and health care were superimposed over the traditional arrangements. At annexation, the Unani and the Ayurvedic systems of medicines were widely practised in the region. Ganesh Das in his *Char Bagh-i panjab* refers to several well-known 'men of medicine' in Gujrat, Sialkot, Wazirabad, Eminabad, Haranpur Sodhian, and Lahore. He gives a long list of the 'unique' among the hakims, *vaids* and *jarrahs* (surgeons) in the city of Lahore under Ranjit Singh.[79] The earliest British surveys testify to the presence of the practitioners of indigenous medicine in urban areas in different parts of the province, with their largest presence, of course, in Lahore and Amritsar.[80] The individual practitioners as well as the institutions imparting instruction in medicine, like the *pathshalas* and *maktabs*, and the establishments belonging to the renunciants of the Udasi and Nirmala orders received material support from the society, and grants of land revenue from the state and its jagirdars.[81] However, the direct involve-ment and control of Ranjit Singh's state was evident only in the case of the *dar-ul-shafa* at Lahore where medicines were distributed at the state's expense. It was initially managed by Faqir Azizuddin. In 1845 it came under the care of the Austrian physician J.M. Honigberger. After the Anglo-Sikh War, Honigberger functioned under the overall supervision of Dr W.L. McGregor of the East India Company. Both Honigberger and McGregor had attended on Ranjit Singh, but the European system of medicine had not struck any roots even in the cities of Lahore and Amritsar, let alone the other parts of his territories.[82]

The situation began to be altered in the very first year of annexation. Steps towards introducing Western medicine in India had already been taken in the 1830s.[83] In 1849, hospitals for indoor treatment were set up for the civilian population at Amritsar, Jalandhar, Multan, and Sialkot.[84] For outdoor treatment, the Board of Administration recommended the construction of dispensaries at most of the 'central stations', or the 'chief cities'. The statistics about the use of dispensaries at Lahore and Amritsar for 1849–52 suggest that the people were slowly beginning to resort to these.[85] In 1853, some 15 dispensaries were sanctioned for the Punjab by the Company's government.[86] During the first decade of colonial rule, the government dispensaries were reported to be functioning even in the relatively distant towns like Peshawar, Bannu, Dera Ismail Khan, Dera Ghazi Khan, Hazara, Rawalpindi, Pind Dadan Khan, and Sialkot.[87]

In 1859, the Punjab became a Lieutenant Governor's province. Dispensaries were now opened in all the district headquarters and a number of other towns. The dispensaries established in cities, middling towns, and small towns varied in status, being class I in cities, class II in medium-size centres, and class III in small towns. In the cities several branch dispensaries were also set up to cover a larger population. Some small towns, like Tank, Bhakkar, Majitha, Phalia, and Sahiwal had dispensaries of the size of the 'branch' dispensaries only.[88] Even a small princely state like Mamdot maintained dispensaries in its towns of Zira, Muktsar, and Jalalabad.[89] All this while, the Christian missionaries were running hospitals, dispensaries, and leper asylums in the province.[90] The 'canal dispensaries' were opened to the public early in the second decade of the twentieth century. At the end of 1919, there were 504 dispensaries in the Punjab, which amounted to one dispensary for every 43,000 inhabitants.[91]

The hospital network also expanded under the Crown and a number of urban centres came to have hospitals by the 1880s. The district headquarters had civil hospitals under the charge of a Civil Surgeon. Some small towns like Sunam also had hospital facilities, though this was not the rule. The states of Patiala, Jind, Nabha, and Kapurthala, among others, had hospitals run by their respective governments. Hospitals for women were opened at Lahore, Amritsar, Sialkot, Rawalpindi, Batala, Peshawar, Narowal, Patiala, Sangrur, Tarn Taran, and Montgomery, among others. Some of them were mission hospitals, as at Batala, Narowal, and Peshawar. Like Simla, the cities of Lahore and Amritsar too came to have a number of hospitals. Leper asylums were established at Sialkot, Lahore, Patiala, Ambala, and Tarn Taran, while the TB sanitaria were set-up in the hills at Murree, Kasauli, and Sheikhbuddin, the last located on the border of Bannu and Dera Ismail Khan districts. Veterinary hospitals were established at Arifwala, Dipalpur, and Pak Pattan, among others.[92] Lahore came to have a mental hospital during the second decade of colonial rule; a mental asylum for the natives had been functioning in the city since the 1860s.[93] It may be of some interest to note that much before the annexation of the Punjab, mental asylums for European officers and troops had been in existence at different places in India, presumably as the price of ruling over a hot and distant country like India.[94] Likewise, lock hospitals were adjuncts of the 'military brothels' in the red light area in the cantonment.[95] According to government statistics, the number of hospitals and dispensaries in the Punjab exceeded 1,000 in 1943.[96]

The new medical institutions would presuppose a large number of native practitioners and a larger number of trained supporting personnel. During the first decade of colonial rule, the new medical institutions were manned by persons trained at the Calcutta Medical College (founded in 1835). In 1860 Lahore Medical School was set-up to train the local people, particularly some of the traditional practitioners, in the Western medical procedures. The school was upgraded in 1870 as a college for training native physicians for manning government medical institutions. As an 'exceptional' measure, it also ran a licentiate course of four years duration for indigenous medical practitioners and produced 'qualified' *vaids* and hakims.[97]

In fact, since 1860 the new administrators had been utilizing the services of the traditional practitioners after giving them elementary training in allopathy, to help facilitate the government's vaccination and anti-cholera measures, and also to 'popularize' Western medical science and culture. Through these 'cultural interlocutors' the British aimed at reaching out to the agricultural classes in the region who were regarded as potential recruits for the British Indian army.[98] Subsequently, however, the indigenous practitioners were virtually excluded from government medical service. The Punjab government decided in 1889 to register only those medical practitioners who had received education in Western medicine. This did not obliterate the *vaids* and hakims from urban areas, but now they functioned increasingly in competition with the allopaths who were being gradually resorted to by the emergent middle classes.[99]

The middle classes themselves were the product of Western education introduced steadily in the territories of the erstwhile kingdom of Lahore. Till its annexation, education and learning had been confined to traditional subjects which, apart from medicine, included jurisprudence, philosophy, astronomy and astrology, mathematics, calligraphy, poetry, and composition. Among the languages studied were Sanskrit, Arabic, Persian, and Gurmukhi. Men of learning were largely based in towns and cities, but some, according to Ganesh Das, lived in villages as well.[100] The early British surveys found many such schools functioning in cities and towns and even some large villages, and attached to mosques, Gurdwaras, temples, and the Udasi establishments.[101] These institutions were patronized by the state and the nobility; sometimes the local community provided support in kind or cash.[102] The larger centres also had accountancy or *mahajani* schools which were of three kinds—*lande, nagari-lande* and *perso-lande.*[103] The first British report on the administration of the Punjab expressed surprise over the prevalence of womens' education 'in all parts of the Punjab'. What made it 'remarkable' was the fact that this phenomenon was reported to be 'almost unknown in other parts of India'. Moreover, the girls and teachers belonged to all the major 'communities' in the region, that is Muslim, Hindu and Sikh.[104]

Colonial rule brought about a significant reorientation in the educational scene, particularly in the urban areas. The earliest report on the administration of the Punjab notices a 'strong desire of learning English' at Lahore and Amritsar where the Punjabi 'noblemen and gentlemen' seemed anxious to even make private arrangements for teaching English to their sons. In response to their keenness, a school 'of a collegiate character' was founded at Amritsar within a year of annexation.[105] In combining vernacular languages with English and European knowledge, it anticipated one of the essential recom-mendations of the Education Despatch of 1854.

Also known as Wood's Despatch (after Sir Charles Wood, President of the Board of Control), this policy document is regarded as a watershed in the history of Indian education.[106] Implementation of its recommendations in the Punjab was characterized broadly by evolution and experimentation, particularly during the early years of colonial rule. Even before the declaration of the new education policy, some government schools had been set-up in the district towns. The process was speeded up after the establishment in 1856 of the Department of Education and appointment of a Director of Public Instruction (DPI). In the same year, the first government girls school was opened at Rawalpindi; there were 17 more by the year end.[107]

Quality education, understandably, came to be centred at Lahore. The Anglo-Vernacular School, later to be called Lahore Zilla School or Government High School, was opened in 1860. This school had five branches in the city and attracted pupils from within and outside the district; they were mainly the sons of well-to-do people in Lahore and the neighbouring countryside. The notables of Lahore persuaded the authorities to provide 'a government-sponsored, western style higher education in the city', in response to which the first Government College was opened in 1864, with the Orientalist Dr G.W. Leitner as its first Principal. By the mid-1860s, the college was offering ancillary lectures in law as well. As noted before, the Lahore Medical School had also been functioning since 1860. For a few years in the mid-1850s (*c.* 1853–8), a school of engineering also functioned in the city to train native surveyors, draftsmen and computators for the Public Works Department (PWD).[108]

The new framework of education was more or less in place by the mid-1860s.[109] In the next decade and a half the schools imparting Western education were gradually classified according to 'stages of instructions' as primary, middle and high. The 1880s saw their increasing transference to the municipalities, albeit under an increasing control of the government.[110] The higher or collegiate education came to be coordinated by a regional university established largely by the efforts of the Anjuman-i Punjab, founded by Leitner in 1865 at Lahore.[111] After education was 'transferred' to a responsible minister in 1921–2 (under the Act of 1919), there was considerable expansion in terms of opening of schools, and also some diversification in the system.[112]

All this while there was a steady erosion of the 'indigenous' educational institutions.[113] This was as much due to withdrawal of direct government support as to the attitude of the urban people who were quick to see the causal connection between Western education and upward mobility. The qualitative efforts in Western education, including higher and professional education, came to be centred on the provincial capital and the divisional and district headquarters, followed at a considerable distance by the towns serving as the tahsil headquarters. Moreover, the secondary and higher education in government institutions was meant for those who could pay the relatively high fees.[114] Fortunately, however, the colonial state was not the sole agency of Western education.

The 'pioneers' in Western education, as also in female education, in the region happened to the American Presbyterian missionaries. The impact of their edeavour was also felt more in cities and towns where they chose to reside for reasons of security and convenience. In 1834, in the very first year of their arrival in the Punjab, they opened an English-medium school at Ludhiana where the British Political Agent was based. Upon the annexation of the Bist Jalandhar Doab in 1846, they opened another mission centre and school at Jalandhar; and a third one at Lahore in 1849, the year of its annexation. By 1907, at Lahore alone, the Presbyterians ran six boys' schools and two girls' schools.[115] They had in the meantime been joined by other missions, and together, they were running 30 girls' schools in 1876.[116] In these early decades, in addition to Lahore and Ludhiana, missionary schools for boys and girls existed at Amritsar, Ambala, Kapurthala, Batala, Pathankot, Dera Baba Nanak, Sialkot, Gujrat, and Rawalpindi, among others.[117] At the core of these institutions was the evangelical programme of the missionaries, supported fairly aggressively by a variety of other activities like publications, famine and orphan relief, medical and zenana missions, itinerant and bazaar preaching, and public debates which, cumulatively, brought about a qualitative change in the urban cultural environment.[118]

The missionaries' criticism of Indian religions combined with some early conversions of well-placed persons and upper-caste students, evoked defensive reactions from the first generation of the English-educated Punjabis. The Societies Registration Act (1860) provided a common framework for 'the rise of organizations diametrically opposed to each other', but sharing broadly the objective of countering the activities of the missionaries.[119] The existing model of the Lahore Brahmo Samaj, founded in 1863, however, was not geared towards this end. Moreover, the Brahmo Samaj was led by babus from Bengal and the Kaisthas from the North-West Provinces; their supercilious attitude offended the upcoming Punjabis. Significant beginnings from within the Punjab were made with the founding of the Anjuman-i Islamia at Lahore (1869), Sri Guru Singh Sabha at Amritsar (1873), and the Arya Samaj at Lahore (1877). These associations were based on communitarian identities respectively as Muslims, Sikhs, and Hindus, and the pattern set by them was replicated, albeit with varying emphases, in something like a wave over the next three decades. By the beginning of the twentieth century, around 60 Anjumans, 260 Arya Samajs, and over 120 Singh Sabhas had been founded in nearly all important urban centres.[120] In addition to socio-religious reform to meet the criticism of the missionaries, the foremost concern of the new associations was to spread modern education combined with religious instruction. This programme also included instruction in the vernacular—Urdu, Hindi, or Punjabi, and the corresponding script—Persian, Devanagari, or Gurmukhi, with which a particular religious community was beginning to identify itself by the 1880s. These voluntary associations opened schools all over the province, but mainly in its urban centres where they had to contend with the missionary endeavour, or to complement the professedly secular enterprise of the religiously neutral government in education.[121]

The voluntary associations took initiative in female education too. In 1911, about 50 girls schools were being run by the Arya Samajs, and 8 by the Singh Sabhas.[122] The Kanya Mahavidyalaya, an enterprise of the Jalandhar Aryas, was the first to offer higher education for girls. It also became the first in the province to start a hostel for girls.[123] Among the Muslims, girls education, though of an elementary kind, was the concern of the Anjuman-i Himayat-i Islam, founded in Lahore in 1884, and its affiliates in Amritsar, Batala and some other urban centres.[124] By the beginning of the twentieth century, boarding schools were functioning, among others, at Lahore, Amritsar, Jalandhar, Sialkot, Ferozepore, and Sangrur. Girl students came to these from the countryside and small towns. Some idea of the changing urban environment can be had from the diversity and number of girls schools at Lahore and Amritsar by the beginning of the twentieth century. Besides a number of municipal or government schools, Lahore had the Cathedral School, St. Anthony's Kincaid Girls' School, Victoria May Christian Girls' High School, Khatri Girls School, Vedic Pathshala, and Donald Town School. Similarly, in Amritsar, the government effort was supplemented by Pandit Baijnath's School, Hindu Sabha School, Mission School, DAV School, Alexandra High School, Anjuman School, and a Sikh boarding school for girls.[125]

An increasing number of students passing out from the new schools were ready for higher education. Lahore, understandingly, offered a wider range. A law school, an Oriental school and the Punjab University College came up in 1870, and the medical school was upgraded the same year. The Punjab University was founded at Lahore in 1882 not only as a degree granting university but also for imparting instruction in Oriental learning. Subsequently, the city came to have the Dayanand Anglo-Vedic (DAV), Dev Samaj and Islamia Colleges. The other well-known colleges run by the voluntary associations were the already noted Kanya Mahavidyalaya at Jalandhar, the Khalsa College at Amritsar, and the Sikh Kanya Mahavidyalaya at Ferozepore. Amritsar came to have a medical school in 1920; and in 1922 McLagan College of Engineering was established in Lahore. The engineering examination had been conducted by the Punjab University College since 1873–4. The Engineering School at Rasul in Gujrat district was started in 1927 to train overseers, sub-overseers and draftsmen. Besides Lahore, the missionaries set-up colleges in Ludhiana, Batala, Sialkot, Rawalpindi, and Peshawar.[126] The princely states could not remain unaffected by these developments, and some of their chief towns—Kapurthala, Nabha, Patiala, and Sangrur—also came to have colleges. By 1941–2, there were 40 colleges in the Punjab with more than one college in cities like Amritsar, Jalandhar, and Ludhiana, but the largest number of colleges were in Lahore.[127] Two altogether different kinds of educational initiatives were represented by the Punjab Agricultural College and Research Institute founded by the government at Lyallpur in 1909, and Hailey College of Commerce established by Sir Ganga Ram at Lahore in 1927.[128] To impart training in new skills and techniques professional and technical institutes were required, initially, by the government and then by the larger society. A teachers' training school was founded at Rawalpindi in 1856 and at Lahore in 1857; normal schools for women were opened in Lahore and Amritsar in 1864; the Mayo School of Art was founded at Lahore in 1875; a Central Training College for secondary school teachers was started in 1881. In the 1880s and 1890s, the Railway Technical School and the industrial schools were established at Lahore, Amritsar and Ludhiana. The 1920s saw the extension of industrial training with the founding of industrial schools at several district and some tahsil headquarters. Some of these schools were teaching more refined techniques in weaving, carpentry, metal work, blacksmithy, tailoring, and pottery making. Numbering 42 by 1939, the industrial schools were meant mainly for urban artisans who were losing employment as a result of the new forces.[129] The relative impact of different educational enterprises varied, but over a period of two or three generations, Western education opened up new vistas and became a major source of social and attitudinal change in the cities and large towns of the Punjab.

IV

There was much in the cultural life of the pre-colonial urban centres that appears to have continued even afterwards, albeit at a somewhat altered pace and with some reorientations. At the same time, the colonial period also saw a qualitative change in the urban modes of recreation, dissemination of information, and collective functioning.

As noticed by Ganesh Das in the year of annexation, several 'annual or seasonal fairs' were held at places of worship.[130] Virtually all urban units had shrines which attracted people from the countryside on the occasion of religious and secular fairs. Given the means of communications in the pre-colonial times, the radius from which people came to an urban centre was relatively small. The early British administrators record such fairs being held in every district of the Punjab. Even at a small centre like Sarhind, the gurdwaras held two fairs annually; Rahon and Phalia had a Baisakhi fair; Jalalpur and Nakodar had fairs on Dussehra; and Gujrat had one on Muharram. Jalandhar had the Baisakhi and Dussehra fairs, in addition to the local fairs at the tombs of Imam Nasiruddin and Pir Sahib. Many other towns held fairs on the occasion of Basant, Holi, and Dussehra.

With the gradual spread of the rail and road network, travel became easier and a much larger number of people began to throng to the cities and towns on such occasions. What to talk of Lahore and Amritsar with several celebrated shrines and places of cultural importance, even small centres increasingly figured on the pilgrimage map of the region. For example, the pilgrims to the *deras* of various sects located at places like Narnaul, Sunam, Bannu, Patiala, and Dera Ghazi Khan, were no longer confined to the locality, but came from different parts of the region.[131] Numbers became so large by the beginning of the twentieth century that to check the spread of epidemics, the government had to restrain the movement of people for large gatherings.[132] Some new kinds of fairs or occasions for gatherings also came up, like the Easter fair organized by the Jalandhar missionaries, and the annual concert of classical music, founded by Harballabh in 1875 in the vicinity of Jalandhar.[133]

In fact, the new environment and the new psychological, social and recreational needs of the increasing number of the educated people presupposed new modes of recreation. The existing gardens laid by the individual members of the erstwhile ruling class and other well-to-do persons were supplemented by the new public parks and gardens laid out in most towns and cities. Gardens for recreation existed, for example, in Lahore, Multan, Amritsar, Rawalpindi, Dera Ismail Khan, Rewari, Gurgaon, and Nabha. Some new places like Okara came to have separate parks for women and children in addition to a public garden. In many district towns, public libraries and reading rooms were set-up by the missionaries, voluntary associations, and the municipalities, as at Lahore, Amritsar, Jalandhar, Simla, Bannu, Peshawar, Ambala, Lyallpur, Sialkot, and Gurdaspur.[134] The organization of *mushairas* or the symposia in Urdu poetry by the local notables or an educational institution in the Punjab was a development of the colonial period. By the 1920s, silent cinema was becoming popular in the cities; the 1930s saw the radio coming in, while the touring theatre (*nautanki*) and circus also appeared in the cities and towns from time to time. Students as well as professional people who were moving outside the walled area took to new sports like hockey, football, tennis, cricket, and volleyball. At the same time, traditional sports like wrestling, kite flying and flying pigeons continued to be enjoyed in the old city.[135] The villagers apparently had a brush with the old and new modes of entertainment whenever they came to the city, or when they were occasionally visited by a touring theatre or *raas-lila* party, or even a motion picture. With all this, the traditional nautch girls and singers (*tawaifs*) also continued to be based in urban areas, though they were increasingly being equated with the common prostitutes.[136]

Nautch as a mode of recreation came to be disfavoured by the new ruling elite of the Punjab, the Sahibs. They preferred outdoor sports or activities in their own exclusive social environment. There were separate parks, clubs and gymkhanas for them not only at bigger civil and military stations like Lahore, Multan, and Ambala with a large European presence, but also at smaller district headquarters like Gujrat and Montgomery. Apart from tennis and cricket which were popularized by them, the Europeans enjoyed badminton, swimming, polo, and races.[137] Large areas were earmarked on the government land for clubs for Europeans in the colony towns of Lyallpur, Sargodha and Montgomery. The club as a place for recreation and social interaction gradually came to be adopted also by the middle-class Punjabis from a professional background. However, they were generally not welcome in the clubs meant for the Sahibs who barely tolerated the Indian officials becoming noticeable in the 1920s. At a few places, like Lahore and Sargodha, the educated natives formed their own clubs. The division between the 'two societies' in their social life was generally maintained. The Model Town at Lahore also came to have a separate club for women, offering facilities for games, but 'no club life'.[138]

The cities also came to have secular social and cultural associations, formed under the Societies Registration Act (1860). These associations facilitated collective action and exchanged and disseminated new ideas not only within a caste group or religious community, but also across these boundaries. The Anjuman-i Punjab (1865) led by Leitner is regarded as the 'originator of modern politics in the region'.[139] However, unlike the Anjuman in which Indian elites were led by the European officers, the later associations were almost entirely the concern of the urban middle classes. For instance, the Lahore Students Association was founded in 1881; the Indian Association, a literary society, was formed in 1883, and the Punjab Science Institute in 1886. In the same year, the Punjab Association was formed in Lahore. The city also came to have the headquarters of the Boy Scouts Association.[140] Some other concerns of the voluntary associations by the 1890s, for example, were promotion of temperance at Dera Ismail Khan, vegetarianism at Jalandhar, and prevention of cruelty towards animals at Batala.[141] By the beginning of the twentieth century, the communitarian associations like the Arya Samajs and Singh Sabhas became increasingly concerned with social issues like the uplift of women and the depressed classes, and famine and orphan relief. Their members came forward at the time of the earthquake of Kangra and the plague epidemic.[142] The last two decades of colonial rule saw the emergence of sports and literary associations like Jagatjit Afghan Club, Bazm-i Iqbal, and Doaba Punjab Kavi Sabha at Jalandhar.[143]

The printing press, which was a necessary adjunct of colonial rule, was a major factor in the new orientation in the social consciousness of the urban Punjabis. Following the missionaries and the government who used the press for evangelical, educational, and administrative purposes, the people tried to make an effective use of the print medium—books, tracts, pamphlets and, above all, newspapers and periodicals—for socio-religious reform. Subsequently, political leaders and journalists sought to influence public opinion through the press. Writers, publishers and printers, and very largely their readership, were concentrated in cities and towns.[144] From the very beginning, Lahore had been the centre of newspaper publishing. The early periodicals like *Kohinoor, Lahore Chronicle,* and the *Civil and Military Gazette* served European interests and readership. The 1870s saw the beginning of the Punjabi initiatives in journalism which soon picked up momentum, with many voluntary associations having their 'own journal broadcasting their point of view'.[145] By 1892–3, over 20 urban centres in the region came to have printing presses. The number of units in Lahore alone was 58, followed by 16 in Amritsar, and 13 in Sialkot. Of these, only five presses were owned by Europeans, including the government. At this time, Lahore published 33 newspapers and 17 periodicals; the respective numbers for Sialkot were 10 and 1; and 4 and 2 for Amritsar.[146] Some of the leading periodicals of the religious reform press were *the Regenerator of the Aryavarta, Arya Musafir, Risalah Anjuman-i Islami Punjab, Khalsa Samachar*, and *Al-Hakam*. The important papers of the predominantly political press in the early twentieth century included *The Tribune, Observer, Akhbar-i Aam, Paisa Akhbar, Zamindar, The Panjabee, Khalsa Advocate*, and the *Pratap*.[147]

There was a steady expansion of the people's enterprise in journalism. According to the census of 1911, 'the number of newspapers and magazines of all classes' rose from 74 in 1891 to 116 in 1901 and to 229 in 1911, resulting in substantial increase in their circulation as well. The census superintendent noticed that the papers were filtering down to 'every village' by this time.[148] By 1918–19, the total number of newspapers and periodicals 'of all kinds' published rose to 264. Of these, 156 were published from Lahore and 43 from Amritsar. The number of papers for the 'other centres of journalistic activity' was: Gurdaspur district, 10; Simla, 9; Ferozepore, 8; Sialkot and Rawalpindi, 5 each; and Gujrat and Gujranwala, 4 each. An overwhelming number of these (176 out of 264) happened to be in Urdu, the language of administration and education in schools since the 1850s.[149] The urban Punjabis used the press creatively for moulding public opinion, initially in the socio-religious sphere and then for political purposes.

The tradition of the urban notables assuming a leadership role in dealing with the state, or its agents like the *kotwal* is old.[150] It was perhaps in this context that the 'Hindu and Muslim notables' of Lahore had invited Ranjit Singh in 1799 to occupy the city so as to relieve them of the oppressive and incompetent rulers.[151] After annexation 'a new framework of consultation between the colonial state and powerful classes within Indian society' was created 'to link them in bonds of sympathy to British rule'.[152] For managing the local affairs and facilitating local taxation, town committees were formed in the 1850s, to be followed by municipalities in the 1860s and 1870s.[153] The government also elicited the opinion of the urban notables representing different religious communities through public commissions like the Hunter Commission (1882) and Aitchison Commission (1887). Thus schooled to act in the public domain, but think in communal terms, the urban centres gradually became the focal points simultaneously of growing politicization and communalization of consciousness. They provided leadership in terms of ideas and action to the rural population as well. Between 1877 and 1941, as many as 24 political organizations functioned in the region for short or long periods, most notably the Lahore Indian Association, Indian National Congress, All India Muslim League, All India Hindu Mahasabha, Central Sikh League, Shiromani Akali Dal, and the Unionist Party.[154]

The urban middle classes were the first to be disillusioned by the colonial political and economic policies, and to be drawn into anti-government protests, triggered off by regional issues like the Alienation of Land Act (1900) and its Amendment (1906). In the backdrop of the agitation against the partition of Bengal (1905), these issues got assimilated with the discontent mounting in rural areas against the Chenab Colony Bill, increase in the Bari Doab Canal rates, and enhancement of land revenue in the Rawalpindi district. Punjabi leaders like Lajpat Rai and Ajit Singh succeeded in linking urban and rural discontent in 1907 which unnerved the provincial government for a while.[155] After World War I, the urban and rural people in the Punjab again came together in the course of the Rowlatt Satyagraha, Jallianwala Bagh agitation, and the Martial Law in 1919, and subsequently, in the Khilafat, Non-Cooperation, and Gurdwara Reform movements. Cumulatively, these movements drew the maximum response of the people in the region, with the leadership as well as most of the rank and file (excepting in case of the Gurdwara Reform), coming from the urban areas.[156] In the late 1920s, the membership of the revolutionary Naujwan Bharat Sabha, led among others, by Bhagat Singh, and the leadership of the Kirti-Kisan (Workers-Peasants) Party also came from amongst the educated urban classes.[157]

The constitutional politics of the 1920s and 1930s was spearheaded by the Unionist Party, professedly a party of the landlords, but even its leaders were based in and operated from cities and large towns. Dominated as it were by the Muslim landlords, the Unionist Party also contributed towards the communalization of provincial politics.[158] The Civil Disobedience (1930–4) and Quit India (1942) movements, therefore, evoked relatively much less response in the Punjab, and that too largely from the non-Muslim population mostly in cities and towns.[159] Even the widespread public demonstrations in the course of the Indian National Army (INA) trials in January 1946 failed to enthuse the Punjabi Muslims.[160] The political activities of both the anti-British and communal varieties remained centred in cities partly in reaction also to the pronounced pro-rural and pro-Muslim stance of the government.

As a whole, in the new political and administrative context of colonial rule, cities provided the training ground for public life, generated ideas, and shaped political attitudes. They were the matrix of cultural reorientation and political articulation, albeit underpinned by a growing communalization of consciousness. Consequently, in less than half a century of colonial rule, large urban centres also became the arena of communal competition which at times spilled into communal rioting, initially over cow killing.[161] In the 1920s, after the withdrawal of Non-Cooperation, riots broke out over different local and communal issues, extending at times to the villages. Finally, in the late 1940s, this situation culminated in the communal riots in nearly all major cities and several towns, enveloping hundreds of villages as well in the process.[162]

V

In retrospect, during a century of colonial rule, the traditional urban functions in the region appear to have been substantially enlarged and qualitatively reoriented. The reorientations in the economic, cultural, and political spheres were so fundamental in nature and far-reaching in effect that it may not be inappropriate to call these revolutionary. The countryside also could not remain unaffected by these developments. The colonial context itself was geared to a greater administrative and economic integration of the countryside with the cities and towns. The nature and degree of this interaction, however, varied with the size, administrative status, and communication linkages of an urban centre. Thus, the maximum concentration of these factors occurred at Lahore, followed at some distance by the divisional headquarters which grew to become cities over the period. As a whole, the range of food items, commodities, raw materials, and manpower received from the countryside became larger than ever before. As the loci of markets, industries, administrative and judicial apparatus, besides the new facilities in health, education and recreation, the larger urban centres became the destination of an ever increasing number of people from villages.

Finally, with greater opportunities for material advancement and meaningful social action, the larger centres came to have an intense and more varied interaction with the countryside. The growing mutual dependence notwithstanding, the city remained the net beneficiary in terms of inflow of commodities, capital, and manpower. Also functioning as a conduit between the villages and the metropolitan economy, the colonial city worked overwhelmingly to the advantage of the latter. Because of the constraints of the colonial situation, and the limited opportunities in the secondary and tertiary sectors, the quality of life offered by the city to the incoming villagers remained far short of the basic civic amenities which were gradually and haltingly becoming available to the upcoming urban middle classes through some kind of urban government.

NOTES

1. By and large, these four functions were performed not only by the cities but also by the middling and small towns, though the scale and complexity would vary substantially with administrative status and size. Cf. Reeta Grewal, 'Urbanization in the Punjab 1849–1947', Ph.D. thesis, GNDU, Amritsar, 1988, pp. 139–40. My earlier position stands substantially modified in the chapter. I gratefully acknowledge the insights and inputs from Professor Indu Banga's forthcoming paper 'Urban Social Transformation in Colonial Punjab'.
2. This understanding of the general movement of goods is based mainly on the information available in the following serial publications of the provincial government: *District Gazetteers* of the Punjab (cited hereafter as *DG*) for the years 1883–4, 1894–5, 1904, 1912, and 1933. *Reports* on Internal Trade and Manufactures of the Punjab for the years 1880–8.
3. *DG Sialkot,* 1894-5, p. 133.
4. *DG Gujranwala,* 1883–4, pp. 60–1.
5. Indu Banga, 'Urban-Rural Interaction: The Upper Bari Doab (*c.*1550–1900)', in Reeta Grewal (ed.), *Five Thousand Years of Urbanization: The Punjab Region,* New Delhi: Manohar, 2005, pp. 134–5.
6. Indu Banga, 'Karachi and its Hinterland under Colonial Rule', in Indu Banga (ed.), *Ports and their Hinterlands in India (1700–1950),* New Delhi:

Manohar, 1992, pp. 343 and 344. In fact, through the mediacy of *mandis*, or collection-distribution points, villages in the Punjab came to constitute the hinterland of Karachi. Ibid., p. 349. Also see n. 13.

7. Rupinder Bal, 'Wheat Production and Structure of Marketing in the Punjab under Colonial Rule (1901–47)', Ph.D. thesis, Panjab University, Chandigarh, 1997, p. 10.
8. *Report on Internal Trade of the Punjab by Rail and River*, 1894–5, p. 5.
9. *Report on Internal Trade and Manufactures*, 1884–5, pp. 18 and 22.
10. Ibid., 1883–4, p. 29.
11. Bal, 'Wheat Production and Structure of Marketing', pp. 113–14, and n. 4.
12. Ibid., p. 115.
13. A *mandi* was 'a set of shops built around three or four sides of a rectangle, a wide brick pavement provided for loading, examining, clearing, weighing and bagging of grain'. L.R. Dawar, *Market Practices in the Punjab*, Lahore: Board of Economic Enquiry Punjab, Publication No. 39, 1934, p. 1.
14. Bal, 'Wheat Production and Structure of Marketing', pp. 116–18.
15. Ibid., p. 123. These *arhtias* belonged to the categories of *kacha, pacca* and *kacha-pacca*, with varying range of services and corresponding commissions. Ibid., pp. 121–3.

    Another report for 1937 gives the total number of *arhtias* as follows: Ludhiana 96, Abohar 94, Okara 80, Lyallpur 74, Jalandhar 73, Gojra 70, Sargodha 60, and Rohtak 57. Kanchan Jyoti, 'The City of Jullundur: A Study in Urban History (1846–1947)', Ph.D. thesis, GNDU, Amritsar, 1988, p. 206 and n. 72.
16. Anand Gauba, *Amritsar: A Study in Urban History (1840–1947)*, Jalandhar: ABS Publications, 1988, pp. 91–4. Jyoti,'The City of Jullundur', pp. 204–5.
17. Imran Ali, *The Punjab Under Imperialism, 1885–1947*, New Delhi: OUP, 1989, pp. 224–5.
18. Ibid., pp. 90–1.
19. Gauba, *Amritsar*, pp. 86–91; Jyoti, 'The City of Jullundur', pp. 227–30. The Amritsar grain exchange started working in 1925. Jalandhar had three such exchanges in the 1930s.
20. Bal, 'Wheat Production and Structure of Marketing', p. 147. *DG Amritsar*, 1914, p. 116.
21. Jyoti, 'The City of Jullundur', pp. 226–31. Gauba, *Amritsar*, pp. 85–95.
22. *DG Sialkot*, 1894–5, p. 133.
23. *Report on Internal Trade and Manufactures in the Punjab*, 1880-1, pp. 16–18. *DG Gujrat*, 1883–4, pp. 88–9.
24. *Monograph on Paper Making and Paper Machie in the Punjab*, 1907–8, p. 8. *Report on Internal Trade and Manufactures in the Punjab*, 1880–1, pp. 17–18.

25. J. Royal Roseberry III, *Imperial Rule in the Punjab: The Conquest and Administration of Multan, 1818-1881*, New Delhi: Manohar, 1987, pp. 220–2 and 234 n. 10.
26. *DG Sialkot*, 1894–5, p. 133.
27. *Monograph on Brass and Copper Ware in the Punjab*, 1886–7, p. 8.
28. Sukhwant Singh, *Agricultural Growth under Colonial Constraints: The Punjab 1849–1947*, New Delhi: Manpreet Prakashan, 2000, pp. 65–6.
29. Ian Johnstone Kerr, 'The Punjab Province and the Lahore District, 1849–1872: A Case Study of British Colonial Rule and Social Change in India', Ph.D. thesis, University of Minnesota, Minnesota, 1975, pp. 325 and 348. Already in the early 1850s, the traditional vegetable gardening caste of Arains in the neighbourhood of Lahore had taken to the production of potato in response to the European demand.
30. Ibid., pp. 348–9, and 389 n. 7. This development, coupled with the regulation of manufacture and sale of spirits by the government forced the Kalals or the distilling caste to turn to other occupations.
31. Jyoti, 'The City of Jullundur', pp. 208–9.
32. Banga, 'Karachi and its Hinterland', p. 34, n. 16. See also, B.S. Saini, *The Social & Economic History of the Punjab 1901–39*, New Delhi: Ess Ess Publications, 1975, p. 319. It may be of some interest to note that kerosene began to be imported in the 1880s. Jyoti, 'The City of Jullundur', p. 201.
33. For imports and exports of Jalandhar see appendices 6A and 6B.
34. Banga, 'Urban-Rural Interaction', pp. 136–42. See also J.S. Grewal, 'Urban Economic Life', in Indu Banga and J.S. Grewal (eds.), *Maharaja Ranjit Singh: The State and Society*, Amritsar: GNDU, 2001, pp. 211–20. See also, Harish C. Sharma, 'Artisans', ibid., pp. 236–45.
35. Harish C. Sharma, *Artisans of the Punjab: A Study of Social Change in Historical Perspective (1849–1947)*, New Delhi: Manohar, 1996, pp. 26–39 and 64–87.
36. A decline in the traditional cotton manufactures due to competition with European goods and factories in Bombay is noted, among others, by *DG Jalandhar*, 1883–4, p. 216; *DG Gurdaspur*, 1914, p. 139; *DG Amritsar*, 1914, p. 108; and *DG Montgomery*, 1933, p. 206.
37. Harminder Singh, 'Industrial Development in the Punjab 1901–47', M.Phil. dissertation, GNDU, Amritsar, 1981, pp. 10 and 48.
38. B.H. Baden Powell, *Handbook of the Manufactures and Arts of the Punjab*, Lahore: Punjab Printing Company, 1872, pp. viii-x. For further detail: *DG Multan*, 1883–4, pp. 105–8. *DG Amritsar*, 1883–4, p. 41. *DG Amritsar*, 1914, p. 108. *DG Lahore*, 1893-4, p.195. The ruling class of the erstwhile kingdom of Lahore had been the biggest patron of silk industry.

Reeta Grewal, 'Polity, Economy and Urbanization: Early 19th-Century Punjab', *Journal of Regional History*, vol. IV, 1984, pp. 56–72.

39. A. Latifi, *The Industrial Punjab: A Survey of Facts, Conditions and Possibilities*, Bombay: Longman's Green and Company, 1911, p. 40. See also, A.C. Badenoch, *Punjab Industries 1911–17*, Lahore: Government Printing, 1917, p. 12.
40. *Monograph on Woollen Manufactures in the Punjab*, 1884–5, pp. 9–10. *DG Jalandhar*, 1883–4, p. 46.
41. *DG Gurdaspur*, 1914, pp. 139–41. *DG Amritsar*, 1914, p. 106. See also, Harminder Singh, 'Industrial Development', pp. 25–6.
42. Latifi, *Industrial Punjab*, p. 150.
43. Badenoch, *Punjab Industries*, p. 15.
44. Harminder Singh, 'Industrial Development', pp. 109–12.
45. *Monograph on Carpet Making in the Punjab*, 1905–6, pp. 6–7. *DG Amritsar*, 1883–4, pp. 112–15. *Report on Internal Trade and Manufactures*, 1880–1, pp. 52–8.
46. *DG Gurdaspur*, 1914, p. 145. Badenoch, *Punjab Industries*, p. 18.
47. Latifi, *Industrial Punjab*, p. 91.
48. *DG Jalandhar*, 1883–4, p. 46. *DG Sialkot*, 1894–5, pp. 127–8. *DG Amritsar*, 1883–4, p. 44. *DG Shahpur*, 1883–4, p. 77. *Monograph on Brass and Copper-Ware in the Punjab*, 1886–7, pp. 3–4.
49. Bal, 'Wheat Production and Structure of Marketing', pp. 55–6.
50. Badenoch, *Punjab Industries*, pp. 34–5.
51. Jyoti, 'The City of Jullundur', pp. 404–6, Appendix V.
52. *Monograph on Wood Manufactures in the Punjab*, pp. 16–17. *Report on Internal Trade and Manufactures in the Punjab*, 1880-1, pp. 53–60. *DG Shahpur*, 1894–5, pp. 76–7.
53. Latifi, *Industrial Punjab*, p. 217.
54. *DG Shahpur*, 1883–4, p. 77.
55. *DG Gujrat*, 1894–5, p. 85. *DG Jalandhar*, 1904, p. 220.
56. Latifi, *Industrial Punjab*, p. 222.
57. *DG Montgomery*, 1933, p. 206.
58. *Monograph on Wood Manufactures in the Punjab*, p. 19. Latifi, *Industrial Punjab*, p. 126.
59. Based on DG series of 1883–4 of Lahore, Gujrat, Sialkot, and Rawalpindi.
60. Latifi, *Industrial Punjab*, pp. 110–16. He remarks, interestingly, that the leather industry was 'killed' by the kerosene tin!
61. Ibid., pp. 106-8. Badenoch, *Punjab Industries*, p. 201.
62. Harminder Singh, 'Industrial Development', pp. 74–5.
63. *DG Multan*, 1883–4, p. 106. *DG Sialkot*, 1894–5, p. 127. *Report on Internal Trade and Manufactures in the Punjab*, 1880–1, p. 50.

64. Latifi, *Industrial Punjab*, pp. 275–6.
65. Badenoch, *Punjab Industries*, p. 38.
66. *DG Sialkot*, 1894–5, p. 126. *DG Multan*, 1883–4, p. 52. For a discussion, Masatoshi A. Konishi, 'Multani Kaghaz: Lesser known Aspect of Multan as a Paper-Making Centre', *Lahore Museum Bulletin*, vol. II, no. 2, 1989, pp. 61–8.
67. *Monograph on Paper Making and Paper Machie in the Punjab*, 1907–8, pp. 6–8. *DG Sialkot*, 1894–5, pp. 126 and 168.
68. Latifi, *Industrial Punjab*, pp. 129, 191–6 and 284–9. Badenoch, *Punjab Industries*, pp. 88–9.
69. Based on the DGs of 1883–4 of Karnal and Hissar.
70. Latifi, *Industrial Punjab*, pp. 138–9.
71. Information on factories has been collected from Table 46 of the DGs of Multan, 1883–4; Jalandhar, 1883–4; Dera Ismail Khan, 1883–4; Lahore, 1883–4 and 1912; Sialkot, 1904 and 1912; Montgomery, 1907 and 1933; Lyallpur, 1912; Ferozepore, 1912; Ambala, 1912; Amritsar, 1914; and the Phulkian States Gazetteer, 1912.
72. J.S. Khanna, 'Lagging Industrial Development in Punjab: An Analysis', *PSE Economic Analyst*, vol. II, 1980, p. 88.
73. D.R. Gadgil, *The Industrial Evolution of India (1860–1939)*; rpt, New Delhi: OUP, 1971, p. 41. Harminder Singh, 'Industrial Development, pp. 2–10.
74. Harminder Singh, 'Industrial Development', pp. 83–4.
75. Kerr, 'The Punjab Province and Lahore District', pp. 385–6.
76. Sharma, *Artisans of the Punjab*, pp. 95–6 and nn. 39 and 42.
77. Harminder Singh, 'Industrial Development', pp. 146–7 and nn. 4–5.
78. Sharma, *Artisans of the Punjab*, pp. 95 and 101–3.
79. *Char Bagh-i Panjab*, Eng tr. and ed. J.S. Grewal and Indu Banga as *Early Nineteenth Century Panjab*, Amritsar: GNDU, 1975, pp. 31, 40, 48, 61, 87, 91, 98 and 118.
80. For example, G.W. Leitner, *Indigenous Education in the Punjab since Annexation and in 1882*; rpt., Patiala: Languages Department Punjab, 1971, pp. 4, 29, 54, 72, 82 and passim.
81. Indu Banga, *Agrarian System of the Sikhs: Late Eighteenth-Early Nineteenth Century*, New Delhi: Manohar, 1978, p. 160 and nn. 59–62. Sulakhan Singh, 'Udasi Establishments under Sikh Rule', *Journal of Regional History*, vol. I, 1980, pp. 70–87. Darshan Singh, 'How did the Nirmalas Preach', *Journal of Sikh Studies*, vol. V, no. 1, 1978, pp. 147–8. See also, Kavita Sivaramakrishnan, 'Addressing the Health of the "Public"—State Authority, Missionaries and Vaids in Punjab Towns and Cities (circa 1880s–1930s)', Ph.D. thesis, Jawaharlal Nehru University, New Delhi, 2003, pp. 18–31.

82. Sasha, 'The State, Society and Epidemics in Colonial Punjab 1849–1947', Ph.D. thesis, Panjab University, Chandigarh, 2003, pp. 9–10.
83. Anil Kumar, *Medicine and the Raj: British Medical Policy in India, 1835–1911*, New Delhi: Sage, 1998, pp. 23–9, 91, 93 and 96.
84. Sasha, 'State, Society and Epidemics', p. 18.
85. *General Report upon the Administration of the Punjab Proper for the Years 1849–50 & 1850–1: Being the first two years after Annexation*, Calcutta: T. Jones, 1853, pp. 151–2. The figures of the patients treated in the 'two chief Dispensaries' were as follows:

Year	Dispensary	No. of patients treated
1849	Lahore	1,369
1850	do	3,560
1851	do	7,770
1851–2	Amritsar	2,800

86. Kumar, *Medicine and the Raj*, p. 96.
87. Sasha, 'State, Society and Epidemics', p. 18. In fact, the British regarded the dispensaries as 'one of the best available means for conciliating and humanizing the lawless tribes beyond the border'. *Report on the Administration of the Punjab and its Dependencies*, 1867–8, p. 106.
88. *Report of the Inspector General of Dispensaries in Punjab 1867*, pp. 8–36.
89. *DG Ferozepore*, 1883–4, p. 85.
90. John C.B. Webster, *The Christian Community and Change in Nineteenth Century North India*, New Delhi: Macmillan, 1976, p. 14, Table 1.
91. *Home Department Proceedings: Medical and Sanitary*, September 1920, no. 6, Punjab State Archive (PSA), Patiala, p. 29.
92. Based on the DGs of different series.
93. *Report on the Administration of the Punjab*, 1867–8, p. 107.
94. Kumar, *Medicine and the Raj*, p. 89.
95. Ibid., pp. 90 and 106-10. The 'military brothels' were maintained for the British troops and regulated by the military authorities who used the lock hospitals to keep the prostitutes (and soldiers) healthy. A lock hospital was opened at the Mian Mir cantonment of Lahore in 1859, and a district lock hospital was established in the Anarkali area in 1879. Kerr, 'Punjab Province and Lahore District', p. 224.
96. The exact number of hospitals and dispensaries in 1943 is reported to be 1065. *Statistics of Hospitals and Dispensaries in the Punjab 1943*, in Sukhdev Singh Sohal, 'Professional Middle Classes in the Punjab', *Journal of Regional History*, vol. III, 1982, p. 77.
97. Kumar, *Medicine and the Raj*, p. 45.

To facilitate vaccination and anti-cholera measures, and also to popularize

Western medical science and culture, the provincial government embarked on an experimental programme of giving 'rudimentary training in government hospitals' to local hakims. This was intended to make up for the shortage of Punjabis trained in allopathy, and help overcome barriers of language, religion, customs and distance. Ibid., p. 46.

98. Ibid., p. 46. After the experience of 1857-8, the Punjab came to have a special importance for the British Indian Army, and this 'policy became enshrined in the mythology of the martial castes theory which maintained that the ethnic origin and racial characteristics of the main groups of Punjabi recruits particularly fitted them for military service'. Ian Talbot, *Punjab and the Raj 1849–1947,* New Delhi: Manohar, 1988, p. 43.
99. Kavita Sivaramakrishnan, 'Addressing the Health of the "Public" ', pp. 125–57.
100. *Char Bagh*, pp. 31–2, 45, 61, 105, 140 and passim.
101. Leitner, *Indigenous Education*, pp. 14, 35, 54, 73, 82 and passim.
102. Banga, *Agrarian System*, pp. 160 and 166. *General Report 1849–50 & 1850–1*, pp. 143–4.
103. Leitner, *Indigenous Education*, p. 11.
104. *General Report 1849–50 & 1850–1*, p. 143.
105. Ibid., p. 144.

The crucial decisions giving an edge to English education, particularly for law courts and government appointments, had already been taken in the 1830s and the 1840s. Aparna Basu, 'The Past, Present and Future of English', in Indu Banga and Jaidev (ed.), *Cultural Reorientation in Modern India*, Shimla: IIAS, 1996, pp. 183–6.

106. Wood's Despatch laid down the broad parameters for the development of Western education for the remainder of the colonial period. Retaining the twin objectives of education in English and 'useful European knowledge', it recommended its 'general diffusion' through the vernacular, a government Department of Education, and an expanding system of grants-in-aid for non-government institutions. For the first time, government schools for girls and teachers training were recommended. The despatch of 1854 also recommended professional education in medicine, engineering, and law, and chairs in modern Indian and classical languages. However, since this educational programme was meant for a colonized people to be trained and tested as 'servants', the universities to be set-up at Calcutta, Bombay, and Madras were visualized mainly as examining bodies. Suresh Chandra Ghosh, *History of Education in Modern India* (*1757–1986*), New Delhi: Orient Longman, 1995, pp. 74–7.
107. H.R. Mehta, *A History of the Growth and Development of Western Educa-*

tion in the Punjab 1846–84, Lahore: Punjab Government Record Office, Monograph 5, 1929, pp. 30–3.

108. Kerr, 'Punjab Province and Lahore District', pp. 364–70. For Leitner's contribution to education also see Nazer Singh, *G.W. Leitner: Founder of Punjab System of Education, including the Punjab University, Lahore*, Patiala: Madaan Publications, 2004, pp. 21–34.

109. According to the Administration Report of 1867-8, the final year before the Department of Education changed its categories, the institutions managed or aided by the government covered the following: colleges (including the government, mission, and Oriental colleges), 3; zilla or district schools, 25; aided schools of a corresponding grade, 8; branch district schools, 49; government town schools, 77; aided schools of a similar grade, 88; aided schools of a lower grade, 93; jail schools, 23; government female schools, 272; aided female schools, 507; government normal teachers training schools, 9; and aided normal female schools, 4. At this time, 4,888 'indigenous schools', were also reported to be in existence. To complete the picture, mention may be made also of '1,555 government village schools'. *Report on the Administration of the Punjab*, 1867–8, p. 91. For some idea of the changes in classification of schools in the decade following, see Kerr, 'Punjab Province and Lahore District', pp. 397–8 n. 61.

110. G.S. Chhabra, *Social and Economic History of the Panjab (1849–1901)*, Jullundur: S. Nagin & Co., 1962, pp. 141–4. In the 1880s there were changes also in the system of examination and grants-in-aid which became more rigorous.

111. Ibid., p. 144. Kerr, 'Punjab Province and Lahore District', pp. 231 and 233–6.

112. Saini, *The Social & Economic History of the Punjab 1901–39*, New Delhi: Ess Ess Publications, 1975, pp. 144–76.

113. Chhabra, *Social and Economic History*, pp. 136–8 and 145. Saini, *Social & Economic History*, pp. 141 and 149.

114. For example, because of the higher fees, the Lahore Zillah School had 'an overtly elitist orientation', and its students came from 'families of some means'. Compared to the local mission school, therefore, students in the government-run school were much less in number, and also less regular in attendance. Kerr, 'Punjab Province and Lahore District', pp. 365, 371 and 372.

In college education too, the per student fee charged in 1897–8 at the Lahore Government College was nearly 2½ times more than that of the local DAV College whose strength was nearly double that of the Government College. Webster, *Christian Community and Change*, p. 157, Table 15.

115. Webster, *Christian Community and Change*, pp. 13, 14, 42, 151 and 167.
116. Ibid., p. 143.
117. Based on the DGs series for 1883–4. For 'the geographical spread' of the Christian missions and their institutions, see C.H. Loehlin, 'The History of Christianity in the Punjab', *The Panjab Past and Present* (*PPP*), vol. VII, pt. I, 1973, p. 218.
118. Webster, *Christian Community and Change*, pp. 93–186. Also see Chapter 2.
119. J.S. Grewal, 'Christian Presence and Cultural Reorientation: The Case of the Colonial Punjab', *Proceedings Indian History Congress*, Calcutta, 1990, pp. 535-42. See also, Geoffrey A. Oddie, 'Constructive "Hinduism": The Impact of the Robert Eric Frykenberg (ed.), Protestant Missionary Movement on Hindu Self-Understanding', in *Christians and Missionaries in India: Cross-Cultural Communication since 1500*, London: Routledge/Curzon, 2003, p. 180.
120. See Ikram Ali Malik, 'Muslim Anjumans and Communitarian Consciousness', in Indu Banga (ed.), *Five Punjabi Centuries: Polity, Economy, Society and Culture, c.1500–1990*; rpt., New Delhi: Manohar, 2000, pp. 121-2. K.C. Yadav and K.S. Arya, *Arya Samaj and the Freedom Movement*, vol. I: *1875–1918*, New Delhi: Manohar, 1988, p. 23, Table 2.2. J.S. Grewal, *The Sikhs of the Punjab*, The New Cambridge History of India; rev. edn., Cambridge: Cambridge University Paperback, 1998, p. 144. A few Singh Sabhas were founded in villages also. Cf. N. Gerald Barrier, *The Sikhs and their Literature*, New Delhi: Manohar, 1970, p. xxv.
121. For the activities of these voluntary associations: Malik, 'Muslim Anjumans', pp. 112–21. Edward D. Churchill Jr., 'Muslim Societies of the Punjab, 1860–90', *PPP*, vol. VIII, pt. I, 1974, pp. 69–91. Kenneth W. Jones, *Arya Dharm: Hindu Consciousness in 19th-Century Punjab*; rpt., New Delhi: Manohar, 1989, pp. 67–154. J.S. Grewal, *Sikhs of the Punjab*, pp. 145–50.
122. Surinder Kaur, 'British Policy Towards Education', pp. 92–3.
123. Jyoti, 'The City of Jullundur', p. 257.
124. Malik, 'Muslim Anjumans', pp. 117–18. Churchill, 'Muslim Societies', pp. 81–2.
125. Surinder Kaur, 'British Policy Towards Education', pp. 92–3.
126. Loehlin, 'History of Christianity in the Punjab', p. 225. Shyamala Bhatia, *Social Change and Politics in Punjab 1898–1910*, New Delhi: Enkay Publishers, 1987, p. 50, Table 2.3. Besides the well-known Forman Christian College, founded initially in 1864, Lahore had Kinnaird College for Women; Rawalpindi had Gordon College; Sialkot had Murray College; and Peshawar had Edwardes College.
127. Surinder Kaur, 'British Policy Towards Education', p. 118.

128. Ibid., pp. 130 and 136. Saini, *Social & Economic History*, pp. 157, 160 and 162. Sohal, 'Professional Middle Classes in the Punjab', *JRH*, vol. III, 1982, pp. 76–7.
129. Saini, *Social & Economic History*, pp. 162–5. For tabulated information on these schools, Badenoch, *Punjab Industries*, Appendix II.
130. *Char Bagh*, pp. 24–5, 86, 120, 133, 140, 142 and passim.
131. Based on DGs series for 1883–4 for various districts.
132. Sasha, 'State, Society and Epidemics', pp. 122-3. The district administration had to often issue a gazette notification to prohibit the booking of train tickets.
133. Kanchan Jyoti, 'Impact of Colonial Rule on Urban Life', in Indu Banga (ed.), *The City in Indian History*; rpt., New Delhi: Manohar, 2005, p. 212. Simultaneously, some new features like public functions, tournaments, brass bands and gramophones got added to the celebration of traditional fairs in Jalandhar. Ibid., pp. 212–13.
134. Based on DGs series for 1883–4 for various districts.
135. Saini, *Social & Economic History*, pp. 129–31. Jyoti, 'Impact of Colonial Rule', pp. 211–12. Prakash Tandon, *Punjabi Saga (1857–2000)*; rpt., New Delhi: Rupa Paperback, 2003, pp. 172–3. Tandon here refers to the city of Lahore.
136. Vidya Rao, 'Thumri and Thumri Singers: Changes in Style and Life-Style', in Indu Banga and Jai Dev (eds.), *Cultural Reorientation in Modern India*, pp. 278–315. Tandon, *Punjabi Saga*, pp. 167–71. Tandon dwells at some length on the changing conditions of the 'courtesans' of Gujrat and Lahore. In the census of 1911, the number of prostitutes in the entire Punjab was reported to be 5,557 which came down to 1,142 in the census of 1931. Saini, *Social & Economic History*, p. 127.
137. This is recorded, among others, by the following: Dennis Kincaid, *British Social Life in India 1608–1937*, London: George Routledge & Sons, 1938, pp. 170–8, 208, 210 and 217–21. Muriel Lester, *My Host the Hindoo*, London: William and Norgate, 1931, pp. 121–30. Mrs Robert Moss King, *Diary of a Civilian's Wife in India 1877–82*, London: Richard Bentley, 1884, p. 157. It must, however, be pointed out that the extent of these recreation facilities was probably determined by 'the quantitative and qualitative difference in the western presence', to borrow a phrase from Ian J. Kerr. 'Urbanization and Colonial Rule in 19th-Century India: Lahore and Amritsar, 1849–1881', *PPP*, vol. XIV, pt. I, 1980, p. 221.
138. Tandon, *Punjabi Saga*, pp. 180 and 217–18. There were 'slight variations' in the 'prescribed' conditions on which clubs for different towns were registered under the Indian Companies Act. *Punjab Colony Manual*, 1933, pp. 254–5.

139. Nazer Singh, *G.W. Leitner*, pp. 16, 21 and 44.
140. *DG Lahore*, 1893–94, pp. 238–9.
141. 'Statement of Scientific and Literary and Charitable Societies in the Punjab, 1892–3', *Report on the Administration of the Punjab and its Dependencies*, 1892–3, Appendix 63.
142. The Lahore and Jalandhar Arya Samajs were the most active in the pursuit of these social causes. For some detail, see, J.S. Grewal and Indu Banga, (eds.), *Lala Lajpat Rai in Retrospect: Political, Economic, Social and Cultural Concerns*, Chandigarh: Panjab University, 2000, pp. 174–258. Jyoti, 'The City of Jullundur', pp. 349–60. See also, Jones, *Arya Dharm*, pp. 202–15 and 218–19. Sasha, 'State, Society and Epidemics', pp. 156–8.
143. Jyoti, 'Impact of Colonial Rule', p. 213.
144. For an overview of these developments, Emmett Davis, *Press and Politics in British Western Punjab 1836–1947*, New Delhi: Academic Publications, 1983, pp. 119–27.
145. Ibid., pp. 32, 84 and 90.
146. 'Statement of Printing Presses in the Punjab for the year 1892–3', *Report on the Administration of the Punjab and its Dependencies for 1892–3*, Appendix 61.
147. Davis, *Press and Politics*, pp. 69-91. Bhatia, *Social Change and Politics*, pp. 64–6. Cf. *Imperial Gazetteer of India*, Provincial Series: Punjab, rpt., New Delhi: Atlantic Publishers, vol. I, p. 144.
148. Quoted in Davis, *Press and Politics*, p. 117.
149. Ibid., Appendix VII, p. 143.
150. See, for example: Abul Fazl, *The Ain-i Akbari*, Eng. tr. H. Blockmann; rpt., New Delhi: D.K. Publishers, 1997, pp. 43-5. S.C. Misra, 'Some Aspects of the Self-Administering Institutions in Medieval Indian Towns', in J.S. Grewal and Indu Banga (eds.), *Studies in Urban History*, Amritsar: GNDU, 1981, pp. 80–90. That the local notables had a say is suggested also by M.P. Singh, *Town, Market, Mint and Port in the Mughal Empire 1556–1707*, New Delhi: Adam Publishers, 1985, pp. 43–4 and 263–77.
151. Sohan Lal Suri, *Umdat-ut-Tawarikh*, Pbi. tr. Amarwant Singh, eds. J.S. Grewal and Indu Banga, Amritsar: GNDU, 1985, p. 49.
152. Ravinder Kumar, 'The Role of Urban Society in Nationalist Politics', in Indu Banga (ed.), *The City in Indian History*, pp. 270 and 271.
153. For a discussion of urban government see Chapter 7.
154. Kirpal C. Yadav, *Elections in Punjab 1920–47*, New Delhi: Manohar, 1987, p. 132.
155. Sri Ram Sharma, *Punjab in Ferment*, New Delhi: S. Chand, 1971, pp. 1–103.
156. See, for example, Ravinder Kumar, 'Urban Society and Urban Politics:

Lahore in 1919', in Indu Banga (ed.), *Five Punjabi Centuries*, pp. 180–220. S.L. Malhotra, *Gandhi and the Punjab*, Chandigarh: Panjab University, 1970, pp. 77–103 and 106–162. Mohinder Singh, *The Akali Movement*, New Delhi: Macmillan, 1978, pp. 97–101.

157. Though not discussed specifically, the urban middle-class background of the revolutionaries and the *Kirti* leadership is quite evident in Kamlesh Mohan, *Militant Nationalism in the Punjab 1919–35*, New Delhi: Manohar, 1985, pp. 78–137. See also, Fauja Singh, *Eminent Freedom Fighters of Punjab*, Patiala: Punjabi University, 1972, pp. 80–3, 86–8, 222–4 and 230.

158. Raghuvendra Tanwar, *Politics of Sharing Power: The Punjab Unionist Party 1923–47*, New Delhi: Manohar, 1999, pp. 60–129. Ian Talbot, *Punjab and the Raj*, pp. 80–99.

159. This is evident from the detailed studies of the Congress in the Punjab: S.L. Malhotra, *From Civil Disobedience to Quit India*, Chandigarh: Panjab University, 1979, pp. 7–48, 137–55 and 160. Ganeshi Mahajan, *Congress Politics in the Punjab 1885–1947*, New Delhi: K.K. Publishers, 2002, pp. 111–22.

160. Satya M. Rai, *Legislative Politics and Freedom Struggle in the Punjab 1897-1947*, New Delhi: ICHR, 1984, pp. 309–12, 314 and 320.

161. 'The first of a series of violent clashes occurred at Multan city' in 1880-1. Roseberry, *Imperial Rule in Punjab*, p. 238. See also, Kirpal Singh, 'The Hindu Muslim Riot in the Punjab 1881', *Proceedings Punjab History Conference*, 6th Session, Patiala, 1971, pp. 288-95. Between 1883 and 1891, at least 15 major riots broke out in different cities and towns of the Punjab over cow slaughter. Sukhdev Singh Sohal, 'Middle Classes and Communalism in the Colonial Punjab', *JRH*, vol. V, 1984, pp. 84–5.

162. Between 1922 and 1927, 4,740 'ordinary' and 'communal' riots were reported largely from urban areas, but also from some villages. Prem Raman Uprety, *Religion and Politics in Punjab in the 1920s*, New Delhi: Sterling, 1980, p. 2. It must be pointed out, however, that instead of looking for causation in the immediate context, or the colonial situation in general, Uprety takes the 'Hindu-Muslim antagonism' to have been 'in existence for a millennium'. Ibid., p. 134. During the 1930s, more villages began to be involved in communal riots. For detail, Naranjan Dass Mohaya, 'The History of Communal Riots in Punjab 1922–47', Ph.D. thesis, Panjab University, Chandigarh, 1984, pp. 15, 123, 125–7, 128, 130–6, 150–5 and passim. During the last year of colonial rule, nearly all the major towns and hundreds of villages became affected. Ibid., pp. 198–269.

APPENDIX 6A

IMPORTS OF JALANDHAR UNDER COLONIAL RULE

From within the Region		From within the Country		From outside India	
Place	Articles of Trade	Place	Articles	Place	Articles
Hinterland covering Jalandhar district	Wheat, rice, milk, ghee cream, vegetables, gur, cotton, timber	Delhi	Gold ornaments, brass and copper vessels, glass, glass bottles, looking glass, chimneys, glazed toys, English piece goods, iron ropes	Kabul	Dry fruit, silk, woollen textiles, copper, horses
Kapurthala	Sugar, hides	Moradabad	Brass utensils	Yarkand	Cotton textiles—Indian and European, silver
Hoshiarpur	Rice, mangoes, ghee timber, hides, lac	Bareilly	Sugar	Bokhara	Silk, gold
		Pilibhit	Sugar		
Ludhiana	Wheat, pulses, hides, gold/silver ornaments	Devband	Sugar	China	Silk, zinc
Amritsar	Rice, brass and copper vessels, iron, camels, hides	Agra	Ropes	Japan	Art silk, leather, celluloid, cycles, cycle parts
		Kanpur	Leather		
Lahore	Oil-seeds	Benaras	Gold and silver thread	Russia	Gold
Lyallpur	Fodder	Jammu-Kashmir	Woollen textiles	Africa	Ivory
Ferozepore	Wheat, pulses, ghee, iron			Java	Sugar

Kangra	Rice, ghee, potatoes, tea	Bombay	Sugar, English piece goods	Australia	Gold and silver ornaments, gold and silver thread
Patiala	Pulses	Ahmedabad	Cotton textiles	Czechoslovakia	Boots, leather
Ambala	Cotton	Calcutta	English piece goods, silk	Germany	Silver, copper, dyes
Gujranwala	Wheat, rice, oil-seeds, brass utensils, iron, henna, gunny bags	Burdwan	Rice	Great Britain	Cotton, textiles, European dyes, iron, cycle, cycle parts
Gujrat	Wheat, rice, ghee, oil-seeds, salt. gunny bags, brass utensils	Assam	Ivory	United States of America	Celluloid toys, rubber
Jhelum	Wheat, bajra, pulses, oil-seeds, ghee, dry fruit, salt, beer, dye, indigo, timber, gunny bags, iron	Guntur	Tobacco		
Multan	Dry fruit, dates				
Karachi	Sugar, kerosene oil				
Peshawar	Woollen garments				

Source: Kanchan Jyoti, 'The City of Jullundur: A Study in Urban History (1846–1947)', p. 191, Table XIVA.

APPENDIX 6B

EXPORTS OF JALANDHAR UNDER COLONIAL RULE

To within the Region		To outside the Region	
Place	Articles	Place	Articles
Hoshiarpur	Gur	Delhi	Wheat, vegetables, hides
Ludhiana	Gur, ghee, silk, locks	Saharanpur	Indian cotton textiles
Amritsar	Silk, ropes	Agra	Wheat
Lahore	English piece goods	Kanpur	Hides
Mian Mir	Pottery		
Ferozepore	Rice, silk	Jammu-Kashmir	English piece goods
Kangra	Wheat, pulses, Indian cotton textiles	Bombay	Loudspeakers
Ambala	Rice	Bikaner	Gur
Hissar	Wheat, fodder	Calcutta	Wheat, loudspeakers
Gujranwala	Tea	Great Britain	Wheat, cooton
Gujrat	Gur, tea	United States of America	Ivory inlaid articles
Chiniot	Hides	Central Asia	Cotton, silk and woollen piece goods
Jhelum	Rice, gur, tea		
Rawalpindi	Gur, leather		
Karachi	Wheat, gur, Indian cotton textiles, locks		
Attock	Gur		
Peshawar	Vegetables, leather		

Source: Kanchan Jyoti, 'The City of Jullundur: A Study in Urban History (1846–1947)', p. 192, Table XIVB.

7

A New Framework for Urban Government

To think of urban government is to think of the municipal system introduced under colonial rule. This does not mean, however, that there was no urban governance before the coming of the British. In fact, urban administration is as old as urbanization itself. Urban centres cannot exist without some kind of authority and organization. Even the British did not introduce municipal committees immediately upon conquering a territory in India. In Lucknow, for example, the nawab, the court, the *kotwal* and his numerous *daroghas* were responsible for 'many of the functions that later formed the core of municipal government'.[1] Furthermore, before the municipal committee was constituted for Lucknow in 1862, there was a managing body, consisting of the Deputy Commissioner as president, the Magistrate of the city as secretary, and the Treasury Officer and a native Extra-Assistant Commissioner as members. In some other cities local leaders were associated with town committees before the introduction of the municipal system. There was, indeed, a pre-municipal phase of urban government in British India which served as the background for the introduction of the municipal system and thus remained relevant for its early evolution. Till the beginning of the twentieth century, the framework for municipal bodies and the underlying principles were being debated and developed for different provinces.[2]

Theoretically, municipal committees have been seen as representative bodies enjoying wide powers of administration and taxation, and functioning as schools for training in government.[3] This assumption appears to be rather oversimplified in the light of recent historical research. It has been pointed out in a social history of Burdwan town that the municipal commissioners who 'supplanted the individual local bosses' and wielded far greater patronage began to seek prestige and power through the municipalities. The new avenues of influence brought many of the old elites together to compete for these 'higher prizes' with the emerging professional middle classes. Apart from this tension between the old and the new elites, it has been argued that the introduction of the elective system became a 'source of tension' between the British and the Indians.[4] Indeed, April 1919 disturbances in Ahmedabad marked the 'transfer of moral authority' from the British government to the Indian National Congress, and the history of the Ahmedabad municipality was henceforth bound up with the national movement.[5] But this was not true of all urban centres, and generally not true of the situation during the nineteenth century. In Lucknow, for example, a growing number of Indian 'collaborators', 'purchased' by favours and concessions, used their influence to oblige their relatives and friends.[6] There was no dearth of 'loyalists' elsewhere, encouraged and supported by the British against their Indian opponents.

Furthermore, communalism or the use of religious identity as the basis of organized politics has been traced to the introduction of the elective principle which 'served to aggravate communal differences'.[7] It is argued that the British ignored the complexity of the cultural life in India and, for political reasons, chose to see the society 'as simple aggregations of Hindus and Muslims' and accorded representation to them on official bodies. The members of the two communities, nominated as members of the municipalities, are thus said to have established themselves as coteries that worked in collaboration with the British in the municipal arena to reap personal rewards.[8] Yet, there was no demand for separate representation when the British decided to introduce separate electorates. In Delhi, for example, the old elites and loyalists wanted weightage for wealth and property, and not for religious communities. The officials nonetheless claimed that communalism was very strong in Delhi. In 1920, they forced the municipality to accept separate electorates on the basis of religion. This was revoked by the municipality itself at a later stage.[9] This was one example of resistance to the introduction of separate electorates for religious communities. But this was not the only one.

The limited achievement or the relative failure of the municipal system has been attributed also to some other kinds of tensions that existed in the municipal bodies.[10] The provision for elections in the municipality of Ahmedabad in the last quarter of the nineteenth century introduced a complication. 'The government of the city was transferred from the Collector and the old urban elite with whom he co-operated to a group of politicians drawn from new business and professional groups, and dependent upon the electoral support of voters who were opposed to changes in their urban environment and to higher taxation'.[11] Here it is the voter and the Collector who stand in the way of reform and change. Understandably, until the second decade of the twentieth century, Ahmedabad's society remained 'socially conservative and politically backward'.[12] This situation changed only after World War I.

Urban improvements were not carried out to the expected degree due as much to the restrictions imposed by the colonial regime as to the cultural factors and personal rivalries.[13] These constraints were both political and financial. Cities have traditionally been centres of civilization and power but in India they were both 'profoundly influential and politically weak'. This paradox is partly explained in terms of the imperatives of colonial rule and the upsurge of nationalism. While it suited the rulers to encourage loyalty and conformity, the stakes of nationalist politics diverted the Indian leaders from pleading the claims of cities for improvements in living conditions. The municipal government in colonial India was far from sovereign even within its own juridical domain. Its functional scope remained extremely limited.[14]

Municipal constitutions and structures in British India evolved with time. Therefore, the development of the system cannot be treated as a monolithic process centrally imposed and centrally governed. Changes in the functions of the municipal bodies, the structure of their management, and the roles of their members have to be seen as much in relation to the regional and local specificities as to the general political dynamics of colonial India. Indeed, some of the historians of the municipal government have tried to identify significant phases. One scholar sees three important phases in the history of the municipal system in India: (i) up to 1882 the municipalities were serving imperial needs; (ii) from 1882 to 1919 they began to function as local self-governments, and (iii) from 1920 to 1937 they were characterized more by the emergence of popular rule.[15] In the history of Ahmedabad, on the other hand, two clear periods have been noticed. From 1817 to 1883 Collectors of varying interests, abilities and devotion ruled over the city in cooperation with the leading citizens, the traditional financial and commercial elites, and the government servants. The second period followed from Lord Ripon's reforms of the local self-government when the municipality was constituted on a more popular basis.[16] However, the year 1919, as noticed before, marked yet another significant phase in the evolution of Ahmedabad municipality.

II

In the context of these perceptions and ideas which underline the complexity of the subject, the general development of the municipal system in the Punjab may be taken up. For about fifteen years after annexation, 'committees of townsmen', constituted by the new rulers looked after the 'local affairs', especially in the headquarters of administrative divisions and districts where the British officers were themselves based.[17]

The town committee in Lahore was replaced by a municipal committee in 1862 after an executive order of the provincial government. The committee consisted of thirteen members to be elected annually by 'delegates or panchayats of trades or callings'. Their religious affiliation was not ignored; seven of them were Hindus, five Muslims, and one Sikh. Loyalty to the British was another criterion; six of the members elected belonged to families which had remained loyal to the British in 1848–9, that is during the rebellions in Multan and Hazara. The committee understood its duties in terms of attending to the needs of the people and promoting their prosperity: 'to improve and extend municipal and conservancy arrangements for their health and safety, and to undertake the management of the Municipal Tax, and the administration of the fund'.[18]

In Amritsar, the town committee consisted of both official and non-official members; the Deputy Commissioner acted as its president, and the Assistant Commissioner as its secretary. The functions of the committee were related to maintenance of law and order, public health and education. The town committee of Jalandhar, consisting of both official and non-official members, concerned itself with watch and ward, health and sanitation, and education. The local committees constituted in other urban centres similarly had simple constitutions and limited functions. The source of their income was the traditional octroi, generally known as the *chungi*.[19]

The basis of the municipalities set-up in the Punjab probably lay in the exigencies of the Police Act of 1861. The Governor-General, Lord

Lawrence, made it quite explicit in 1864: 'Municipalities shall raise (in any manner they decide) funds for the *police* and for *conservancy* and such other funds as the members may think fit to expend on works of improvement, education and other local objects; and the cost of the Municipal Police shall be a *first charge* [italics added] on all such funds'.[20] However, the report of the Royal Army Sanitation Commission, published in 1863, had already suggested to all provincial governments that they should set-up municipalities for improving sanitary conditions in the towns to obviate disease and epidemics. The details of police charges were nevertheless specified by the Punjab government. Comprehensive by-laws concerning other functions were worked out by the newly established Delhi municipality. These were generalized for the province as a whole in the Punjab Municipal Act of 1867.[21] It provided for three classes of municipal committees, and became the basis of establishing municipal bodies in the province. This Act reduced official representation to one-third, and introduced the principle of election in addition to nomination.[22]

The functions of the municipal committees to be set up were clearly outlined in the Act:

> Every Committee, so far as the Municipal Fund at their disposal will permit, shall after providing out of such funds for a police establishment in manner hereinafter mentioned, keep the public streets, roads, drains, tanks and water-courses of the town for which they are appointed clean and repaired, and may cause such streets and roads, or any of them, to be watered and lighted, and may construct new streets, drains, tanks and water-courses, and may provide for the management of poor houses, dispensaries, market-places and other works of general utility, and generally may do all acts and things necessary for the purposes of conservancy and local improvement, and may also make provision, by the establishment of new schools or aiding of already existing schools or otherwise, for the promotion of education in the town for which such Committee is appointed.[23]

In 1870, the government under Lord Mayo laid emphasis on the management of funds for 'education, sanitation, medical charity and local public works' by encouraging 'local interest, supervision and care'. This concern was reflected partially in the Punjab Municipal Act of 1873. All official members were to be replaced by non-official native members and every rate-paying householder was to be given the right to vote, and local funds were separated from the provincial funds.[24]

Under the principle of local self-government first enunciated by Lord Ripon in 1881, the Resolution of 1882 stressed its value 'as an instrument of political and popular education'. The primary functions of the municipalities and the principal sources of their revenues were also specified. The municipalities were to have greater independence in disbursing their finances and also to fend for themselves to secure them. These changes were reflected in the Punjab Municipal Act of 1884 which was one among a series of provincial legislation that was passed in Madras, North-West Provinces and Oudh.[25] The reforms proposed by Lord Ripon were considerably whittled down in the course of their interpretation by the provincial bureaucracy. After 1884, the grants-in-aid from the imperial and provincial governments began to decrease. Even though the representation of the elected component was raised to two-thirds, and even the president and the vice-president could be elected in principle, in actual practice it made no significant difference.[26]

The Punjab Municipal Act of 1891 repealed the Act of 1884 but retained most of its basic features. It was meant to make 'better provision' for the administration of municipalities of the province: 'Every committee shall from time to time elect one of its members to be president and the member so elected shall, if approved by the local government in the case of a first class committee, or by the Commissioner in the case of a second class committee, become president of the committee'. However, what was given by the right hand was taken back by the left. The same clause added that a committee could request the local government or the Divisional Commissioner to appoint a president from amongst its members.[27] The Deputy Commissioner too was among the official members. The Act of 1891 emphasized that every committee shall, unless relieved of this obligation by the local government, maintain a sufficient police establishment within municipal limits and for the performance of other duties imposed on it by the Act. This police could consist of watchmen, or of a part of the general police force, or of both, but even if it consisted wholly of watchmen it was to function 'under the orders' of the District Superintendent of Police, subject to the 'general control' of the District Magistrate.[28] The Act also retained the general control of the Commissioner or the Deputy Commissioner over the first or the second class municipal committees. Apart from the three classes of municipalities, a fourth category was created as the 'notified area', denoting a habitation of less than 10,000 persons and having at least a bazaar, as well as a committee of its own.[29]

The Punjab Municipal Act of 1911 was meant to make still 'better provision' for the administration of municipalities. The municipality was clearly defined as a legal entity: a body corporate, with a common seal and perpetual succession, to acquire and hold property, to enter into contracts, and to sue and be sued in its corporate name. The president elected from amongst its members was still to be approved by the local administration or the Commissioner. A government official in municipal employement in accordance with the Act of 1884 could not be dismissed without the approval of the provincial government. The Deputy Commissioner and the Commissioner still exercised control over the municipality. They had the powers to dismiss an employee of a municipal committee, inspect and survey any building occupied by a committee, inspect its books and documents, receive periodic reports, and suspend the execution of any resolution or order of a committee. In an emergency, they could execute any work at the committee's expense to ensure that it worked efficiently in accordance with the laws and rules in force. A committee could be superseded for incompetence or abuse of power. The 'notified area committees' were placed under a still tighter control.[30]

The Government of India Act of 1919 made the municipal administration a 'transferred' subject. In the last quarter of the colonial rule, thus, municipalities became the concern of elected ministers. The Municipal Act of 1911 was amended successively in 1919, 1922, 1934, 1937 and in 1940, and it was partly repealed in 1920 and 1923. Nevertheless, the general control of the provincial government over the municipalities was retained, and they could function only within the overall context of colonial rule.[31]

III

The number of municipalities and notified area committees in the Punjab began to increase from about the third quarter of the nineteenth century. Already, before the Act of 1867, there were more than two scores of municipal committees. The Act became the basis of about a hundred municipalities. In Lahore, for example, the municipal government formalized in 1862 was replaced in 1867 by a new committee formed in accordance with the new Act. Among the other committees in the district of Lahore which came to be based on this Act were Kasur (1867), Khem Karan (1869), and Sharakpur (1874).[32] By the beginning of the 1880s, municipalities had been formed in 55 per cent of the cities and towns of the region.[33] These municipalities were established at urban centres of different sizes spread all over the province, as at Kaithal, Phillaur, Ferozepore, Kartarpur, Qila Sobha Singh, Gujranwala, Khushab, Dera Ghazi Khan, and Dera Ismail Khan.[34]

By the end of the nineteenth century, municipalities came into existence in the cities and most of the large and middling towns, besides a few small centres. The notified area committees were formed in many small towns as at Majitha, Ramdas, Mitranwali, and at Okara and Chichawatni in the canal colony areas.[35] By 1891, municipalities had been set up in 89 per cent of urban units. In later years, on an average about 60 per cent of the urban units maintained their municipal councils.[36] The princely states lagged behind in this respect, and a beginning was made by Patiala in 1904 by forming urban committees.[37]

There was no substantial difference in the powers of the municipalities over the years. The extension of municipal regulations relating to the elective principle, larger proportion of non-official members, and increased powers remained restricted. Out of about 30 members in the municipal committees of Lahore, Amritsar and Multan, two-thirds were elected since the 1890s.[38] In the medium size towns, the number of elected members ranged from eight to twenty. In some of them, like Jalandhar, Sialkot, Montgomery and Kasur, even two-thirds of the members were elected.[39] At the same time, in some other medium-sized towns, like Panipat, Gujranwala and Dera Ghazi Khan, two-thirds of the members were nominated by the government.[40] This was true of the small towns too. The number of municipal members in the small towns ranged from six to sixteen. In a few of them, however, like Patti, Khudian, Jamke, Pasrur, and Dunyapur, two-thirds of the members were elected.[41] In most of the small towns, municipal members were partly nominated, but there were some centres like Nuh, Kohat, Abbottabad, and Pak Pattan in which official members alone formed the urban council.[42] The notified area committees were generally composed of government officials only.[43]

Government presence and control was an essential feature of the urban bodies. At the district headquarters, the Deputy Commissioner was the president of the municipal committee; his place was taken by the Tahsildar in the small towns, as at Nawanshahr, Patti, and Kamalia.[44] This position continued till the early twentieth century. Presidents were rarely elected in the medium and small size towns. In the cities too the elected president was in actual fact a government nominee and entirely supported by the officials. Other official members in the municipalities included the Assistant Commissioner, Civil Surgeon, Superintendent of Police, Executive Engineer, and Inspector of Schools in large towns, as in Gujrat, Gujranwala and Karnal.[45] In the small towns, ex-officio members headed by the Tahsildar also included the Hospital Assistant and Headmaster of the government school, as at Baffa, Nawanshahr, Kamalia, and Patti.[46] This position continued up to the 1940s. Thus, till the end of colonial rule, the government remained well in control of the urban bodies.

In fact, right from the beginning, the government had arrogated to itself the authority to cancel any resolution or election of the municipalities if it was considered detrimental to 'public interest'.[47] The local administrators did not hesitate to invoke this provision in the Act of 1867 to interfere in the affairs of the municipal committees. Often petty considerations weighed with the government's representatives in overriding decisions related to minor matters falling within the jurisdiction of municipal committees. At Rohtak, for example, the municipality was not allowed to treat the services of a clerk and *muharrir* as pensionable. The local administrators vetoed the appointment of a teacher at Gujranwala and postponed an increase in salaries to provide for famine relief work. At Bannu, the resolution for appointing licensed weighmen was overruled. Till the end of the nineteenth century, the municipalities and notified area committees exercised only a limited control through by-laws and various rules and regulations concerning day-to-day life in the town, like sanitary conditions and construction of public buildings and conveniences.[48] For these too, the municipalities were often overruled by the government. As noted before, the election of non-official presidents during the second decade of the twentieth century made no real difference in this respect. They did not really 'control' the local bodies in the sense in which the Act of 1911 spelled it out.

IV

The activities and functions of the municipal bodies were determined virtually by the requirements of the colonial government. It delegated its own functions to the municipalities and made them responsible for the maintenance of law and order through the municipal police which was created in most urban units by the end of the nineteenth century. In the 1860s, the municipalities had also been entrusted with the extension of schemes relating to conservancy, drainage, water supply, public health, and public safety. These were to be paid for by the sums realized from the collection of octroi, the main source of income of the municipality. The municipalities were required also to support some local educational institutions under the over all control of the government.

As a matter of fact, there was no marked difference in the activities and functioning of the municipalities of different sizes. Essential works such as drainage, conservancy, water supply, construction of school buildings, markets, slaughter houses, and paving of roads began in almost all urban centres in the 1860s and 1870s. For water supply generally wells were provided, though at some places, tanks were built, and later on, hand pumps were installed. Conservancy work was undertaken, and efforts were made to improve drainage at most places. The native states also carried out similar activities. In notified area towns, like Chichawatni and Okara, markets and slaughter houses were built. Grain markets were constructed in centres like Mithankot, Gujrat, and Lyallpur.[49] One of the new colony towns, Lyallpur had most of these amenities soon after its establishment in the 1890s.[50] But it was nearly two decades later that a medium-size town like Montgomery came to have electricity. For small towns like Okara and Pak Pattan, this facility was under consideration as late as the early 1930s.[51] Other facilities such as fire fighting units were also created by stages in different urban centres. On the whole, relatively speaking, the provision of modern amenities in the cities and new colony towns was qualitatively better and came at a faster pace.

The officially approved by-laws relating to various aspects of urban life were adopted by nearly all local bodies. In the small towns of Nakodar, Phillaur, Rahon, and Kartarpur, among others, rules for warehouses were made. At Rohtak, by-laws regarding the inspection of slaughter houses were passed; Jhang-Maghiana regulated vaccinations; Dera Baba Nanak made rules to control 'houses of ill-fame'; while many other urban centres passed by-laws on storing of kerosene oil, disposal of dead animals, prohibition of the use of unwholesome water, and on refunds of octroi. Municipalities were authorized to prohibit use of insanitary wells, control cattle and other fairs, and regulate the rates of hired carriages. The power to allow or refuse services of teachers and other professionals in municipal establishments also rested, at least in theory, with the local bodies.[52] However, the actual exercise of these powers or implementation of the by-laws was far from satisfactory, as much because of official control, as because of lack of suitable supervisory staff and adequate funds.

In the sphere of education, delegated under the revised provisions for grants-in-aid, municipalities could make a limited contribution. It was only in cities like Lahore and Amritsar, and some medium towns like Jalandhar and Gujranwala, that a number of schools were provided separately for girls.[53] In Amritsar, the municipal committee ran an industrial school as well.[54] The municipalities of small towns maintained schools for boys only, as at Chunian, Jandiala, Kartarpur, and Gurdaspur, among others.[55] These schools were largely of the primary level, and the municipality's role was limited to the provision of funds, having no say in their functioning.

The history of the municipality of Patti is illustrative of the process of education generated by municipalities of small towns in the Punjab. Patti was a pargana town before 1849. After annexation, it was relegated more or less to the position of a village in the tahsil of Kasur. Before 1875, however, it regained its position and a municipal committee was established at Patti. Like committees elsewhere, education was one of its concerns. In 1881, its population was about 6,400 which rose to over 10,400 by 1921, and to about 17,600 in 1941. This growth had some bearing on the development of education as well. In 1883, the town had a vernacular middle school but it was transferred to a village in the same district, that is Lahore. The municipality of Patti could have its vernacular middle school back only in the first decade of the twentieth century. In the second decade, a primary school for girls was opened. In the third decade, the vernacular middle school became Anglo-vernacular, and three primary schools for boys were opened. The Anglo-vernacular school became high school in the 1930s when a new primary school was added. In 1941, the high school was taken over by the district board. The committee tried to accommodate Hindu, Muslim and Sikh preferences by opening Hindi, Urdu and Gurmukhi schools for girls, but none of these was successful. Apparently, the municipal committee of Patti could not keep pace with the aspirations of the people, and for education they turned to the local Arya Samaj which established its high school in the 1910s. The Arya school for girls was started as a primary school in 1928. The Arya institutions had the largest number of students and qualified teachers; sometimes the entire aid fund of the municipality was absorbed by the Arya schools.[56]

In the sphere of public health, the municipalities were obliged to contribute to the government dispensaries and hospitals within their limits. In the city of Amritsar, for instance, the municipality supported two branch dispensaries as well as a midwife hospital.[57] At Jalandhar, a hospital and dispensary were maintained by the local body.[58] In many small towns like Bannu, Tarn Taran and Pak Pattan also, such support was given by the municipalities.[59] As may be expected, the local bodies had no control over the management or functioning of the dispensaries and hospitals.

The same was true of police arrangements. Till the second decade of the twentieth century the municipalities were responsible for maintaining the police within their jurisdiction. But the police, though financially maintained by the municipality, was under the direct control of the police authorities at the provincial and district levels. Furthermore, in almost all the urban centres, the work of the municipal police was considered to be inefficient due to their small numbers. The cities like Multan and Lahore were slightly better off, with a smaller ratio between the police and the population.[60] Understandably, the cantonments and 'military' towns like Haripur, Abbotabad, and Murree were better provided in terms of police arrangements.[61] In fact, the cantonments were reported to have the largest proportion of policemen during the early decades of colonial rule.[62]

V

The funds allocated for various functions of the municipalities reflected the priorities of the colonial government, and were utilized for pre-selected services, that is the police, public health, and sanitation. In 1869-70, for instance, the largest proportion of the municipal in-come—about 20 per cent—was spent on the police force; about 11 per cent on sanitary arrangements; and only 1.5 per cent on education.[63] By the end of the nineteenth century, the highest expenditure was on public works and health, amounting to about 46 per cent;

15 per cent on administration; nearly the same amount was spent on public safety; and about 13 per cent was allocated for education.[64] In 1926–7, the municipalities of the Punjab spent over 22 per cent on public works and health; about 25 per cent on administration; and nearly 8 per cent each on education and municipal constructions.[65] Thus, from a marked expenditure on municipal police in the 1860s, the municipalities moved gradually to spending more on other heads by the end of the nineteenth century. However, the public works often included government buildings and structures like the town hall. The maintenance of the administrative staff took up the largest proportion of the municipal funds in the early twentieth century. Education remained less important throughout the period, ostensibly because there were other government and non-govern-ment institutions imparting education.[66] This pattern of expenditure is noticeable in the municipalities of all classes in the region.

For specific examples of the relative allocation and the bearing of the colonial context, Amritsar, Jalandhar and Lyallpur municipalities may be taken up in greater detail. Each represented one of the three classes of municipalities in the region. In Amritsar during 1895–9, over 39 per cent of the municipal income was spent on public health; about 23 per cent on administration, and around 13 per cent each on education and public safety. By 1911–12, these proportions rose to 59 per cent in the case of public health, but decreased to 8 per cent on administration and to nearly 7 per cent on education.[67] On the other hand, Jalandhar, a second class municipality till the early years of the twentieth century, but a divisional headquarters from the beginning, was spending over 52 per cent on public health, and about 15 per cent each on administration and education, and about 14 per cent on public safety.[68] A small but planned town like Lyallpur which served the Lower Chenab Colony, and which had a third class municipality allocated 71 per cent to public health, and about 5 per cent each to education and public safety.[69]

Municipal funds depended largely on octroi which, as suggested before, accounted for over 50 per cent of the income of most of the urban bodies till the end of the nineteenth century. In the medium and small towns, octroi remained the major source of income in the twentieth century as well.[70] Even in 1946–7, 54 per cent of municipal income in the Punjab came from octroi. Cities like Lahore and Amritsar could develop new sources of income with taxes on water, electricity, licenses, and houses. After 1910, in the cities at any rate, the income from additional sources exceeded that from octroi.[71]

In small and medium towns some income was obtained from miscellaneous sources like fines and sale of sweepings gathered by the municipal sweepers, besides trees, grass and wood, and fees from buildings, lands, and gardens.[72] At a new place like Chichawatni, a terminal tax was imposed on trade goods. In the new towns of Okara and Arifwala, agricultural land within the town limits was leased out to enhance income.[73] However, the proportion of income from licenses and fees remained minimal till the 1940s, being 0.34 per cent and 1.16 per cent, respectively.[74]

The increase in municipal income kept pace with a hike in the per head rate of taxation in the municipal areas. In 1883–4, the per capita rate of tax in most towns ranged from 4 to 6 annas.[75] The succeeding decade had a tax range of Rs. 1–4–5 to Rs. 10–2–1.[76] In the early twentieth century, a per head increase in the rate of taxation was noted, among others, at Bannu, Gurdaspur, Dinanagar, Batala, and Pathankot.[77] On the whole, there was not much difference in the rates of taxation in the cities, medium towns and small towns. The highest rate was at those places where the government established its 'official' settlement as at Simla and Edwardesabad (Bannu).[78]

VI

Looking at the Punjab in the context of British India, it may be noted that the constitution of municipalities in all provinces was broadly similar, with variations only in the proportion of elected members. In 1881–2, for example, compared to the Punjab, the proportion of partially elected municipalities was much larger in other provinces, with the exception of Bengal.[79] This situation changed by the mid-1920s when almost all provinces had around 75 per cent of the elected members on their urban bodies (Table 7.1).[80]

However, till the early 1920s, the chairmen were mostly officials. In the 1930s, even when a large proportion of the chairmen in most provinces, including the Punjab, were 'non-official', it made no difference to the ground situation, because they functioned virtually under official control.[81]

TABLE 7.1: PERCENTAGE OF PARTIALLY ELECTED MUNICIPALITIES IN PROVINCES

Province	1881–2	1925–6
Central Provinces	100	77.4
North-West (later United) Provinces	70	86.9
Madras	25	76.7
Bombay	6.1	78.3
Punjab	*2.5*	*72.3*
Bengal	2.2	64.2

Source: R.L. Khanna, *Municipal Government and Administration in India*, Chandigarh: Mahindra Capital Publishers, 1967, pp. 10 and 29.

With regard to municipal finances, the Punjab remained at the middling level, with four provinces having higher income and expenditure than the region. Municipal expenses were generally less than the income except in the United (formerly North-West) Provinces, Bengal and the Punjab in 1918, and UP and Madras in 1937 (Table 7.2).

Most of the small urban committees in the Punjab depended on octroi for their income, whereas in some other provinces the propor-

TABLE 7.2: MUNICIPAL FINANCES OF VARIOUS PROVINCES

Province	1881–2		1937	
	Income	Expenditure	Income	Expenditure
	(in lakhs)		(in crores)	
Punjab	*27.10*	*24.21*	*1.72*	*1.70*
Bengal	24.98	22.03	1.01	1.03
Bombay	29.60	27.71	2.03	1.86
Madras	13.68	13.32	2.28	2.36
NW (later United) Provinces	30.79	29.06	1.78	1.89

Source: R.L. Khanna, *Municipal Government and Administration in India*, Chandigarh: Mohindra Capital Publishers, 1967, pp. 10 and 31.

tion of octroi in the total income was much less. For example, it was around 32 per cent in the Central Provinces and Bombay against 54 per cent in the Punjab. It had the minimum income from house tax and professional taxes both of which constituted a much larger resource in the other provinces. There was no change in this situation till the end of colonial rule.[82] The per head rate of taxation in urban areas also varied in different provinces over the period. In 1881–2, the Punjab had the highest rate of taxation, a position which it continued to occupy till the 1920s. By 1946–7, however, its rate of taxation was exceeded by four other provinces (Table 7.3).

The existence of the largest proportion of cantonments and hill stations or 'official' urban settlements in the Punjab region probably accounted for a relatively high percentage of local taxation till the 1920s. It may not be irrelevant to mention that, compared to some other provinces, a larger percentage of urban population in the Punjab had access to 'protected water supply' and 'medical institutions'.[83] Paradoxically, during the phase of provincial autonomy, the Punjab was ruled by the professedly pro-rural Unionist Party under which 'there was no significant effort at reform of municipal government'. This situation appears to be in marked contrast to the municipal legislation in other provinces like CP, Bihar, UP, Bombay and Madras.[84]

TABLE 7.3: PER HEAD RATE OF TAXATION IN 1881–2 AND 1946–7

Province	1881–2 (in Rs.)	1946–7 (in Rs.)
Bombay	1-3-6	5-15-6
Punjab	*1-7-7*	*3-10-6*
Central Provinces	1-0-6	6-13-6
NW (later United) Provinces	0-12-0	6-10-0
Madras	0-11-0	6-1-4

Source: R. Argal, *Municipal Government in India*, 3rd edn, Allahabad: Agarwal Press, 1967, p. 24, n. 6. Hugh Tinker, *The Foundation of Local Self-Government in India, Pakistan and Burma*, Bombay: Lalvani Publishing House, 1967, p. 331.

VI

It may now be instructive to turn to the case studies of the cities of Jalandhar and Amritsar, covering the entire period of colonial rule. The municipal committee of Jalandhar, established in 1868 and placed in the second class, was supposed to have a good proportion of 'elected' members. All the thirteen non-official members, however, were actually nominated with an eye on their religious affiliation: seven of them were Hindus, four were Muslims, and two Sikhs. Before long, the number of members increased to fifteen, out of which two were officials, three nomi-nated, and ten elected. Elections were held only after the Act of 1884. Secret ballot was introduced in 1917. In 1896, two more members were added to the elected category. The Deputy Commissioner and the Civil Surgeon ceased to be members in 1919 and 1920 so that in these years there was no official member: four were nominated and eighteen were elected. In 1924, the number of the nominated members was reduced to three and that of the elected increased to twenty-two. During this year, elections were held for all the members at one time, which was not done before.[85]

The qualifications of members for the Jalandhar municipality were fixed for the first time in 1920. In 1923, the criteria were relaxed: the value of immoveable property was reduced from Rs. 4,000 to 1,500, land revenue paid was reduced from Rs. 40 to 15, and the level of education was lowered from BA to Intermediate. In the 1940s, there was a further reduction to Rs. 500 in the value of property as a criterion. All along there were some other categories of persons who could contest elections: a government employee receiving Rs. 50 a month; a pensioner receiving Rs. 30 a month; an income tax payee; a pleader of the Lahore High Court; and a doctor with a medical degree. Between 1924 and 1947, out of the total of sixty-seven elected members, twenty-seven were pleaders—four of them remaining on the committee for twenty years. There were five retired government servants, three contractors, two doctors, and one headmaster. From amongst traditional occupations, there were nine traders, five zamindars, two *sahukars* and one hakim. One woman was nominated in 1936. The occupations of the remaining eleven members are not known. Out of the fifty-four members whose religious affiliation is known, twenty-nine were Muslims, twenty-four Hindus, and there was a lone Christian.[86]

The number of voters increased from 2,700 in 1896 to 32,643 in

1940. The percentage of voters in the total population rose from 5 to 43. The Muslims increased their voting strength more than the Hindus. In 1896 only 10 per cent of the Muslims were eligible to vote; in 1936, this figure rose to 39 per cent. The percentage of Hindus also was 39 per cent in 1936, but their total population was less than 10,500, whereas the Muslim population was almost 19,000. Successive revisions of the voting qualifications were helpful to the Muslims. In 1924, for the first time, all matriculates and persons having passed an oriental examination were made eligible to vote. However, women, who formed 45 per cent of the population of Jalandhar, were not enfranchised. In fact, a resolution moved in 1937 to this effect was defeated. Even among the male population, 47 per cent did not possess the right to vote.[87]

Jalandhar had five voting wards in 1896. The number rose to six in 1916, and to twelve in 1924. The Muslims were in majority in eight wards. In 1896, four Muslims and six Hindus were elected. In 1916, they were equal in proportion. In 1924, the number of Muslim and Hindu members became fourteen and eight respectively; in 1946, the gap became wider, with nineteen Muslims against ten Hindus. Significantly, Jalandhar municipality never opted for separate electorates for Muslims. This did not mean, however, that people were not influenced by communitarian concerns or that there was no tension between Hindus and Muslims. The municipality provided separate schools for Muslims and Hindus, and employed Muslim and Hindu servants for these. Hindu-Muslim tension became evident in the municipal elections of the 1890s. In 1919, the Hindus demanded seats on the basis of their voting strength and the Muslims on the basis of their numbers. The Unionist ministry formed in 1923 supported the latter view, and seats were allocated on that basis in 1924. In the early 1940s, in the wake of the demand for Pakistan, the two segments appeared to be keen to inflate their numbers, charging each other of manipulation. There was some tension also between the British authorities and the Indian leaders of Jalandhar, particularly in the last fifteen years of colonial rule. During the individual satyagrah of the Congress in 1941, three members of the municipality resigned on the issue of participation in World War II without prior consultation with the national leaders.[88]

In 1919, on the persistent demand of the members, the Deputy Commissioner as president of the municipality was replaced by an elected member. Secret ballot for the election of the vice-president and the secretary as well as the president was introduced in 1923. The office-bearers were assisted by a medical officer, appointed for the first time in 1915. The municipality worked through a number of sub-committees. But this was not something new. As early as 1888, four standing sub-committees had been created to handle finance, sanitation, education, and public works. To these were added two more in 1919: the sub-committees for building and hackney carriage.[89] .

The primary concerns of the Jalandhar municipality were public health and sanitation, education, public works, and public safety. The first included conservancy, drains, slaughter houses, unadulterated edibles and pure water, medical facilities, and collection of vital statistics. These functions required the appointment of sanitary inspectors and the employment of sweepers and supervisory staff. Baskets and donkeys for removing the nightsoil were replaced later by handcarts and bullock-carts. The drainage system was completed in 1925–6, but not for all localities. Tubewells came into use increasingly from the 1920s, but remained insufficient. Licenses were issued to sellers of both *halal* and *jhatka* meat. Milk products, sweets, fruits, sherbets, and bakeries were inspected from time to time to ensure wholesomeness. Hand pumps were introduced and bathing or washing on the wells was prohibited. Preventive and curative measures were adopted to reduce tuberculosis, malaria, cholera, small pox, and the plague. A hospital and a few dispensaries were opened. Some measures were adopted to deal with stray animals. Registers of deaths and births had begun to be maintained since the 1860s. Steps were taken also for the upkeep of burial and cremation grounds.[90]

Some idea of the relative importance of the various functions of the municipality can be formed from the expenditure incurred on them during 1891–6 and 1941–7. The total expenditure on public safety, public health, education, and public works in Jalandhar ranged from around Rs. 316,000 in 1891–6 to around Rs. 2,728,000 in 1941–7. Its break up under different heads has been rounded off in Table 7.4.

There were variations in the intervening period. For example, the expenditure on public safety was even less than 8 per cent of the total during 1911–16, 1921–6 and 1936–41. Percentage of expenditure on public health exceeded 40 in 1906–11, 1926–31, 1931–6 and 1936–41; it exceeded even 55 per cent in 1911–16 and 1921–6. On educa-

TABLE 7.4: EXPENDITURE OF JALANDHAR MUNICIPALITY, 1890s AND 1940s

Head	1891–6		1941–7	
	(in Rs.)	%	(in Rs.)	%
Public Safety	52,000	16.34	235,000	8.61
Public Health	111,000	35.00	1,021,000	37.43
Education	63,000	19.92	320,000	11.73
Public Works	33,000	10.36	300,000	10.18

Source: Kanchan Jyoti, 'The City of Jullundhar: A Study in Urban History (1846–47)', Ph.D. thesis, GNDU, Amritsar, 1988, Table XXV.

tion, however, it ranged from 5 to 11 per cent during the intervening decades.

The municipality constructed some public buildings and conveniences in Jalandhar, like the town hall, school buildings, slaughter houses, tanks, public urinals and latrines, a *dhobi ghat,* and a few parks. Some public buildings were repaired from time to time, like the offices of the Commissioner, the Deputy Commissioner, the Magistrate, and the Tahsildar. Roads were paved by bricks or stones, and later on coal-tarred. In the 1940s, the city had 10.5 miles (over 18 km) of roads. The unpaved streets were sprinkled with water. A couple of lorries were purchased in 1927 and 1940 for watering roads and extinguishing fires. Despite by-laws, unplanned construction and encroachment on public land could not be checked. The Improvement Trust of Jalandhar came up only in 1946.[91]

Public safety came to include lighting arrangements in addition to the maintenance of police and fire fighting arrangements. The police was not under the control of the municipality which bore its expenditure nonetheless. In 1935, the police personnel consisted of 133 Inspectors, Deputy Inspectors, constables and watchmen. The town had been relieved of expenditure on police in 1911, but not of policing the *bastis* or suburbs around. Oil lamps for lighting were replaced by kerosene lamps towards the end of the nineteenth century. The town came to have electricity in 1925, but not its suburbs. The municipality continued to hold some fairs and festivals. A municipal library was opened in 1943.[92]

The municipal income came from three major sources: tax-revenue, non-tax revenue, and grants-in-aid. In 1891–6, the total revenues of the Jalandhar municipality amounted to around Rs. 324,000. In 1941–7, this sum rose to about Rs. 2,980,000. Tax revenues (octroi and toll tax) brought in the largest share, ranging from 44 to 80 per cent of the total income. The percentage of non-tax revenue (*tehbazari* and wheel tax) rose from 16.81 to 31.9 per cent, never going below 16 per cent throughout the period. The grants-in-aid from the provincial government for education, public health, and public works came generously only on a few occasions. In 1891–6 and 1896–1901 their percentage in the total income was around 17 per cent. But the highest was in 1916–21, a little over 25 per cent, and the lowest was in 1941–7, forming only 4.32 per cent of the total income. A few other small sources of income tapped from time to time were taxes on buildings and lands (1921–31), sale of immovable property (1921–6), and registration of dogs (1941–7).[93]

On the whole, the municipality of Jalandhar did not have a very large income from the sources it could tap. Members were reluctant to impose new taxes because of the pressure of the voters who were rather unwilling to pay. House tax had actually to be withdrawn in 1925–6. A few of the minor resources were appropriated by the provincial government. But even the limited resources were not effectively used. Cases of embezzlement and misappropriation of funds came to light in 1930, 1935 and 1937. Corruption could be a cause of inefficiency. The Commissioner, Deputy Commissioner and the Executive Engineer did not hesitate to intervene in the affairs of the municipality even after 1919–20. In 1939, a candidate rejected by the voters was nominated by the government. In 1940, the president of the municipality was forced to suspend a resolution by which the committee had increased the pay of its employees. In 1942, the Commissioner of the division threatened to suspend the committee when its members voted for the removal of the executive officer.[94]

In the case of Amritsar, which had a first class municipal committee, only a few significant points may be noted. Elections were introduced in 1868 itself. In the early 1870s, the elected members were somewhat restive over the imposition of house tax. The city was divided into 12 wards in 1872, and the 'rate paying' householders were entitled to vote. Separate electorates for Muslims and Sikhs were introduced in

1917. In 1918–19, there was a demand for an elected president. The Deputy Commissioner felt obliged to contest and he won by 13 votes to 8 votes. But the Rate-Payers Association approached the provincial governor not to approve of the election. The Deputy Commissioner resigned in 1921. Till 1947, however, the officials remained keen to get 'loyalists' elected to presidentship. They could find such candidates in Sir Gopal Das Bhandari, Khan Sahib Khwaja Muhammad Ghulam Sadiq, Khan Bahadur Mir Hidayat Ullah, and Rai Bahadur Prakash Chand Mehra. In 1937 a 'communal pact' was worked out to have Muslim, Hindu and Sikh presidents in turn. On the basis of the census of 1931, the number of seats was raised to thirty. Out of these, twenty-two seats were to be filled by electing a fixed number of Muslims, Hindus and Sikhs. For the nominated members also their religious affiliation was kept in view. One representative of the labour was added in 1938, and women became entitled to vote in 1940.[95]

The sources of income and heads of expenditure of the municipality of Amritsar were very much similar to those of the Jalandhar municipality. The total income of the municipality of Amritsar, however, far exceeded that of Jalandhar, increasing from about Rs. 3,758,000 in 1900–4 to about Rs. 13,610,000 in 1935–40. The most important source of income was octroi, rising from Rs. 200,000 a year in 1870–4 to about Rs. 873,000 in 1941–5. In the period from 1869–72 to 1910–14, octroi ranged between 95 to about 50 per cent of the total income. But, after World War I, this percentage began to decline, from 43.4 per cent in 1915–19 to 33.5 per cent in 1940–5. There was a rise now in income from electricity which had been introduced in 1915. By 1935-6, it was more than Rs. 920,000. In 1946–7, electricity earned nearly Rs. 1,120,000 for the municipality. It may be added that a hospital for women was opened at Amritsar in 1917, and the number of municipal schools for girls rose to 29 by 1947. The allocations of the municipality of Amritsar were broadly similar to those of the municipality of Jalandhar (Table 7.5).[96]

The city of Amritsar was much larger than Jalandhar. Its municipality had more money and functioned on a larger scale. It was also perhaps a little more liberal. But it was not free from official intervention. In 1941, the elections to the municipality were postponed. These were the war years. The election of Diwan Chand as president was cancelled on the assumption that he was not a 'loyalist'. Eleven members walked

TABLE 7.5: PERCENTAGE OF EXPENDITURE OF THE AMRITSAR MUNICIPALITY

Head	1900–1	1910–11	1920–1	1930–1
Public Safety	14.62	12.43	2.57	3.56
Public Health and Conveniences	38.63	47.65	44.81	33.97
Public Instructions (Education)	13.18	6.13	5.94	10.16

Source: Anand Gauba, *Amritsar: A Study in Urban History (1840–1947)*, Jalandhar: ABS Publications, 1988, Table 6.

out of the meeting but the remaining seventeen elected Sardar Harnam Singh Ramgarhia who was acceptable to the authorities. In 1947, Sardar Gurbux Singh was disqualified to be a member for five years. Not very serious cases of intervention in themselves, these were symbolic enough of the general attitude of the colonial administrators.[97]

Communal undercurrents in the affairs of municipalities have been noticed in both Jalandhar and Amritsar. This was becoming a general phenomenon in the 1920s. In 1913, a meeting of Muslims in Lahore asked the government to extend separate electorates to all local bodies in proportion to the population of each community. Fazl-i Husain, the first minister in the government, was generally in favour of such demands. A resolution to this effect was moved by Khawaja Dil Muhammad in a meeting of the Lahore municipality. It was passed by the casting vote of its president who happened to be Muslim. When there was a split in the committee, several important members resigned from it, like Ruchi Ram Sahni, Dr Gopi Chand Bhargava, and Ram Bhaj Datt Chaudhary. This led to bitterness. By 1926, over 50 municipalities had separate electorates for Muslims. Half of these had Hindu majorities, but a score of these urban centres had Muslim majorities. More than a score of Sikhs also came to be represented on a number of municipalities despite their small proportion in urban population.[98]

In sum, Anand Gauba is quite appreciative of the work done by the Amritsar municipality. It turned a city of large ponds (*dhabs*) into a city of gardens. The city came to have paved streets with side drains. Sanitary improvements and health care resulted in the growth of population. The supply of tap water, building of metalled roads, public buildings like the municipal hospital and the Prince of Wales Hospital, and new market centres changed the physical appearance of the city. The municipal committee made substantial contribution towards spreading the light of education, especially among the girls. Literally, too, Amritsar became the best lit city of the province.[99]

Kanchan Jyoti is less enthusiastic but nonetheless appreciative of the work of the Jalandhar municipality. Despite limited powers and meagre resources, it made a beginning towards improvement in the health of the people which came to be reflected in the growth of population by natural increase. Haphazard growth of the city was checked. The supply of electricity and school education were significant new developments. Even though the gap between the felt needs and the available amenities remained wide, by catering to the needs of the common people the municipality signified a qualitative change in urban government.[100]

VIII

On the whole, it is clear that municipal administration represented a new form of urban government in the colonial Punjab. The introduction of a formal and partially elected body, covering the entire urban area, was a beginning in popular, representative local government. Direct services of public health, public works, public safety, and education by the city administration were unknown in earlier times. Under the British, new sources of income were also tapped, though octroi remained a major part of the municipal resources. At the same time, and despite constitutional concessions, control of the colonial state over the administration of towns and cities remained intact; in their structure and functioning, the municipalities were virtually an extension of the provincial government. The district officer as the chairman 'often of one or more municipalities in the district was just as much the eyes, ears and arms of the Provincial Government' as when functioning as revenue officer or District Magistrate.[101] The concessions given under the dyarchy were neutralized by 'the weapon of supersession' which was 'freely used'.[102]

It has been observed that the colonial government made half-hearted attempts to create local institutions which it tended to centralize. Western forms of local government without local autonomy were 'superimposed upon native institutions for purposes of commercial gain or political control'.[103] The municipal committees were required to carry out the functions delegated by the government without the corresponding powers. 'The association of Indians with administration', in fact, enabled the government to tap the local sources of revenue.[104] Within these constraints, the only sphere where the municipalities could make a minor contribution was education, and that too at the primary level. Most of the municipal activity in the so-called improvement of towns was in terms of essential public services which should normally have been provided by a modern government. The municipal funds were largely poured into these schemes for 'improvement', leaving little for developmental activities.

Moreover, the intricacies of the Western system of urban government and its underlying values could not be absorbed by the people, because the system had 'not grown from below'.[105] The emphasis of the government remained more on controlling and using the influential urban classes rather than on training them in self-government. It is not surprising, therefore, that a large number of municipalities in the province failed even to hold the statutory number of meetings.[106] Furthermore, infighting and factionalism, nepotism, personal and communal animosity, embezzlement and graft, besides financial mismanagement did not allow the municipalities to function constructively.[107] Cases of collusion between the octroi contractors and municipal members were often reported. Examples of members of the committee selling plots at cheaper rates to their relatives were also known.[108] The rigid framework of municipal administration as erected by the government prevented growth or innovation. Financially, the municipality was always dependent on the government which did not allow any radical schemes of taxation or social development. Nor was there a legislature or judiciary of the municipality.

It is not surprising that the urban government in the sense of a distinct body of elected towns people working autonomously for the betterment of their environment did not emerge. Cities remained subservient to the colonial administration, and this legacy has continued well into the post-Independence period.[109] Jawaharlal Nehru's comment on the municipal administration remains apt: 'The framework was neither democratic nor autocratic; it was a cross between the two and had the disadvantages of both'.[110]

NOTES

1. Veena Talwar Oldenburg, *The Making of Colonial Lucknow 1856–1877*, Princeton, New Jersey: Princeton University Press, 1984, pp. 76 and 77. See also, author's 'Urbaniztion in Medieval India', in J.S. Grewal (ed.), *The State and Society in Medieval India*, History of Science, Philosopy and Culture in Indian Civilization, vol. VII, pt. 1, New Delhi: OUP, 2005, pp. 417–18.
2. Christine Furedy, 'Contrasting Models in the Development of Municipal Administration in Calcutta', in Donald B. Rosenthal (ed.), *The City in Indian Politics*, Faridabad: Thomson Press, 1976, pp. 153–5.
3. Shriram Maheshwari, *Local Government in India*; rpt. of 9th edn., Agra: Lakshmi Narain Agarwal, 2002, pp. 7 and 14. Maheshwari calls the municipal system 'a product of the nineteenth century liberalism'. Ibid., p. 9.
4. Indrani Ganguly, *The Social History of a Bengal Town*, Bombay: Himalaya Publishing House, 1987, p. 103.
5. Kenneth L. Gillion, *Ahmedabad: A Study in Indian Urban History*, Berkeley: University of California Press, 1968, pp. 168 and 169.
6. Oldenburg, *Colonial Lucknow*, p. 84.
7. Narayani Gupta, *Delhi Between Two Empires 1803–1931: Society, Government and Urban Growth*, New Delhi: OUP, 1981, p. 232.
8. Oldenburg, *Colonial Lucknow*, p. 81.
9. Gupta, *Delhi Between Two Empires*, p. 142.
10. Ganguly, *A Bengal Town*, pp. 103–4.
11. Gillion, *Ahmedabad*, p. 109.
12. Ibid., p. 7.
13. Ganguly, *A Bengal Town*, pp. 104–5.
14. Rodney W. Jones, *Urban Politics in India: Area, Power, and Policy in a Penetrated System*, New Delhi: Vikas, 1975, pp. 1, 7 and 11.
15. R.L. Khanna, *Municipal Government and Administration in India*, Chandigarh: Mohindra Capital Publishers, 1967, pp. 19–21. Cf. Maheshwari, *Local Government*, pp. 14–22.
16. Gillion, *Ahmedabad*, p. 118.
17. *Imperial Gazetteer of India, Provincial Series: Punjab*; rpt., New Delhi: Atlantic Publishers, 1991, vol. I, pp. 123–4.
18. Quoted in Ian Johnstone Kerr, 'The Punjab Province and the Lahore District, 1849–72: A Case Study of British Colonial Rule and Social Change in India', Ph.D. thesis, University of Minnesota, Minnesota, 1975, pp. 119–20.
19. Respectively, Anand Gauba, *Amritsar: A Study in Urban History* (*1840–1947*), Jalandhar: ABS Publications, 1988, pp. 159–61. Kanchan Jyoti,

'The City of Jullundur: A Study in Urban History (1846–1947)', Ph.D. thesis, GNDU, Amritsar, 1988, p. 280.

20. *Gazette of India Extraordinary*, 14 September 1864, p. 13, quoted in Gupta, *Delhi Between Two Empires*, p. 70.
21. Khanna, *Municipal Government and Administration*, p. 8.
22. Gauba, *Amritsar*, pp. 162-3. *Imperial Gazetteer*, vol. I, p. 124.
23. Section 9 of Act XV of 1867, quoted in Kerr, 'Punjab Province and Lahore District', p. 122.
24. Khanna, *Municipal Government and Administration*, pp. 9–10. Gauba, *Amritsar*, p. 165.
25. *Imperial Gazetteer: Punjab*, vol. I, p. 124. Khanna, *Municipal Government and Administration*, pp. 11–13.
26. Khanna, *Municipal Government and Administration*, pp. 14–15. Maheshwari, *Local Government in India*, p. 19.
27. *Punjab Municipal Act, 1891*, Clause 15(1).
28. Ibid., Clause 79(1).
29. Ibid., Clause 176(1) and Clause 210(1).
30. Bhagatjit Singh Chawla (ed.), *Punjab Municipal Act, 1911: With Short Notes*, Chandigarh: Chawla Publications, 1994, pp. 123–30 and passim. See also, R. Argal, *Municipal Government in India*, 3rd edn., Allahabad: Agarwal Press, 1967, p. 32. Khanna, *Municipal Government and Administration*, p. 28.
31. Chawla, (ed)., *Punjab Municipal Act, 1911*, pp. 1–2. It may be interesting to note that despite successive amendments—over a dozen during the colonial period, and nearly three dozen in the post-Independence period—the essential nature of the government's control over the municipalities has remained unchanged. Bhagatjit Singh, *The Punjab Municipal Act: A Commentry*, Chandigarh: Chawla Publications, 1994, pp. 374–87.
32. *DG Lahore*, 1883–4, pp. 196–9. Chunian, however, was constituted a municipality in 1866. Ibid., pp. 194–6. See also, Kerr, 'Punjab Province and Lahore District', pp. 104–5.
33. Calculated from Table IV, *Census of the Punjab, 1881*. Cf. *Imperial Gazetteer, Punjab*, vol. I, p. 124.
34. Information collected from the DGs of the Punjab for the year 1883–4.
35. *DG Amritsar*, 1914, pp. 159–61. *DG Montgomery*, 1933, pt. A, p. 287. In 1904, there were 48 notified area committees. *Imperial Gazetteer: Punjab*, vol. I, p. 124.
36. Calculated from Table IV, *Census of the Punjab* for the years 1891, 1901, 1911, 1921, and 1931.
37. *Phulkian States Gazetteer*, 1904, pt. A, p. 201. Significantly, this was during the minority of Maharaja Bhupinder Singh when his administration was directly supervised by the British.

38. *DG Lahore*, 1883–4, p. 310. *DG Multan*, 1883–4, p. 154. *DG Amritsar*, 1883–4, p. 63.
39. *DG Sialkot*, 1894–5, p. 169. *DG Jalandhar*, 1883–4, p. 66. *DG Jalandhar*, 1904, part A, p. 285. *DG Montgomery*, 1898–9, p. 231. *DG Lahore*, 1893–4, p. 332.
40. *DG Karnal*, 1883–4, p. 259. *DG Gujranwala*, 1883–4, p. 84. *DG Dera Ghazi Khan*, 1883–4, p. 136.
41. *DG Sialkot*, 1894–5, pp. 172–3. *DG Dera Ghazi Khan*, 1883–4, p. 136. *DG Lahore*, 1893–4, p. 334. *DG Multan*, 1883–4, p. 159.
42. *DG Gurgaon*, 1883-4, p. 144. *DG Kohat*, 1883–4, p. 183. *DG Hazara*, 1883–4, p. 211. *DG Montgomery*, 1898–9, p. 67. See also, Amarnath, *Development of Local Self Government (1849–1900)*, Monograph 8, Lahore: Punjab Government Record Office Publication, 1929, Appendix IV.
43. As, for example, in Okara. *DG Montgomery*, 1933, p. 287.
44. Respectively: *DG Hazara*, 1883–4, pp. 210–12. *DG Lahore*, 1893–4, p. 334. *DG Montgomery*, 1898–9, p. 228.
45. *DG Gujrat*, 1883-4, p. 115. *DG Gujranwala*, 1883–4, p. 84. *DG Karnal*, 1883–4, p. 254. See also, Amarnath, *Local Self Government*, p. 27.
46. *DG Hazara*, 1883–4, p. 210. *DG Lahore*, 1893–4, p. 334. *DG Montgomery*, 1898–9, p. 228.
47. Under section 232 of the Act of 1911, the Deputy Commissioner of Amritsar, or any other district officer and the Governor of the province could take such a step in public interest. Gauba, *Amritsar*, p. 174 and n. 61. See also, Chawla (ed.), *Punjab Municipal Act, 1911*, p. 124.
48. *Review of Municipal Administration in the Punjab*, 1893–4, pp. 7–8. Ibid., 1899–1900, p. 6.
49. *Local Improvement Report*, 1863–4, pp. 13–15. Ibid., 1864–5, pp. 3–12. *Review of Municipal Administration in the Punjab*, 1899–1900, p. 6. *Report on the Working of Municipalities in the Punjab*, 1926–7, pp. 304.
50. *Gazetteer of the Chenab Colony*, 1904, pt. A, p. 150.
51. *DG Montgomery*, 1933, pt. A, p. 288.
52. *Review of Municipal Administration in the Punjab*, 1899–1900, p. 5. *DG Jalandhar*, 1904, pt. A, p. 286. *DG Lahore*, 1893–4, p. 317.
53. *DG Lahore*, 1883–4, p. 195. *DG Gujranwala*, 1883–4, p. 86. *DG Jalandhar*, 1904, pt. A, p. 279. *DG Amritsar*, 1914, pp. 171–2.
54. *DG Amritsar*, 1914, p. 171.
55. *DG Lahore*, 1893–4, p. 215. *DG Amritsar*, 1914, p. 169. *DG Jalandhar*, 1904, pt. A, p. 273. *DG Guranwala*, 1914, pt. A, p. 191.
56. This statement is based on the proceedings of the Municipal Committee of Patti from 1907 to 1947.
57. *DG Amritsar*, 1883–4, p. 71.
58. *DG Jalandhar*, 1904, pt. A, p. 280.

59. *DG Bannu,* 1907, pt. A, p. 134. *Gazetteer of the Chenab Colony,* 1904, pt. A, p. 163. *DG Montgomery,* 1933, pt. A, p. 304.
60. *Report on Police Administration in the Punjab,* 1869, pp. 54, 56, 74, 87 and passim. Ibid., 1870, pp. 52, 55, 57, 59, 61 and passim. Ibid., 1873, pp. 228, 263, 273, 282 and passim.
61. Ibid., 1873, pp. 58, 82, 90, 100, 112 and 124.
62. Ibid., pp. 310, 342 and 368. Cf. *Imperial Gazetteer,* vol. I, Table XIV: 'Police Statistics'.
63. Calculated from figures available in the *Punjab Local Improvement Report,* 1869-70, pp. 4 and 13.
64. Calculated from statistics given in the *Review of Municipal Administration in the Punjab,* 1899-1900, p. 26.
65. Calculated from figures in the *Report on the Working of Municipalities in the Punjab,* 1926-7, p. 2.
66. This is evident from the meagre amounts spent on education by the municipalities. For details on expenditure on public instruction, see all District Gazetteers series of the Punjab: Table 51/52.
67. Based on *DG Amritsar* 1912, pt. B, Table 46.
68. Based on *DG Jalandhar* 1904, pt. A, p. 285.
69. Based on the *Gazetteer of the Chenab Colony,* 1904, pt. A, pp. 149–50.
70. In Sialkot, for instance, octroi accounted for 50 per cent, and in Daska 52 per cent of the municipal income: *DG Sialkot,* 1894–5, pp. 172–3.
71. R. Argal, *Municipal Government in India,* pp. 171–7. Gauba, *Amritsar,* p. 202. During 1940–5, octroi constituted 33.5 per cent of the income of the municipal committee of Amritsar. During 1910–14, this percentage was 49.5.
72. *DG Jalandhar,* 1883–4, p. 30. *DG Hazara,* 1883–4, p. 213. *DG Amritsar,* 1892–3, p. 64. *DG Kapurthala,* 1904, pt. A, p. 45. *DG Amritsar,* 1914, p. 160.
73. *DG Montgomery,* 1923, pt. A, p. 75.
74. Argal, *Municipal Government,* p. 198.
75. In the urban areas of Jalandhar district, the average rate of taxation was 6 annas and 6 pies per head, while it was 4 annas at many places in Amritsar district. *DG Jalandhar,* 1883–4, p. 13. *DG Amritsar,* 1883–4, pp. 73–6.
76. Most of the towns had more than a rupee as the rate of taxation. In Rawalpindi, it exceeded Rs. 2, while in Edwardesabad (Bannu) it was more than Rs. 3. Simla had the highest tax at Rs. 10–2–1: *Review of Municipal Administration in the Punjab,* 1893–4, p. 9. Incidentally, in British times a rupee had 16 annas, and ananna had 12 pies/4 paisas.
77. In Bannu, the tax was raised to Rs. 3–7–0 from 0–14–10; in Gurdaspur from 1–4–2 to 1–8–3; in Dera Baba Nanak from 1–5–6 to 1–12–2, and in Dinanagar from 1–7–11 to 2–4–8. *DG Bannu,* 1907, p. 128. *DG Gurdaspur,* 1914, p. 182.

78. *Review of Municipal Administration in the Punjab*, 1893–4, p. 9.
79. The elective system was not regarded as much of a success in British India, except in the Central Provinces and North-West (later United) Provinces. Argal, *Municipal Government*, p. 15.
80. Of the remaining provinces in 1925–6, Bihar and Orissa had 77.9 per cent elected members, and their percentage in Assam was 78.1. Khanna, *Municipal Government and Administration*, p. 29.
81. Ibid., pp. 20 and 29. Even after local self-government became a 'transferred' subject under the Act of 1919, there remained a very high proportion of non-official chairmen, ranging from 60 to 96 per cent in 1925–6. Their number in the Punjab was 72 out of 101 in 1918–19, and 90 out of 104 in 1925–6.
82. For a discussion of the relative position of various municipal taxes, Argal, *Municipal Government*, pp. 171–97.
83. Khanna, *Municipal Government and Administration*, p. 36.
84. Ibid., pp. 34–5.
85. Jyoti, 'The City of Jullundur', pp. 281–2.
86. Ibid., pp. 283–4 and Appendix VI.
87. Ibid., pp. 284–7.
88. Ibid., pp. 288–9 and 375–81.
89. Ibid., pp. 290–1.
90. Ibid., pp. 292–310.
91. Ibid., pp. 310–14.
92. Ibid., pp. 314–16.
93. Ibid., pp. 319–31 and Tables XXVII, XXVIII and XXIX.
94. Ibid., pp 330–2.
95. Gauba, *Amritsar*, pp. 163–73.
96. Ibid., pp. 201–14 and 216–18.
97. Ibid., p. 174.
98. Prem Raman Uprety, *Religion and Politics in the Punjab in the 1920s*, New Delhi: Sterling,1980, pp. 52–62.
99. Gauba, *Amritsar*, pp. 215 and 219.
100. Jyoti, 'The City of Jullundur', p. 333.
101. Argal, *Municipal Government*, p.25.
102. Khanna, *Municipal Government and Administration*, p. 30. For example, during 1935–7, eight municipalities were superseded in the Punjab. Their number was ten in the province of Bombay, nine in Madras, six in UP, and one in Bengal.
103. Harold F. Alderfer, *Local Government in Developing Countries*, New York: McGraw Hill, 1964, pp. 2 and 228.
104. *Report of the Taxation Enquiry Commission, 1953–54*, vol. III, p. 336 quoted in Maheshwari, *Local Government*, pp. 16–17.

105. A. Avasthi, *Municipal Administration in India*, Agra: Lakshmi Narain Agarwal, 1972, p. 523.
106. *Report on the Working of Municipalities in the Punjab, 1926–7*, p. 1.
107. Khanna, *Municipal Government and Administration*, p. 30.
108. *Punjab Local Government Report, 1869–70*, p. 17. Ibid., *1872–3*, p. 21.
109. Rosenthal, *City in Indian Politics*, pp. 7–11. See also, Alderfer, *Local Government in Developing Countries*, p. 229. In this comparative study of local government, Alderfer comes to the conclusion that the national government in the former colonies has controlled the municipal government 'down to the minutest detail, has reduced its powers to the very minimum, and has impoverished it financially by absorbing its natural sources of revenue'. A legacy, indeed, of colonialism!
110. Jawaharlal Nehru, *An Autobiography*, rpt., New Delhi: OUP, 1982, p. 142.

8

Colonialism and Urbanization: An Overview

Urbanization in the Punjab region goes back to the prehistoric times. The region continued to be relatively more urbanized from the early historical to the late medieval times. Even the phase of decline of the Mughal empire saw the founding of new towns or the revival of old ones to serve as the headquarters of the emergent principalities during the late eighteenth century. In the kingdom of Ranjit Singh new urban centres came into existence and the existing ones expanded in size and population. Towards the end of his reign, there were two 'cities' (Lahore and Amritsar), several middling urban centres, and a large number of small towns.

These urban centres were located mostly in the relatively well-endowed upper *doabs,* or close to the rivers, or on the trade routes. The hill towns were situated in the valleys. The location of urban centres was dictated by the natural advantages and constraints of the terrain, but their relative size in the urban hierarchy depended mostly on their economic functions. Of crucial importance was their place in the collection-distribution network, the market for manufactures, and the easy availability of raw materials. The administrative position of an urban centre and its proximity to the seat of authority also made a difference to its size and functions. Thus, from a nearly stagnant and dilapidated condition in the late eighteenth century, Lahore grew as the capital of the supra-regional state of Ranjit Singh. Amritsar, likewise, grew as his second capital, but more as a centre of trade and manufactures, and the premier sacred place for the Sikhs. All these factors made it the largest city of the north-west at the beginning of colonial rule.

I

The Punjab was the last region to be annexed to the British Indian empire in 1849, followed soon by the Crown taking over the reins from the East India Company. Industrial capitalism was at its peak in Great Britain, and its representatives in India were suffused with a confidence and idealism not experienced before. With the modern science and technology at their disposal, they could master the hills and the plains and tame the rivers to tap the unrealized potential of the region. Within the first decade of annexation, therefore, work on the railway, metalled roads and canals began. In due course, the north-west came to have one of the best transportation networks in the subcontinent. Its irrigation system and the canal colonies came to be regarded as unique feats of modern technology and social engineering to the benefit ultimately of the colonial state. After the establishment of its direct rail link with the Punjab in 1878, Karachi grew to be the fourth largest port in India. By the early twentieth century, the new means of irrigation and transport-ation and the resultant external trade had probably touched even the remotest villages in the region, let alone its urban centres.

Furthermore, the frontier location of the region and its contribution to the British Indian Army on the basis of the so-called 'martial castes' imparted to it a special place in the defence of the subcontinent. A number of cantonments were created in the hills and the plains in the region to house the large number of British troops and officers and to station the Indian soldiers and the supporting personnel. The British civilian officers and other Europeans stayed in the secure and clean environment of the civil station, at a comfortable distance from the natives. Yet, the British depended on the old urban centres for services and supplies as well as for mediating with the subject people. The control and sanitation of the indigenous urban centres were considered to be of crucial importance to the small number of white men, including the troops, living in the European enclaves. The introduction of the municipal government was intended essentially to meet these requirements through the urban notables.

II

The well-connected and economically well-developed urban centres at annexation were particularly well-suited to serve as administrative headquarters. Most of the towns performed administrative functions now as before, but the difference of degree was important. Just as the control of the state increased steadily so did the importance of towns and cities as seats of power. The *subas* or the provinces of the kingdom of

Lahore were replaced by seven large administrative units called 'divisions' which varied in number over time. A number of erstwhile parganas or talukas at the secondary level were grouped into districts, each of which had three or four tahsils. With its headquarters generally in a centrally located town, each tahsil administered a group of villages, besides a few small urban units. This framework remained intact up to 1947, with some territorial changes over the period, like creation of the North-West Frontier Province in 1901 and the separation of the Delhi territory in 1912, besides some minor adjustments of the district and tahsil boundaries. With the exception of the towns founded by the British specifically as seats of authority, like Gurdaspur in the upper Bari Doab and Lyallpur in the Chenab Colony, the functions of the district headquarters which were the most important administrative units, were discharged by the previously existing towns which grew in almost direct proportion to the number of government functionaries and departments, as well as to the new communication linkages.

In addition to the offices and institutions necessary for discharging the basic functions of the state—revenue collection, law and order and justice, including jails—several new departments, aimed at the control and utilization of the natural and human resources of the region, functioned from the district headquarters, such as Engineering, Forest Conservation, Railway, Post and Telegraph, Customs, Canals and Irrigation, Colonization, besides Education and Health. Institutions dealing with some of these functions were established in small urban centres as well, depending upon their location. While cantonments were generally attached to the divisional and district headquarters, new sites in the hills were especially chosen to serve as military stations and health resorts for Europeans, at places also serving as the summer headquarters for the district and divisional administration and the provincial government. The district headquarters were provided with dual linkages—rail as well as road, as also did the 'colony' towns and cantonments. The small urban centres generally outside the administrative hierarchy had road connections only unless located along the rail route. Nearly all of them came to include post and telegraph connections. The towns outside the new communication network tended to relapse into villages.

The new idiom of governance represented by the colonial state, as well as the requirements of domination and management of the natives, dictated the introduction of Western systems of education and health care. The process of education was initiated by the American Presbyterian missionaries who first came to Ludhiana in 1834. They were followed by several other missionaries most of whom preferred to live in the relatively secure and comfortable urban environment, especially in the district headquarters. They established educational institutions, printing presses and philanthropic institutions for evangelical purposes. To counter the activities of the missionaries the educated Punjabis set-up their own cultural institutions in urban areas under the Societies Registration Act (1860) as the Muslim Anjumans, Singh Sabhas, Arya Samajs and the Sanatan Dharm Sabhas. The spread of culturally safe modern education for both boys and girls, though more for the former, was one of their major concerns. Barring a few schools, most of the government and denominational schools, including those for girls, and all institutions of higher, professional and technical education, came to be located in cities and towns. Incidentally, with relatively higher fees, the government institutions catered to the better-placed sections of society. Notwithstanding the few dispensaries in the newly conquered tribal tracts, most of the government dispensaries and certainly all government, mission, and other charitable hospitals were also based in the urban areas. In addition to their contribution towards the emergence of the new professions and rise of the middle classes, the facilities for Western education and even health care available in larger urban units drew people from villages and small towns to the cities and middling centres.

III

The colonial context accelerated the pace of urbanization in several respects. Demographically, the total number of urban people in the region increased from 2.5 million in 1881 to 5.5 million in 1941, raising the proportion of urban population from less than 10 to nearly 14 per cent of the total. The process of increase in urban population picked up in the 1920s.

Much of the increase during the twentieth century was due to migration of men in the 20–40 age group from the countryside to cities and large towns, which accounted for the increasing ratio of able-bodied males in the urban population. The cantonments and 'colony' towns had a very low sex ratio. Their special character accounted for a much higher literacy rate. On the other hand, a substantial majority of those who migrated to cities and large towns in search of employment were illiterate. Thus, while the urban areas recorded an increase in the total number of literate males, literacy among the urban population was not increasing at the same pace. As a whole, more men were literate than women, more women were married than men, and there were more widows than widowers.

The pattern of urban centres altered substantially during this period. The number of cities increased from 2 to 9 and came to be located in different parts of the plain areas. Town of classes II to V also increased their relative proportions, but the smallest towns of class VI decreased in number from 104 in 1881 to 62 in 1941. The region's population tended to be drawn towards its cities and middling centres. Consequently, the number of people living in small towns as a whole was substantially reduced and the urban pyramid appears to have become heavier towards the middle and the top. The 130 new towns that came into existence under colonial rule mostly happened to be small cantonments and hill towns located in the Simla hills and the north-west frontier region, and the *mandis* in the canal-irrigated tracts in the west and the south-east, or along the railway.

However, there was no radical increase in the total number of towns. There were 240 'urban' units in the Punjab in 1881, and their number was no more than 275 in 1941. This was because the process of deurbanization went on simultaneously. Significantly, nearly 60 per cent of the old urban centres remained in existence throughout the period.

Nevertheless, significant changes took place in the physical form and size of urban centres. Since the British chose to live in the civil stations and cantonments outside the walls, minimum of improvements were introduced in the old towns: widening of roads, construction of a circular road around, the railway station and a new railway suburb, besides a grain *mandi* nearby. To meet the requirements of the British, a whole new complex of buildings, symbolic of colonial presence, were added to the larger centres: generally, the town hall and the clock tower and, occasionally, Queen Victoria's statue in the walled area, while government offices, post and telegraph offices, hospitals, dispensaries, educational institutions, Christian compounds, churches, cemeteries, parks, clubs, libraries, race courses, new bazaars, bus stands, factories, and new residential localities outside the walls. Physically, and in terms of morphology, the 'native' and the anglicized parts remained separate, but functionally they formed a single whole. The maximum change took place in the cities, some of which had expanded four or five times in population and size.

The planning and layout of the new urban forms, which housed the Europeans, Anglo-Indians and later, some well placed Indians, were influenced by considerations of efficiency, comfort, convenience, and distance from the natives. The civil stations and cantonments were characterized by spacious bungalows, wide roads, generous water supply, civic amenities, and a low density of population, besides much less density of built-up area than the old city. The hill stations replicated most of these features, albeit on a smaller scale, and as permitted by the terrain.

The 'colony' town, a planned model settlement, on the other hand, was created for an entirely different purpose. Founded at the specifically chosen sites in the canal irrigated tracts, these centres combined features of the old and new towns, housing the grain market as well as other bazaars, light manufactures and residential blocks organized, interestingly, along caste or community lines. The colony towns had their suburbs in the railway station and the civil lines. Functionally, the new urban enclaves and towns showed a specific land use pattern whereas the indigenous but anglicized towns had an overlapping land use.

IV

Colonial presence brought about a substantial reorientation in the traditional urban functions and the lifestyles, behaviour and attitudes of the urban people, particularly the new urban middle classes.

As a result of the increased agricultural production following canalization and commercialization of agriculture, local trade was diverted to new urban centres with modern transportation facilities. This realignment of urban trading in agricultural produce was more or less stabilized by the early 1920s when most urban units situated along the rail routes directly entered the trade network, functioning as focal points for local, regional and export trade at the cost of the previously dominant large towns and even cities. Modern banking and joint stock companies and agency houses and, later the grain exchanges, appearing in cities for the first time, largely subserved the external and overseas trade of the region.

The pattern of urban manufactures was reoriented in the face of competition from goods produced in factories in the UK and other parts of India. Some of the traditional manufactures like paper and work in textiles, metals, wood, and leather declined because of their inability to withstand competition with mill-made goods. Occasional readjustments were made by the craftsmen in techniques, designs and even raw materials, but such reorientations were rather limited in scale. The few factories set-up in the Punjab region were connected largely with colonial economy and lifestyles, like cotton ginning, pressing and baling, hosiery and textiles, glass and chemical works, woollen mills, sports goods, breweries and distilleries. The few mechanical and electrical goods factories and iron foundries as also some mills catering for the regional and local market were essentially consumer goods industries. Their potential, including that of the railway workshops, for generation of wealth and employment remained extremely limited.

The traditional cultural functions of the urban centres as centres of pilgrimage and recreation, and sources of ideas and information, were substantially reoriented under colonial rule. The printing press and the newspapers and periodicals aided the spread of education and dissemination of new ideas, beginning with the programmes of social and religious reform, women's upliftment, and social welfare undertaken by voluntary associations.

Functioning collectively, and often as pressure groups, the people connected with these associations or societies were made conscious of the significance of numbers in the evolving cultural, administrative, and political context of colonial rule.

By the end of the nineteenth century, municipalities of three different 'classes' were established in most of the cities and towns of the Punjab. During the early twentieth century there was an increase in the number of elected members. In the 1920s, municipalities in many cities came to have elected non-official presidents. However, the divisional and district administrators continued to exercise control over municipal bodies through constitutional and extra-constitutional means. The income of the municipalities from octroi, accounting for over 50 per cent of their resources, was never sufficient to meet the expenditure on public works like roads, water supply, sanitation, electricity, primary and secondary education, and law and order. The police was controlled by the administration, though the municipality bore the expenses. The Improvement Trusts created towards the end of colonial rule were controlled by the administrators much more effectively than the municipalities, so that what was given by the right hand was taken back by the left. The municipalities never really became 'self-governments', but they did become arenas of politics, and even of communal competition.

Urban centres in fact became the focal points of the growing politicization and communalization of consciousness among the middle classes of the region. Separate electorates were introduced first for municipal elections in the Punjab in the 1880s. This tended later to assimilate the local politics with provincial politics. Political activities in the Punjab by and large remained centered in urban areas at least partly because of the small numbers of the urban electorates, and the pronounced rural bias of the British government and the ruling Unionist Party. Rather, politics originated and culminated in the cities which were the headquarters of the major political parties, and also associated with the landmarks in the freedom struggle. However, where the cities popularized positive ideas like swadeshi, self-help and freedom from foreign rule, they also nurtured communal competitiveness which surfaced as communal rioting in urban centres of the region, and led, finally, to widespread riots before and after Partition. Trans-migration on large scale changed the demographic and occupational structure of towns and cities after Independence, a setback that served as an incentive for new experiments in urbanization.

V

Cumulatively, urbanization in the Punjab region reflects an interplay of spatial, technological, institutional, economic, social, and cultural changes within the overall context of colonialism in its mature phase. The various sub-regions and social classes were affected differently by the urban processes. Their direction, content and pace were guided by colonial requirements of administrative centralization, military control, cultural domination, and economic exploitation which virtually turned the region into an appendage of the metropolitan economy. The export market controlled by the urban middlemen, and supported by the new communication linkages, strengthened the interaction between urban and rural areas, but functioned mostly to the latter's disadvantage. The rural people migrating to cities generally remained underemployed in the face of the slow growth of industry, and limited opportunities in the tertiary sector. By and large, the new professional middle classes, traditional business communities, and big landlords appear to have been the beneficiaries of colonial urban development and the lifestyle changes stimulated by it.

There was a wide divergence also in the experiences of different kinds of urban centres The pace of change was much faster in the directly administered areas than the princely territories. The old cities, middling centres and small towns in the British territories differed in terms of the 'improvements' in their living conditions. As a whole, there was a wide gap between the quality of life available in the pre-existing urban units and the new urban forms. Moreover, displacement and deprivation of the local people of their lands and way of life were integral to the processes underpinning the creation of the civil station, cantonment, hill station, and the colony town.

Finally, changes in the urban forms, patterns, population, functions, and government were sufficiently significant as to be called revolutionary. Yet, all of these cannot necessarily be construed as development in the accepted sense of the term. Urbanization tended to benefit only a few sections of the Punjabi society, and even among them to discourage secular and modernizing tendencies, simultaneously facilitating colonial control over the people. If there was an urban policy, it was marked by manipulation and control and adhocism and convenience.

The states of Punjab, Haryana and Himachal Pradesh in the post-colonial period have registered substantial urban development, but like the colonial state they do not as yet seem to make a distinction between the development policies *per se* and urban policies in particular, with a clear vision of a coordinated change for the better.

Glossary

akhara:	a wrestling ground in common usage, the term was applied in the period of Sikh rule to some of the monastic centres established by the Udasis who treated the *Adi Granth* as a religious text.
arhatia:	one who takes commission (*ahrat*) on the sale of a commodity, especially agricultural produce, in a market.
Baisakhi:	the first day of the month of Baisakh which is observed as a festival. Also spelt as Waisakhi.
baoli:	a step well.
Basant:	a spring festival celebrated in various ways, especially by kite-flying.
basti:	a settlement; a residential locality.
bulbul chashm:	nightingale-eyed; a cloth of good quality.
bunga:	a building, especially a structure built around the Harmandir in Amritsar during the late eighteenth or the early nineteenth century by the Sikh *sardars* for accommodating visitors to the sacred place.
chungi:	octroi or duty levied on goods entering or leaving a town.
dar-ul-shafa:	the house of health, a hospital.
daryai:	a plain silk cloth.
deodhi:	the entrance hall of a large mansion. The term was also used for the ruler's palace during the period of Sikh rule.
dera:	an encampment; an army unit; a place used permanently as a religious establishment.
dhab:	old ponds.
dharmsala:	a Sikh place of worship later called gurdwara, a rest house for travellers.
dhobi ghat:	the place where professional washermen wash and clean the clothes of others.
doab:	a tract between two waters or rivers, an interfluve.

Dussehra: the festival celebrated in commemoration of Ravana's defeat and death at the hands of Rama, as the triumph of good over evil.

ghat: a river bank; a ferry.

gulbadan: literally, rose-body; a striped silken cloth.

halal: lawful; the meat of an animal slaughtered in the Islamic way.

Holi: a festival celebrated in spring by throwing coloured water and powder over one another, carrying the implication of mutual goodwill, irrespective of social distinctions.

hukka: a device for smoking tobacco, the hubble bubble.

ijaradar: the holder of a contract (*ijara*), generally authorized to collect revenues from a specified area on the condition of paying a specified sum, but not exceeding the prescribed rates for the locality.

jhatka: the meat of an animal slaughtered with a single stroke of the sword or another instrument; presumably an old, pre-Islamic, practice in India, but presently associated with Sikhs.

katra: a locality in a city, generally with a single entrance and initially under the control of a single person, often having its own local market.

khanqah: a hospice established by a Sufi *shaikh*; the term continued to be used after the death of the founding *shaikh*, or even when there was no *shaikh* to guide the disciples.

kotwal: literally the holder of a fort, generally the keeper of law and order in a city.

kuppa: a container for oil and the like.

lacha: a piece of cloth, generally worn round the waist as a dress.

lande: the script used by the trading communities, varying in form from area to area.

lungi: a piece of cotton cloth with silk border, generally used as a dress worn round the waist.

Mahajani school: the indigenous school where account-keeping and practically useful learning was imparted, in addition to literacy.

mahal: a fiscal unit for the collection of revenue or customs on behalf of the state.

maktab: a school where elementary education in Arabic and Persian was imparted.

mandi: a market; generally for agricultural produce.

mazar: a tomb, a structure raised over a grave, generally used for the tombs of the saints visited by way of pilgrimage.

mille: thousand in French.

Muharram: the month of the Hijri year in which processions in commemoration of the martyrdom of Ḥasan and Husain, the sons of Caliph Ali and Fatima, the daughter of the Prophet Muhammad, are taken out.

muharrir: a professional writer of reports in an office; a clerk.

mushaira: an informal competition at which poets recite their poems in the presence of an appreciative audience.

nautanki: a touring theatre of the traditional kind.

Nirmalas: the ascetics and renunciants belonging to the *nirmala* order among the Sikhs.

Nizamat: the area under the jurisdiction of a *nazim*; a district in a princely state.

pashmina: from *pashm*, the wool of a Tibetan goat.

pathshala: an elementary school.

Pir: a guide; a *shaikh*; a saint.

qanungo: an official who kept all records related to land revenue and who was generally familiar with the local customs.

qasba: a term used for a small town as distinct from a city (*shahr*).

Raas-lila: the dance-drama depicting episodes from the life of Krishna, especially in relation to the milkmaids (*gopis*).

rehat: a way of life, especially the way of life enjoined upon the Khalsa of Guru Gobind Singh.

sahukar: one who pursues the profession of a *sahu* and advances money to his agents for trade; a moneylender; a rich merchant.

salu: a piece of cloth dyed in a deep and fast colour to be used as a dress by women, especially brides.

samadhi: a structure raised over a spot of cremation of a religious or a secular personage.

saraï: a resting place for travellers.

Sehajdhari: a Sikh who has not been baptized through the rite of the double-edged sword and who, consequently, does not follow all the injunctions of the Khalsa way of life (*rehat*).

sepidar: a person who performed customary services for his patrons to be paid in kind; there were several categories of such traditional service performers in a village and, therefore, the whole system was known as the *sepidari* system.

shahr: a city as distinct from a small town (*qasba*); the two terms were sometimes used interchangeably.

Shivdwara: literally, the door of Shiva, a temple dedicated to Shiva as the deity.

susi: a smooth cloth with coloured stripes used for making trousers for women.

taluka: an area under the jurisdiction of a particular person; spelt as the *ta'alluqa* in the Persian, and used in the early nineteenth century as the equivalent of pargana.

tawaif: a professional singer and dancer.

tehbazari: the cess paid to the original proprietor of land on which shops were built or trade was carried on by others.

Thakurdwara: literally, the door of the Master; a temple dedicated to Vishnu as the deity.

Thana: a garrison post in pre-colonial times, and a police post under colonial rule.

Udasis: renunciants belonging to the Udasi order, tracing their origin to Guru Nanak through his son Sri Chand, and living in their own establishments.

vaid: a practitioner of traditional Indian medicine.

wali: a friend, a friend of God; one who has attained the knowledge of God; a Sufi saint with whom miracles are associated.

Bibliography

PRIMARY SOURCES

Census Reports

Census of India, 1881, London 1883.
Census of India, 1891, London 1893.
Census of India, 1901, Calcutta 1903.
Census of India, 1911, Calcutta 1913.
Census of India, 1921, Calcutta 1923.
Census of India, 1931, Delhi 1933.
Census of India, 1971, Census Centenary Monograph No. 1, New Delhi: Registrar General of India, 1972.
Census of India: Indian Census in Perspective, New Delhi: Registrar General of India, Ministry of Home Affairs, 1971.
General Report on the Administration of the Punjab Territories, No. 6, Selection of Records of the Government of India, 1855 (containing the first Census of the Punjab).
Reports on the Census of the Punjab taken on 10th January 1868, Lahore 1870.
Reports on the Census of the Punjab, 1881, 2 vols., Lahore, 1883.
Reports on the Census of the Punjab, 1891, 2 vols., Calcutta, 1982.
Reports on the Census of the Punjab, 1901, 2 vols., Lahore, 1902.
Reports on the Census of the Punjab, 1911, 2 vols., Lahore, 1912.
Reports on the Census of the Punjab, 1921, 2 vols., Lahore, 1922.
Reports on the Census of the Punjab, 1931, 2 vols., Lahore, 1933.
Reports on the Census of the Punjab, 1941, 2 vols., Delhi, 1941

District and State Gazetteers

District Gazetteer Ambala, 1883–4, 1904, 1912.
District Gazetteer Amritsar, 1883–4, 1892–3, 1912, 1941.
District Gazetteer Attock, 1907.
District Gazetteer Bannu, 1883–4, 1907, 1913.
District Gazetteer Dera Ghazi Khan, 1883–4, 1893–4, 1904, 1912.
District Gazetteer Dera Ismail Khan, 1883–4, 1907–8, 1911–12, 1913.
District Gazetteer Ferozepore, 1883–4, 1904, 1913, 1914.
District Gazetteer Gujranwala, 1883–4, 1893–4, 1904, 1911–12.

District Gazetteer Gujrat, 1883–4, 1892–3, 1904, 1912.
District Gazetteer Gurdaspur, 1883–4, 1891–2, 1904, 1912, 1914
District Gazetteer Gurgaon, 1883–4, 1912.
District Gazetteer Hazara, 1883–4, 1907, 1913
District Gazetteer Hissar, 1883–4.
District Gazetteer Hoshiarpur, 1883–4, 1912.
District Gazetteer Jalandhar, 1883–4, 1904, 1912.
District Gazetteer Jhang, 1883–4, 1904, 1907, 1912.
District Gazetteer Jhelum, 1883–4, 1905,1912.
District Gazetteer Karnal, 1883–4, 1912.
District Gazetteer Kohat, 1883–4, 1914.
District Gazetteer Lahore, 1883–4, 1893–4, 1904, 1912.
District Gazetteer Lyallpur, 1912.
District Gazetteer Mianwali, 1904, 1912, 1916.
District Gazetteer Montogomery, 1883–4, 1898–9, 1913, 1933.
District Gazetteer Multan, 1883–4, 1912.
District Gazetteer Muzaffargarh, 1883–4.
District Gazetteer Peshawar, 1883–4, 1897–8, 1904, 1912–13.
District Gazetteer Rawalpindi, 1883–4, 1912.
District Gazetteer Rohtak, 1883–4.
District Gazetteer Shahpur, 1883–4, 1913.
District Gazetteer Sialkot, 1894–5, 1904, 1912.
Gazetteer Chenab Colony, 1904.
Phulkian States Gazetteer, Patiala, Nabha and Jind, 1904, 1909.
State Gazetteer, Faridkot, 1904, 1907, 1913.
State Gazetteer Jind, 1913.
State Gazetteer Kalsia, 1904, 1912.
State Gazetteer Kapurthala, 1904, 1912.
State Gazetteer Loharu, 1904, 1907, 1912.
State Gazetteer Nabha, 1913.
State Gazetteer Patiala, 1913.

MONOGRAPHS ON INDUSTRIES

Monograph on Cotton Manufactures in the Punjab, 1884, Lahore: Civil and Military Gazette Press, 1885.
Monograph on Woollen Manufactures of the Punjab, 1884–5, Lahore: Civil and Military Gazette Press, 1886.
Monograph on Silk Industry in the Punjab, 1885–6, Lahore: Civil and Military Gazette Press, 1887.

Monograph on Brass and Copper Ware in the Punjab, 1886–7, Lahore: Civil and Military Gazette Press, 1888.

Monograph on Wood Manufactures in the Punjab, 1887–8, Lahore: Civil and Military Gazette Press, 1889.

Monograph on Gold and Silver Works in the Punjab, 1888–9, Lahore: Civil and Military Gazette Press, 1890.

Monograph on Fibrous Manufactures, 1889–90, Lahore: Civil and Military Gazette Press, 1891.

Monograph on Pottery and Glass Industry of the Punjab, 1890–1, Lahore: Civil and Military Gazette Press, 1892.

Monograph on Leather Industry of the Punjab, 1891–2, Lahore: Civil and Military Gazette Press, 1893.

Monograph on Ivory Carving, 1900, Lahore: Civil and Military Gazette Press, 1901.

Monograph on Stone Carving and Inlaying in the Punjab, 1904–5, Lahore: Punjab Government Press, 1906.

Monograph on Carpet Making in the Punjab, 1905–6, Lahore: Civil and Military Gazette Press, 1907.

Monograph on Iron and Steel Industries in the Punjab, 1906–7, Lahore: Civil and Military Gazette Press, 1908.

Monograph on Paper Making and Paper Mache in the Punjab, 1907–8, Lahore: Civil and Military Gazette Press, 1908.

Monograph on Wire and Tinsel Industry in the Punjab, 1908–9, Lahore: Civil and Military Gazette Press, 1909.

Government Reports

Report on the Administration of the Punjab, and its Dependencies for the years 1867–8, 1868–9, 1872–3, 1875–6, 1901–2, 1909–10, 1920–1, 1929–30, 1934–5, Lahore.

Report on the Chenab, Jhelum and Chunian Colonies for 1901–2 to 1918–19, 2 vols., Lahore.

Report on the Vocational Education in India (Delhi, Punjab and United Pro-vinces) with a Section on General Education and Administration, 1939.

Report of the Inspector General of Dispensaries in the Punjab, 1867.

Report on the Punjab Internal Trade by Rail and River, 1888 to 1921–2.

Report on Punjab Internal Trade of the Punjab by Rail and River, 1921–2.

Report on the Internal Trade and Manufacture of the Punjab for 1880–1, 1881–2, 1882–3, 1883–4, 1884–5, 1885–6, 1886–7, 1887–8.

Reviews on Municipal Administration in the Punjab in 1893–4, 1898–9, 1899–1900.

Report on the Working of the Municipalities in the Punjab for the years 1899–1900, 1901–2, 1902–3, 1903–4, 1904–5, 1905–6, 1906–7, 1907–8, 1908–9, 1909–10, 1910–11, 1911–12, 1912–13, 1913–14, 1914–15, 1915–16, 1916–17, 1917–18, 1918–19, 1919–20, 1920–1, 1921–2, 1922–3 , 1923–4, 1924–5, 1925–6, 1926–7.

Provincial Reports: Municipalities, 1888–9, 1907–8 to 1915–16.

Punjab Municipal Act, 1891.

Punjab Municipal Act, 1911.

CONTEMPORARY WORKS

Amarnath, *Development of Local Self Government (1849-1900)* Monograph 8, Lahore: Punjab Government Record Office Publication, 1929.

Arora, Faqir Chand, *Commerce by River in the Punjab,* Monograph 9, Lahore: Punjab Government Record Office Publication, 1930.

Baden Powell, B.H., *Handbook of the Manufacturers and Arts of the Punjab,* Lahore: Punjab Printing Company, 1872.

Badenoch, A.C., *Punjab Industries, 1911–7,* Lahore: Government Printing, 1917.

Baquir, Muhammad, *Lahore: Past and Present,* Lahore: Punjab University Press, 1952.

Bruce, J.F., *History of the University of the Punjab,* Lahore: University of Punjab, 1952.

Buck, Edward J., *Simla Past and Present,* Calcutta: Thacker Spink & Co., 1904.

Calvert, H., *The Wealth and Welfare of the Punjab: Being some Studies in Punjab Rural Economics,* Lahore: Civil and Military Gazette Press, 1922.

Carthill, Al, *Madampur,* London: William Blackwood & Sons, n.d.

Darling, Malcolm Lyall, *The Punjab Peasant in Prosperity and Debt*; rpt., New Delhi: Manohar, 1977 (1st pub. 1925).

Douie, James, *The Punjab, North-West Frontier Province and Kashmir*; rpt., New Delhi: Low Price Publications, 1994 (1st Pub. 1916).

Ganesh Das, *Char Bagh-i Panjab* (Persian), Kirpal Singh (ed.), Amritsar: Khalsa College, 1965.

———, *Char Bagh-i Panjab,* Eng tr. and ed., J.S. Grewal and Indu Banga, as *Early 19th Century Punjab,* Amritsar: Guru Nanak Dev University (GNDU), 1975.

Kincaid, Dennis, *British Social Life in India 1608–1937,* London: George Routledge & Sons, 1938.

King, Mrs. Robert Moss, *Diary of a Civilian's Wife in India 1877–82,* London: Richard Bentley, 1884.

Latif, Syed Muhammad, *Lahore—Its History, Architectural Remains and Antiquities,* Lahore: np, 1892.

Latifi, A., *The Industrial Punjab: A Survey of Facts, Conditions and Possibilities,* Bombay: Longman's Green and Company, 1911.

Leitner, G.W., *Indidgenous Education in the Punjab Since Annexation and in 1882*; rpt., Patiala: Language Department Punjab, 1971(1st pub. 1883).

Lester, Muriel, *My Host the Hindoo,* London: William and Norgate, 1931.

Mehta, H.R., *A History of the Growth and Development of Western Education in the Punjab 1846–84,* Monograph 5, Lahore: Punjab Government Record Office Publication, 1929.

Ross, David, *The Land of Five Rivers and Sindh*; rpt., Patiala: Language Department, Punjab, 1970.

Shah, K.T., *Industrialization of the Punjab,* Lahore: Punjab Government Printing, 1941.

Suri, Sohan Lal, *Umdat-ut-Tawarikh* Punjab tr. from Persian Amarwant Singh, ed. J.S. Grewal and Indu Banga, Amritsar: GNDU, 1985.

Thorburn, S.S., *The Punjab in Peace and War*; rpt., Patiala: Language Department Punjab, 1970.

Trevaskis, Hugh Kennedy, *Punjab of Today: An Economic Survey of the Punjab in Recent Years 1890–1923,* Lahore: Civil and Military Gazette Press, 1931.

SECONDARY WORKS

Books

Alam, S. Manzoor (ed.), *Urbanization in Developing Countries,* Hyderabad: Osmania University, 1976.

Alderfer, Harold F., *Local Government in Developing Countries,* New York: McGraw Hill, 1964.

Ali, Imran, *The Punjab under Imperialism, 1885–1947,* New Delhi: Oxford University Press (OUP), 1989.

Argal, R., *Municipal Government in India,* 3rd edn., Allahabad: Agarwal Press, 1967.

Avasthi, A., *Municipal Administration in India,* Agra: Lakshmi Narain Agarwal, 1972.

Bagchi, Amiya Kumar, *The Evolution of the State Bank of India: The Era of the Presidency Banks, 1876–1920,* vol. II, New Delhi: Sage/SBI, 1997.

Banerjee, Himadri, *Agrarian Society of the Punjab (1849–1901)*, New Delhi: Manohar: 1982.

Banerjee, Prajananda, *Calcutta and Its Hinterland: A Study in Economic History of India 1833–1900*, Calcutta: Progressive Publishers, 1975.

Banga, Indu (ed.), *Ports and Their Hinterlands in India, 1700–1950*, New Delhi: Manohar, 1992.

______ (ed.), *Five Punjabi Centuries: Polity, Economy, Society and Culture, c. 1500–1900*; rpt., New Delhi: Manohar, 2000.

______ (ed.), *The City in Indian History*; rpt., New Delhi: Manohar, 2005.

Barrier, N. Gerald, *The Sikhs and Their Literature*, New Delhi: Manohar, 1970.

Basu, Dalip K. (ed.), *The Rise and Growth of the Colonial Port Cities in Asia*; rpt., Berkeley: University of California Press, 1983.

Bhatia, Shyamla, *Social Change and Politics in Punjab, 1898–1910*, New Delhi: Enkay Publishers, 1987.

Blake, Stephen P., *Shahjahanabad: The Sovereign City in Mughal India, 1639–1739*; 1st Indian edn., New Delhi: Foundation Books, 1993.

Bose, Ashish, *Urbanization in India—An Inventory of Source Material*, New Delhi: Academic Books, 1970.

______, *Studies in India's Urbanization 1901–71*, New Delhi: Tata McGraw Hill, 1973.

______, *India's Urbanization 1901–2001*; 2nd rev. edn., New Delhi: Tata McGraw Hill/Institute of Economic Growth, 1978.

______, *Bibliography on Urbanization in India 1947–76*, New Delhi: Tata McGraw-Hill, 1976.

Bose, Ashish, P.B. Desai and S.P. Jain, *Studies in Demography*, London: George Allen and Unwin, 1970.

Breese, Gerald, *Urbanization in Newly Developing Countries*, New Delhi: Prentice Hall of India, 1978.

Carter, Harold, *The Study of Urban Geography*, London: Arnold Heinemann, 1972.

Chakrabarti, Dilip, *The Archaeology of Ancient Indian Cities*, New Delhi: OUP, 1997.

Champakalakshmi, R., *Trade, Ideology and Urbanization: South India, 300 BC to AD 1300*, New Delhi: OUP, 1996.

Chandna, R.C. and Manjit S. Sidhu, *Introduction to Population Geography*, New Delhi: Kalyani Publishers, 1980.

Chandra, Satish, *Fernand Braudel on Towns*, Occasional Papers Series 11, Chandigarh: Urban History Association of India, 1992.

Chattopadhyaya, Brajadulal, *The Making of Early Medieval India*; rpt., New Delhi: OUP, 1999.

Chaudhuri, M.K. (ed.), *Trends of Socio-Economic Change in India*, Simla: Indian Institute of Advanced Study, 1969.

Chawla, Bhagatjit Singh, *The Punjab Municipal Act: A Commentry*, Chandigarh: Chawla Publications, 1994.

Chhabra, G.S., *The Social and Economic History of the Punjab (1849–1901)*, New Delhi: Sterling Publishers, 1962.

Cox, Peter R., *Demography*, Cambridge: Cambridge University Press, 1976.

Dagar, Rainuka, *Identifying and Controlling Female Foeticide and Infanticide in Punjab*, Chandigarh: Institute for Development and Communication, 2002.

Datta, V.N., *Amritsar: Past and Present*, Amritsar: Municipal Committee, 1967.

Davies, Philip, *Splendours of the Raj: British Architecture in India, 1660 to 1947*, New Delhi: Dass Media, 1985.

Davis, Emmett, *Press and Politics in British Western Punjab 1836–1947*, New Delhi: Academic Publications, 1983.

Dickinson, Robert E., *City and Region: A Geographical Interpretation*, London: Routledge & Kegan Paul, 1972.

Dyos, H.J. (ed.), *The Study of Urban History*, London: Edward Arnold, 1971.

Ferriera, J.V. and S. S. Jha (eds.), *The Outlook Tower*, Bombay: Popular Prakashan, 1976.

Fox, Richard G., *Lions of the Punjab: Culture in the Making*, Berkeley: University of California Press, 1985.

Gadgil, D.R., *Sholapur City: Socio-Economic Study*, Poona: Gokhale Institute of Politics and Economics, 1965.

———, *The Industrial Evolution of India in Recent Times (1860–1939)*; rpt., New Delhi: OUP, 1971.

Gallion, Arther B. and Simon Eisner, *The Urban Pattern*, New Delhi: OBS Publishers and Distributors, 1984.

Ganguly, Indrani, *The Social History of a Bengal Town*, Bombay: Himalaya Publishing House, 1987.

Gauba, Anand, *Amritsar: A Study in Urban History (1840–1947)*, Jalandhar: ABS Publications, 1988.

Ghosh, A., *The City in Early Historical India*; rpt., Shimla: Indian Institute of Advanced Study, 1990.

Ghosh, Suresh Chandra, *History of Education in Modern India (1757–1986)*, New Delhi: Orient Longman, 1995.

Ghurye, G.S., *Cities and Civilization*, Bombay: Popular Prakashan, 1962.

Gibbs, Jack P., *Urban Research Methods*, New Delhi: Affiliated East West Press, 1966.

Gillion, Kenneth L., *Ahmedabad: A Study in Indian History*, Ahmedabad: New Order Book Company, 1968.

Gilmartin, David, *Empire and Islam: Punjab and the Making of Pakistan*, Berkeley: University of California Press, 1988.

Goswamy, Kshama, *Nagarikaran aur Hindi Upanyas* (Hindi), New Delhi: Jayashri Prakashan, 1981.

Grewal, J.S., *In the By-Lanes of History: Some Documents from a Punjab Town*, Shimla: Indian Institute of Advanced Study, 1975.

———, *The Sikhs of the Punjab*, The New Cambridge History of India; rev. edn., Cambridge: Cambridge University Press, 1998.

———, *Maharaja Ranjit Singh: Polity, Economy and Society*, Amritsar: GNDU, 2001.

Grewal, J.S. and Indu Banga (eds.), *Studies in Urban History*, Amritsar: GNDU, 1981.

Grewal, Reeta, (ed.), *Five Thousand Years of Urbanization: The Punjab Region*, New Delhi: Manohar/Institute of Punjab Studies, 2005.

——— and Sheena Pall (eds.), *Precolonial and Colonial Punjab: Society, Economy, Politics and Culture*, New Delhi: Manohar, 2005.

———, and Sheena Pall (eds.), *Five Centuries of Sikh Tradition: Ideology, Society, Politics and Culture*, New Delhi: Manohar, 2005.

Gupta, Narayani, *Delhi Between Two Empires 1803-1931*, New Delhi: OUP, 1981.

Havell, E.B., *Benares: The Sacred City*, Calcutta: Thacker Spinks and Co., 1968.

Hoselitz, Bert F., *Sociological Aspects of Economic Growth*, New Delhi: Amerind Publishing Company, 1975.

Hoti, Prem Singh, *General Hari Singh Nalva* (Punjabi); rpt. Ludhiana: Lahore Book Shop, 1937.

Humes, Samuel and Eileen M. Martin, *The Structure of Local Government Throughout the World*, The Hague: Martinus Nijhoff, 1961.

Jones, Emrys, *Towns and Cities*, London: OUP, 1966.

Jones, Kenneth W., *Arya Dharm: Hindu Consciousness in the 19th Century Punjab*, rpt., New Delhi: Manohar 1989.

Jones, Rodney W., *Urban Politics in India*, New Delhi: Vikas, 1975.

Kanwar, Pamela, *Imperial Simla: The Political Culture of the Raj*, New Delhi: OUP, 1990.

———, *Essays on Urban Patterns in Nineteenth Century Himachal Pradesh*, Shimla: Indian Institute of Advanced Study, 1999.

Kessinger, Tom G., *Vilyatpur, 1848–1968: Social and Economic Change in a North Indian Village*; Indian edn., New Delhi: Young Asia Publications, 1979.

Khanna, R.L., *Municipal Government and Administration in India*, Chandigarh: Mohindra Capital Publishers, 1967.

King, Anthony D., *Colonial Urban Development: Culture, Social Power and Environment*, London: Routledge & Kegan Paul, 1976.

Kumar, Anil, *Medicine and the Raj: British Medical Policy in India, 1935–1911*, New Delhi: Sage, 1998.

Kumar, Dharma (ed.), *Cambridge Economic History of India 1750–1947*, Cambridge: Cambridge University Press, 1983.

Lowenstein, Louis K., *Urban Studies*, New York: The Free Press, 1971.

Mahajan, Ganeshi, *Congress Politics in the Punjab 1885–1947*, New Delhi: K.K. Publishers, 2002.

Maheshwari, Shriram, *Local Government in India*; New Delhi: Orient Longman, 1976.

Malhotra, S.L., *Gandhi and the Punjab*, Chandigarh: Panjab University, 1970.

———, *Gandhi: An Experiment with Communal Politics*, Chandigarh: Panjab University, 1975.

———, *From Civil Disobedience to Quit India*, Chandigarh: Panjab University, 1979.

Mathur, Y.B., *British Administration of Punjab 1849–75*, New Delhi: Surjeet Book Depot, n.d.

Meyer, Harold M. and Clyde F. Kohn, *Readings in Urban Geography*, Allahabad: Central Book Depot, 1967.

Mishra, Kamala Prasad, *Banaras in Transition 1738–95: A Socio-Economic Study*, New Delhi: Munshiram Manoharlal, 1975.

Mishra, R.P., *Million Cities of India*, New Delhi: Vikas, 1978.

Misra, B.B., *The Administrative History of India 1834–1949*, London: OUP, 1970.

Mitra, Ashok, *Delhi: Capital City*, New Delhi: Thomson Press Ltd., 1970.

———, *India's Population: Aspects of Quality and Control*, New Delhi: Abhinav Publishers, 1975.

Mohan, Kamlesh, *Militant Nationalism in the Punjab 1919–35*, New Delhi: Manohar, 1985.

Mukerjee, S.N., *Calcutta: Myths and History*, Calcutta: Subaranrekha, 1977.

Nair, Janaki, *Women and Law in Colonial India: A Social History*, New Delhi: Kali for Women, 1996.

Nath, R., *Agra and Its Monumental Glory*, Bombay: Taraporewala, 1977.

Oldenburg, Veena Talwar, *The Making of Colonial Lucknow 1856–77*, Princeton: Princeton University Press, 1984.

Pahl, R.E., *Reading in Urban Sociology*, Oxford: Pergamon, 1969.

Pirenne, Henri, *Medieval Cities*, New Jersey: Princeton, 1969.

Postgate, J.N., *Early Mesopotamia: Society and Economy at the Dawn of History*, London: Routledge, 1992.

Prabha, K., *Towns: A Structural Analysis: A Case Study of Punjab*, New Delhi: Inter India, 1979.

Premi , M.K., A. Ramanamma and Usha Bambawal, *An Introduction to Social Demography*, New Delhi: Vikas, 1983.

Pubby, Vipin, *Shimla Then and Now*: Indan edn., New Delhi: Indus Publishing Company, 1996.

Quinn, James A., *Urban Sociology*, New Delhi: Eurasia Publishing House, 1967.

Rai, Satya M., *Legislative Politics and Freedom Struggle in Punjab 1897–1947*, New Delhi: ICHR, 1984.

Ramachandran, R., *Urbanization and Urban Systems in India*; 6th imp, New Delhi: OUP, 1997.

Ramegowda, K.S., *Urban and Regional Planning*, Mysore: Unviersity of Mysore, 1972.

Rao, M.S.A. (ed.), *Urban Sociology in India*, New Delhi: Orient Longman, 1974.

Rao, V.L.S. Prakasa, *Urbanization in India: Spatial Dimensions*, New Delhi: Concept Publishing Company, 1983.

Ray, A.K., *A Short History of Calcutta*; Indian edn., Calcutta: Rddhi India, 1982 (1st pub. 1902).

Roseberry, III, J. Royal, *Imperial Rule in Punjab: The Conquest and Administration of Multan, 1818–81,* New Delhi: Manohar, 1987.

Saberwal, Satish (ed.), *Process and Institution in Urban India*, New Delhi: Vikas, 1978.

Sachdeva, Veena, *Polity and Economy of the Punjab During the Late Eighteenth Century*, New Delhi: Manohar, 1993.

Sahai, Jugendra, *Urban Complex of an Industrial City*, Allahabad: Chugh Publications, 1980.

Saini, B.S., *The Social and Economic History of the Punjab* (*1901–39*), Delhi: Ess Ess Publications, 1975.

Saxena, Sudha, *Trends of Urbanization in Uttar Pradesh*, Agra: Satish Book Enterprise, 1970

Sharma, Harish C., *Artisans of the Punjab: A Study of Social Change in Historical Perspective* (*1849–1947*), New Delhi: Manohar, 1996.

Sharma, K.D., *Urban Development in Metropolitan Shadow*, New Delhi: Inter India Publications, 1985.

Sharma, Sri Ram, *Punjab in Ferment*, New Delhi: S. Chand, 1971.

Simmons, J.W. and L.S. Bourne, *Systems of Cities: Readings in Structure, Growth and Policy*, New York: OUP, 1978.

Singh, Fauja (ed.), *Sirhind Through the Ages*, Patiala: Punjabi University, 1972.

———, *Eminent Freedom Fighters of Punjab*, Patiala: Punjabi University, 1972.

Singh, Fauja (ed.), *The City of Faridkot*, Patiala: Punjabi University, 1976.

——— (ed.), *The City of Amritsar*, Patiala: Punjabi University, 1977.

——— (ed.), *Patiala and Its Historical Surroundings*, Patiala: Punjabi University, 1982.

Singh, Ganda (ed.), *The Singh Sabha and Other Socio-Religious Movements in the Punjab 1850–1925*, (*The Panjab Past and Present*, vol. VII, pt 1, 1973); rpt., Patiala: Punjabi University, 1984.

Singh, Joginder, *The Sikh Resurgence*, New Delhi: National Book Organization, 1997.

Singh, Mohinder, *The Akali Movement*, New Delhi: Macmillan, 1978.

Singh, M.P., *Town, Market, Mint and Port in the Mughal Empire 1556–1707*, New Delhi: Adam Publishers, 1985.

Singh, Navtej, *Starvation and Colonialism: A Study of Famines in the Nineteenth Century British Punjab*, New Delhi: National Book Organization, 1996.

Singh, Nazer, *G.W. Leitner: Founder of Punjab System of Education, including the Punjab University, Lahore*, Patiala: Madaan Publications, 2004.

Singh, Sukhwant, *Agricultural Growth and Colonial Constraints: The Punjab 1849–1947*, New Delhi: Manpreet Prakashan, 2000.

Smith, T. Lynn, *Fundamentals of Population Study*, Chicago: J.B. Lippincott Company, 1960.

Sohal, Sukhdev Singh, *The Making of the Middle Classes in the Punjab (1849–1947)*, Jalandhar: ABS Publications, 2008.

Spate, O.H.K. and A.T.A. Learmonth, *India and Pakistan: A General and Regional Geography*, 3rd edn., London: Methuen & Co., 1967.

Surendra Gopal, *Patna in the 19th Century*, Calcutta: Naya Prakashan, 1982.

Talbot, Ian, *Punjab and the Raj 1849–1947*, New Delhi: Manohar, 1988.

Tandon, Prakash, *Punjabi Saga (1857–2000): The Monumental Study of Five Generations of a Remarkable Punjabi Family*; rpt., New Delhi: Rupa, 2003.

Tanwar, Raghuvendra, *Politics of Sharing Power: The Punjab Unionist Party 1923–1947*, New Delhi: Manohar, 1999.

Thakur, Vijay Kumar (ed.), *Towns in Pre-Modern India*, Patna: Janaki Prakashan, 1994.

Tinker, Hugh, *The Foundation of Local Self Government in India, Pakistan and Burma*, Bombay: Lalvani Publishing House, 1967.

Turner, Roy (ed.), *India's Urban Future*, Bombay: OUP, 1962.

Tuteja, K.L., *Sikh Politics, 1920–1940*, Kurukshetra: Vishal Publications, 1984.

Tyrwhitt, Jacqueline, *Patrick Geddes in India*, London: Lund Humphries, 1947.

Uprety, Prem Raman, *Religion and Politics in Punjab in the 1920s*, New Delhi: Sterling, 1980.

Verma, D.C. and Sukhbir Singh, *Haryana*; 4th edn., New Delhi: National Book Trust, 2001.

Walia, Amrit, *Development of Education and Socio-Political Change in the Punjab 1882–1947*, Jalandhar: ABS Publications, 2005.

Webster, John C.B., *The Christian Community and Change in Nineteenth Century North India*, New Delhi: Macmillan, 1976.

Yadav, Kirpal C., *Elections in Punjab 1920–1947*, New Delhi: Manohar, 1987.

Yadav, K.C. and K.S. Arya, *Arya Samaj and the Freedom Movement*, vol. I: 1875–1918, New Delhi: Manohar, 1988.

ARTICLES

Ahmed, Qazi S., 'Distribution Pattern in Pakistan', *Pakistan Geographical Review*, vol. VII, no. I, 22, January 1967.

Anal, Awadesh Kumar Singh, 'Begusarai: A Study in Urban Morphology', *The Deccan Geographer*, vol. IX, no. 1, January–June 1972.

Balandiers, G., 'The Colonial Situation: Theoretical Approach', in Immanuel Wallerstein (ed.), *Social Change: The Colonial Situation*, New York: John Wiley, 1966, pp. 34–61.

Banga, Indu, 'Polity, Economy and Urbanization in the Upper Bari Doab', in J.S. Grewal and Indu Banga (eds.), *Studies in Urban History*, Amritsar: GNDU, 1981, pp. 192–205.

———, 'The Emergence of Hindu Consciousness in Colonial Punjab', in P.C. Chatterjee (ed.), *Self-Images, Identity and Nationality*, Shimla: Indian Institute of Advanced Study, 1989, pp. 201–17.

———, 'Karachi and its Hinterland under Colonial rule', in Indu Banga (ed.), *Ports and their Hinterlands, 1700–1950*, New Delhi: Manohar, 1992, pp. 337–58.

———, 'Ecology and Land Rights in the Punjab', *Journal of Punjab Studies*, vol. 11, no. 1, Spring 2004, pp. 59–76.

———, ' Urban-Rural Interaction: The Upper Bari Doab (c.1550–1900)', in Reeta Grewal (ed.), *Five Thousand Years of Urbanization: The Punjab Region*, New Delhi: Manohar, 2005, pp. 129–44.

Basu, Aparna, 'The Past, Present and Future of English', in Indu Banga and Jaidev (eds.), *Cultural Reorientation in Modern India*, Shimla: Indian Institute of Advanced Study, 1996, pp. 176–97.

Bose, Ashish, 'A Note on the Definition of "Town" in the Indian Census', *The Indian Economic and Social History Review*, vol. I, no. 3, January–March 1964.

Brush, John E., 'The Morphology of Indian Cities', in Roy Turner (ed.), *India's Urban Future*, Berkeley: California University Press, 1962, pp. 224–36.

Chopra, Kusum, Atiya Habeeb Kidwai and Subhash Marcus, 'Urbanization Process in the Undivided Punjab', in Reeta Grewal (ed.), *Five Thousand Years of Urbanization: the Punjab Region*, New Delhi: Manohar/Institute of Punjab Studies, 2005, pp. 175–98.

Churchill Jr., Edward D. 'Muslim Societies of the Punjab, 1860–90', *The Panjab Past and Present*, vol. VIII, pt. 1, 1974, pp. 69–91.

Dagar, Rainuaka, 'Patriarchal Structure and Violence against Women', in J.S. Grewal and Indu Banga (eds.), *Punjab in Prosperity and Violence: Administration, Politics and Social Change, 1947–97*, New Delhi: K.K. Publishers/Institute of Punjab Studies, 1998, pp. 187–206.

Davis, Kingsley, 'The Origin and Growth of Urbanization in World', *American Journal of Sociology*, vol. LX, no. 6, March 1955.

———, 'Foreword', Jack P. Gibbs (ed.), *Urban Research Methods*, New Delhi: Affiliated East West Press, 1966.

Dossal, Mariam, 'Managing Cities: Professional Expertise, Popular Participation and Political Will', Section III: Modern India, Sectional President's Address, *Proceedings Indian History Congress*, Amritsar, 2002, pp. 457–85.

Furedy, Christine, 'Contrasting Models in the Development of Municipal Administration in Calcutta', in Donald B. Rosenthal (ed.), *The City in Indian Politics*, Faridabad: Thomson Press, 1976, pp. 152–72.

Gosal, Gurdev Singh, Urbanization in the Punjab 1881–1961, *Research Bulletin of the Panjab University*, vol. XVII, June 1966, pp. 1–26.

———, 'Spatial Perspective on Literacy in India', *Population Geography*, vols. 1 & 2, June–December 1979, pp. 41–67.

———, 'Agricultural Development and Urbanization, 1921–81', in Indu Banga (ed.), *Five Punjabi Centuries*, rpt., New Delhi: Manohar, 2000, pp. 358–74.

Grewal, J.S., 'Ramdaspur to Amritsar: From a Town to a City', in J.S. Grewal and Indu Banga (eds.), Studies in *Urban History*, Amritsar: GNDU, 1981, pp. 115–22.

———, 'The Making of the Sikh Self-Image before Independence', in P.C. Chatterjee (ed.), *Self-Image, Identity and Nationality*, Shimla: Indian Institute of Advanced Study, 1989, pp. 187–200.

———, 'Christian Presence and Cultural Reorientation: The Case of the Colonial Punjab', *Proceedings Indian History Congress*, Calcutta: 1990, pp. 535–42.

———, 'Cultural Reorientation in India under Colonial Rule', in Indu Banga and Jaidev (eds.), *Cultural Reorientation in Modern India*, Shimla: Indian Institute of Advanced Study, 1996, pp.13–23.

———, 'Urban Economic Life', in Indu Banga and J.S. Grewal (eds.),

Maharaja Ranjit Singh: The State and Society, Amritsar: GNDU, 2001, pp. 211–20.

———, 'Batala as a Medieval Town', in Reeta Grewal and Sheena Pall (eds.), *Precolonial and Colonial Punjab: Society, Economy, Politics and Culture*, New Delhi: Manohar, 2005, pp. 113–42.

Grewal, J.S. and Veena Sachdeva, 'Urbanization in the Mughal Province of Lahore (*c.*1550–1850)', in Reeta Grewal (ed.), *Five Thousand Years of Urbanization: The Punjab Region*, New Delhi: Manohar/Institute of Punjab Studies, 2005, pp. 107–27.

Grewal, Reeta, 'Polity, Economy and Urbanization: Early 19th Century Punjab', *Journal of Regional History*, vol. IV, 1983, pp. 56–72.

———, 'The Pattern of Urbanization in the Punjab under Colonial Rule', *Journal of Regional History*, vol. V, 1984, pp. 69–82.

———, 'Women in the Colonial City: Demographic Study of Punjab', in Kiran Pawar (ed.), *Women in Indian History: Social, Economic, Political and Cultural Perspectives*, Patiala: Vision and Venture, 1996, pp. 213–20.

———, 'Urban Revolution under Colonial Rule', in Indu Banga (ed.), *Five Punjabi Centuries: Polity, Economy, Society and Culture, c.1500–1990*; rpt., New Delhi: Manohar, 2000, pp. 438–54.

———, 'Urbanization in Medieval India, in J.S. Grewal (ed.), *The State and Society in Medieval India*, History of Indian Science, Philosophy and Culture in Indian Civilization, vol. VII, pt. 1, New Delhi: OUP, 2005, pp. 396–429.

Grewal, Reeta and J.S. Grewal, 'Urbanization in Colonial Punjab', in Reeta Grewal (ed.), *Five Thousand Years of Urbanization: The Punjab Region*, New Delhi: Manohar/Institute of Punjab Studies, 2005, pp. 145–66.

Gupta, J.K., 'Urbanization in Punjab: Problems and Prospects', in Reeta Grewal (ed.), *Five Thousand Years of Urbanization: The Punjab Regions*, New Delhi: Manohar/Institute of Punjab Studies, 2005, pp. 239–53.

Harris, Chauncy and Edward Ullman, 'The Nature of Cities', in Harold Mayer and Clyde F. Kohn (eds.), *Readings in Urban Geography*, Allahabad: Central Book Depot, 1967.

Heitzman, James, 'Urbanization and Political Economy in, Early South India, during the Cola Period', in Kenneth W. Hall (ed.), *Structure and Society in Early South India*, New Delhi: OUP, 2001, pp. 117–56.

Jyoti, Kanchan, 'Impact of Colonial Rule on Urban Life', in Indu Banga (ed.), *The City in Indian History*, rpt., New Delhi: Manohar, 2005, pp. 207–30.

Kant, Surya, 'Urbanization in Himachal Pradesh: Analysis of Patterns and Trends (1901–2001)', in Reeta Grewal (ed.), *Five Thousand Years of*

Urbani-zation: The Punjab Region, New Delhi: Manohar/Institute of Punjab Studies, 2005, pp. 199–221.

Kerr, Ian J., 'Urbanization and Colonial Rule in the 19th Century', *The Panjab Past and Present*, vol. XIV, pt. I, April 1980, pp. 210–24.

Khan, Sanaullah, 'Girls Education in the Punjab', *The Panjab Past and Present*, vol. 7, pt. 1, April 1973.

King, Anthony D., 'India's Urban Past', *Quarterly Review of Historical Studies*, vol. III, no. 4, 1968–9.

———, 'Colonial Cities: Global Pivots of Change', in Robert Ross and Gerard J. Telkamp (eds.), *Colonial Cities*, Dordrecht: Martinus Nijhoff Publishers for the Leiden University Press, 1985, pp. 7–32.

Khanna, J.S., 'Lagging Industrial Development in Punjab: An Analysis', *PSE Economic Analyst*, vol. II, 1980, pp. 88–126.

Konishi, Masatoshi A., 'Multani Kaghaz: Lesser Known Aspect of Multan as a Paper-Making Centre', *Lahore Museum Bulletin*, vol. II, no. 2, 1989, pp. 61–8.

Krishan, Gopal, 'Social Parameters of Punjab Urbanization since Independence', in Reeta Grewal (ed.), *Five Thousand Years of Urbanization: The Punjab Region*, New Delhi: Manohar/Institute of Punjab Studies, 2005, pp. 225–38.

Krishan, Gopal and Surya Kant, 'Administrative Space', in J.S. Grewal and Indu Banga (eds.), *Punjab in Prosperity and Violence: Administration, Politics and Social Change, 1947–97*, New Delhi: K.K. Publishers/Institute of Punjab Studies, 1998, pp. 1–22.

Kumar, Ravinder, 'The Changing Structure of Urban Society in Colonial India', *Indian Historical Review*, vol. V, nos. 1–2, July 1978–January 1979, pp. 200–15.

———, 'Urban Society and Urban Politics: Lahore in 1919', in Indu Banga (ed.), *Five Punjabi Centuries: Polity, Economy Society and Culture, c.1500–1990*; rpt., New Delhi, Manohar, 2000, pp. 180–220.

———, 'The Role of Urban Society in Nationalist Politics', in Indu Banga (ed.), *The City in Indian History*, rpt., New Delhi: Manohar, 2005, pp. 265–78.

Loehlin, C.H. 'The History of Christianity in the Punjab', *The Panjab Past and Present*, vol. VII, part 1, 1973, pp. 203–30.

Malik, Ikram Ali, 'Muslim Anjumans and Communitarian Consciousness', in Indu Banga (ed.), *Five Punjabi Centuries: Polity, Economy, Society and Culture, c.1500–1990*; rpt., New Delhi: Manohar, 2000, pp. 112–25.

Mehta, M.J. 'Business Environment and Urbanization: Ahmedabad in the 19th Century', in J.S. Grewal and Indu Banga (eds.), *Studies in Urban History*, Amritsar: GNDU, 1981, pp. 123–34.

Misra, S.C., 'Some Aspects of the Self-Administering Institutions in Medieval Indian Towns', in J.S. Grewal and Indu Banga (eds.), *Studies in Urban History*, Amritsar: GNDU, 1981, pp. 80–90.

———, 'Urban History in India: Possibilities and Perspectives', in Indu Banga (ed.), *The City in Indian History*; rpt., New Delhi: Manohar, 2005, pp. 1–8.

Mukerji, Karunamoy, 'Land Prices in Punjab', in M.K. Chaudhuri (ed.), *Trends in Socio-Economic Change in India, 1871–1961*, Shimla: Indian Institute of Advanced Study, 1969, pp. 529–47.

Neild, Susan M., 'Colonial Urbanism: The Development of Madras City in the 18th and 19th Centuries', *Modern Asian Studies*, vol. 13, no. 2, 1979, pp. 217–46.

Oddie, Geoffrey A., 'Constructing "Hinduism": The Impact of the Prostestant Missionary Movement on Hindu Self-Understanding', in Robert Eric Frykenberg (ed.), *Christians and Missionaries in India: Cross-Cultural Communication since 1500*, Grand Rapids, Michigan/Cambridge UK: William B Eerdmans Publishing House, 2003, pp. 155–82.

Pall, Sheena, 'Lala Lajpat Rai and the Punjab National Bank', in J.S. Grewal and Indu Banga (eds.), *Lala Lajpat Rai in Retrospect: Political, Economic, Social and Cultural Concerns*, Chandigarh: Panjab University, 2000, pp. 40–50.

Rahi, J.S., 'Socio-Cultural Change in Amritsar as Reflected in Punjabi Fiction', in Reeta Grewal (ed.), *Five Thousand Years of Urbanization: The Punjab Region*, New Delhi: Manohar 2005, pp. 167–73.

Rao, Vidya, 'Thumri and Thumri Singers: Changes in Style and Life-Style', in Indu Banga and Jaidev (eds.), *Cultural Reorientation in Modern India*, Shimla: Indian Institute of Advanced Study, 1996, pp. 278–315.

Ray, Pranabranjan, 'Urbanization in a Colonial Situation: Serampre', in M.S.A Rao (eds.), *Urban Sociology in India*, Delhi: Orient Longman, 1974, 119–50.

Rezavi, S. Ali Nadeem, 'Uniqueness of the Eastern "Imperial City"? Testing the Model with Fathpur Sikri', in Krishna Mohan Shrimali (ed.), *Reason and Archaeology*, New Delhi: Association for the Study of History and Archaeology, 1998, pp. 103–17.

Schultz, Stanley K., 'An Approach to a Theory of Urbanization', in J.S. Grewal and Indu Banga (eds.), *Studies in Urban History*, Amritsar: GNDU, 1981, pp. 8–17.

Sen, Sunil, 'Industrialization and Economic Growth in India 1849–1947', in N.R. Ray (ed.), *Western Colonial Policy*, Calcutta: Institute of Historical Studies, 1981, vol. I, pp. 95–108.

Sharma, Harish C., 'Changing World of the Artisans, 1849–1947', in Indu Banga (eds.), *Five Punjabi Centuries: Polity, Economy, Society and Culture, c. 1500–1990*; rpt., New Delhi: Manohar, 2000, pp. 496–508.

———, 'Artisans', in Indu Banga and J.S. Grewal (eds.), *Maharaja Ranjit Singh: The State and Society*, Amritsar: GNDU, 2001, pp. 236–45.

Sharma, K.D., 'Cantonment Towns of India: Islands in the Urbanization Stream', in Jaymala Diddee and Vimla Ranga Swamy (eds.), *Urbanization: Trends, Perspectives and Challenges*, Jaipur: Rawat Publications, 1993, pp. 145–63.

Singh, Darshan, 'How did the Nirmalas Preach', *Journal of Sikh Studies*, vol. V, no. 1, 1978.

Singh, Joginder, 'The Sikh Community: Demography and Occupational Change, 1881–1931', in Indu Banga (ed.), *Five Punjabi Centuries: Polity, Economy, Society and Culture, c. 1500–1990*; rpt., New Delhi: Manohar, 2000, pp. 471–95.

Singh, Kirpal, 'The Hindu-Muslim Riot in the Punjab 1881', *Proceedings Punjab History Conference*, Patiala, 1971, pp. 288–95.

Singh, Sulakhan, 'Udasi Establishments under Sikh Rule', *Journal of Regional History*, vol. I, 1980, pp. 70–87.

Sircar, D.C., 'Foundation of Early Indian Cities and Towns', in Vijay Kumar Thakur (ed.), *Towns in Pre-Modern India*, Patna: Janaki Prakashan, 1994, pp. 90–104.

Smailes, A.E., 'The Indian City: A Descriptive Model', *Geographic Zeit Schrift*, vol. 57, 1969.

Sohal, Sukhdev Singh, 'Professional Middle Classes in the Punjab', *Journal of Regional History*, vol. III, 1982, pp. 72–86.

———, 'Middle Classes and Communalism in the Colonial Punjab', *Journal of Regional History*, vol. V, 1984, pp. 83–96.

———, 'Emergence of the Middle Classes and Forms of Political Articulation', in Indu Banga (ed.), *Five Punjabi Centuries: Polity, Economy, Society and Culture, c. 1500–1990*; rpt., New Delhi: Manohar, 2000, pp. 455–70.

Thakur, Renu, 'Urban Centres in the North-West (*c.* AD 600–1200)', in Reeta Grewal (ed.), *Five Thousand Years of Urbanization: The Punjab Region*, New Delhi: Manohar/Institute of Punjab Studies, 2005, pp. 79–89.

Ullman, Edward, 'A Theory of Location for Cities', in Harold Meyer and Clyde F. Kohn (eds.), *Readings in Urban Geography*, Allahabad: Central Book Depot, 1967, pp. 202–9.

Wirth, Louis, 'Urbanism as a Way of Life', *The American Journal of Sociology*, vol. XIIV, no. 1, July 1938, pp. 1–24.

PH.D. THESES AND M.PHIL. DISSERTATIONS

Bal, Rupinder, 'Wheat Production and Structure of Marketing in the Punjab under Colonial Rule(1901–47)', Ph.D. thesis, Panjab University, Chandigarh, 1997.

Bhalla, Rupali, 'Urbanization in Post-Independence India: A Comparative Study of Punjab and Haryana upto 1991', Ph.D. thesis, Panjab University, Chandigarh, 2000.

Bhardwaj, Dharmvir, 'Communalism in South-East Punjab (1920–47)', Ph.D. thesis, Maharishi Dayanand University, Rohtak, 1997.

Dhami, Dilbagh Singh, 'Cantonment Towns in India: Some Locational and Population Attributes', M.Phil. dissertation, Panjab University, Chandigarh, 1985.

Gill, Madanjeet, 'Administration of Justice in the Punjab 1849–1947', M.Phil. dissertation, GNDU, Amritsar, 1988.

Grewal, Reeta, 'Polity, Economy and Urbanization: Early 19th Century Punjab', M.Phil. dissertation, GNDU, Amritsar, 1983.

———, 'Urbanization in the Punjab, 1849–1947', Ph.D. thesis, GNDU, Amritsar, 1988.

Jyoti, Kanchan, 'Jullundur 1846–1947: An Urban History', Ph.D. thesis, GNDU, Amritsar, 1988.

Kerr, Ian Johnstone, 'The Punjab Province and the Lahore District, 1849–1872: A Case Study of British Colonial Rule and Social Change in India', Ph.D. thesis, University of Minnesota, Minnesota, 1975.

Mohaya, Naranjan Dass, 'The History of Communal Riots in Punjab 1922–47', Ph.D. thesis, Panjab University, Chandigarh, 1984.

Rezavi, Syed Ali Nadeem, 'Urban Middle Classes in Mughal India', Ph.D. thesis, Aligarh Muslim University, Aligarh, 2006.

Sasha, 'Social History of the Plague with Special reference to Medieval and Modern Punjab', M.Phil. dissertation, Panjab University, Chandigarh, 1999.

———, 'The State, Society and Epidemics in Colonial Punjab, 1849–1947', Ph.D. thesis, Panjab University, Chandigarh, 2003.

Sharma, Anshu, 'Early Twentieth Century Landscape and Ecology of Shimla Town', M.Phil. dissertation, Panjab University, Chandigarh, 1987.

Singh, Harminder, 'Industrial Development in the Punjab 1901–47', M.Phil. dissertation, GNDU, Amritsar, 1981.

Singh, Navtej, 'Famines in the Punjab, 1858-1901', Ph.D. thesis, Panjab University, Chandigarh, 1986.

Sivaramakrishnan, Kavita, 'Addressing the Health of the "Public"—State Authority, Missionaries and Vaids in Punjab Towns and Cities (circa 1880s–1930s)', Ph.D. thesis, Jawaharlal Nehru University, New Delhi, 2003.

Index